MICHAEL LEE
BACK from the BRINK

TONY McDONALD

PKBA K

First published in England in 2010 by

RETRO SPEEDWAY

Tel: 01708 734 502
www.retro-speedway.com

Printed in Great Britain by CPI Antony Rowe.

Distributed by Retro Speedway
103 Douglas Road, Hornchurch, Essex, RM11 1AW, England.
Email: editorial@retro-speedway.com

ISBN: 978-0-9559340-5-6

To Michael, Nicky, Andy, Val and all the Lee family.

Acknowledgements

This book wouldn't have been possible without the help of so many others who I need to thank before we go any further. The biggest 'thank you' must, of course, go to Michael and Nicky for their help and total support throughout, and for allowing me the freedom and scope to obtain such diverse and wide-ranging opinions without interference.

I'd also like to say a huge thanks to Mike's parents, Andy and Val, for their unfailing patience and co-operation in answering many difficult questions about their son, which can't have been easy. They both fully deserve to enjoy the rest of their lives in peace and happiness!

Also, to Michael's second son, Jordan, for being a 'chip off the old block' in terms of his frankness, willingness and courage to respond readily to even more of my awkward questions.

Many people who played a part in Michael's racing career also kindly gave up their time to provide accounts of their working relationship with him, or helped by providing quotes or invaluable research for the book. I'd sincerely like to thank the following (in alphabetical order):
Eddie Argall, John Berry, Terry Betts, Eric Boocock, Nigel Boocock, Barry Briggs, Randall Butt, Richard Clark, Peter Collins, Phil Collins, Cyril Crane, Dennis Hicks, Danny King, Steve Magro, Ivan Mauger, Neil Middleditch, Con Migro, Martin Neal, Martin Rogers, Mike Rumens, Reg Fearman, Rick Frost, Bruce Penhall, Gareth Rogers, Laurence Rogers, Malcolm Simmons, Chum Taylor, Ian Thomas, Tai Woffinden and Doug Wyer.

Without pictures, the words are almost meaningless, so please take a bow: John Somerville (John Somerville Collection), Mike Patrick (www.mike-patrick.com), Alf Weedon, Ken Carpenter, John Hipkiss, Doug Booth, Steve Magro, Bill and Wayne Meyer, Dave Fairbrother, Kevin Goodacre and Stephen Waller (www.stephenwaller.com) for taking and/or supplying the 150-plus images included in this book. Sincere apologies to anyone who may have been unintentionally overlooked.

Another word of gratitude too to Michael and his mum Val for the kind loan of their personal pictures and for giving me access to the family scrapbooks.

And to my loved ones and colleagues at Retro Speedway for making the seemingly impossible, possible: Susie, Anne Walker and Glen, the designer.

The following should be recognised for their useful reference purposes:
Bibliography: As Luck Would Have It – Len Silver (Retro Speedway); Backtrack (Retro Speedway); Booey: Around in Circles - Eric Boocock (Retro Speedway); Confessions of a Speedway Promoter – John Berry (Retro Speedway); Five-One magazine (Pinegen); Forty Years On: King's Lynn Speedway – Martin Rogers with Chris Hornby (Doonvilla); In My View – Martin Rogers (Marlin Publications); Mike The Bike (DVD, Retro Speedway); Simmo: The Whole Truth - Malcolm Simmons (Retro Speedway); Speedway Mail; Speedway Star; The Complete History of the British League, Peter Oakes (Front Page Books); Wheels and Deals – Ian Thomas (Pinegen).

Websites: www.internationalspeedway.co.uk; www.speedway.org.

Contents

Michael, the Grand Prix engine tuner, with Tai Woffinden at the start of the 2010 GP season.

Introduction

THE prisoner being driven away from Newmarket Magistrate's Court in the back of the prison service van was feeling anxious about what would happen next.

He had been refused bail and had to accept that he was on his way back to jail, where he'd spent the previous two weeks on remand after being arrested by police and found in possession of an "astronomical amount" of drugs.

Soon after the meat-wagon left the court, it reached the main A12 road and looked as if it was about to head back towards Norwich.

Michael Lee knew Norwich quite well. He'd spent two previous prison sentences in Norfolk's capital city for minor drugs offences and was sent back there again, only this time for committing a much more serious crime that would ultimately carry a three-year sentence.

By now 40-years-old, he'd lost a lot of weight and was feeling tired, hungry and dejected at being denied bail. He knew he was heading back to his cell. But it soon became clear to him that it wasn't the familiar one he'd left behind in Norwich that morning.

The vehicle slowed at the main junction and turned right. As it did so, he managed to catch sight of one of those familiar green road signs through a tiny window.

Alarm bells started ringing in his head. It read: 'LONDON A12'.

"Hey! Where the f*** are we going?" he shouted with panic in his voice. "Where are you taking us now?" The two other prisoners sharing the squalid, cramped conditions with him were equally frightened and confused.

Within the next few hours Michael Lee, the 1980 World Champion and one of the greatest speedway riders of his generation, would be arriving through the gates at Brixton prison in South London, one of the most notorious jails in Britain and home to murderers, psychopaths, rapists, paedophiles, armed robbers, junkies and all the other dregs of society.

But what was he doing there among the low-life?

How had it come to this?

Michael had been dubbed a so-called 'bad boy' and 'rebel' of speedway following a number of high profile brushes with authority that led to a year's ban from the track and countless other problems that brought about the premature end of a once great racing career.

When he fell out of love with speedway in the early 80s and, in his eyes, the sport turned its back on him, he felt isolated and persecuted by officialdom.

He needed to replace the thrill of racing a 500cc bike with a new adrenalin buzz, so he turned to a new lifestyle dominated by drugs.

Michael literally produced hundreds of his own cannabis plants, took amphetamines and snorted cocaine "by the bucketful" on such a large scale and for so long that he is convinced he would be dead by now if he hadn't come to his senses in time.

He became such a "full-on" cog in the drugs underworld that for a while he made a very lavish living as a drug-dealer, comfortably earning thousands of pounds a week.

He loved the lifestyle, the fast cars and the parties – a far cry from his golden days on the track where he was idolised by thousands.

But he wasn't a murderer!

And Brixton prison wasn't for him.

So how did it come to this?

Following a series of revealing interviews with Michael and members of his close family, friends, team-mates, rivals and others who knew him best, his astonishing story can now be fully told.

The King's Lynn and England legend – one of only six Englishmen to have lifted the world title and twice a World Team Cup winner too – recalls all the exhilarating highs and depressing lows of his turbulent life, on and off the track.

It's been a heck of a rollercoaster journey and, at times, a very painful and emotional one – not only for Mike, but also for his loved ones. Especially his parents, Andy and Valerie, who have seen the best and worst of him for more than 50 years but have stuck by him through it all. With Michael's soul laid bare, this book can't have been easy for them to read.

But at times it's been a very rewarding adventure, too, with many highlights to remember along the way. Michael won more races in his first year of racing than many riders have managed in their entire career.

He has turned his life around completely through sheer hard work and dedication, his renewed passion for speedway and his mechanical engineering skills, he has established himself as one of the most respected and successful engine tuners in the business, with more than 15 star riders now putting their trust in him to produce the goods.

In recent years a couple of respected promoters have recruited him as their Technical Advisor, tapping into his enormous wealth of experience both on the track and in the workshop.

In 2010 he was back among the big-time on the Grand Prix circuit.

It's been a remarkable turnaround.

When Michael and I first spoke about turning his compelling story into a book, he had it in mind that it would be a straightforward ghosted autobiography, with me putting his thoughts and memories into words. The problem with that limited approach is Michael's natural humility – he wouldn't have wanted to dwell on his many achievements as one of Britain's all-time greats in the way some others like to boast about themselves. One of the things this modest man is not very good at is talking about himself – well, not in a positive way!

It's one of his most endearing qualities that he appears almost embarrassed to recall his finest moments and the countless brilliant things he did on a bike, but record them we must and I hope the biography approach has enabled me, along with the input of numerous others who have contributed, to do full justice to just how good a rider he was from such a very young age.

I hope the book will answer questions and provide an insight into a very talented and gifted rider who has divided opinion almost since the day he burst onto the scene as a child prodigy. Michael will always possess strong views, while others also have the right to express theirs. You can make up your own mind.

As an authorised account of his life, Michael naturally had the final right of veto on any comments that he didn't particularly like or agree with – and I'm sure there are opinions voiced by others here that will have made him wince or cringe with embarrassment as he and his partner Nicky proof-read the finished version.

But it's typical of the brutal honesty he has shown throughout this soul-searching process that he didn't ask me to alter or delete a single negative word written about him from any of the following pages. That takes admirable strength of character and we should respect him all the more for his willingness to accept criticism from others.

Probably Michael's biggest achievement is that he has survived the worst times and is still here to tell the story! Not only that, but he has re-emerged as a much stronger, mature and wiser individual. With the help of certain people and due to the manner in which he has responded to their trust, he has regained his dignity and self-respect and turned his whole life around.

When you think how badly out of control his life became after he quit racing, he really has come back from the brink.

Tony McDonald
Hornchurch, Essex
June 2010

World Champion in 1980, but survival and his re-emergence has been an equally great achievement for Michael.

Field of Dreams

Born to race

Chapter 1

MICHAEL ANDREW LEE was born in Cambridgeshire on December 11, 1958. It was a Thursday and there wasn't much else of note happening in the world some 13 years after the end of WW2. The most famous other person born on this day is musician Nikki Sixx, bassist and songwriter for the American heavy rock band Motley Crue. No, I'd never heard of him either.

Elsewhere, Jermain Jackson was probably singing his way through his fourth birthday as the third eldest of those precocious kids from one of the world's most famous musical families. American heiress Christina Onassis was eight that day and singer Brenda Lee was blowing out 24 candles.

And as bookmaker Joe Coral turned 62 years of age on that Thursday, you bet he couldn't have imagined the significance of events going on in East Anglia. On the couch at 50 Woodlands Park, in the small village of Girton, five miles north-west of Cambridge, a future star was born.

Valerie Lee was 20-years-old when she gave birth to her first child. Although she and husband Andy were by then married and living in a bungalow at nearby Hauxton, it was at his mother Alice Lee's house where their son entered the world in which the price of an English home was less than £2,500.

Val explains: "Andy's mum was a lovely grandma to the kids. It was quite common for children to be born at home in those days and as she was offering, I went there to have the baby.

"Michael's was a breech birth and I had a terrible time. In those days there was only the local district nurse to take care of you. Ours was a great character who kept pigs. I'll never forget Andy's mum coming in and telling me the nurse was having problems with her pigs and that she would 'be along in a minute'. Of course, I was in agony.

"The nurse arrived in an old mac and wellington boots. Talk about hygiene! There was nothing like oxygen or epidurals available in those days.

"Michael was about a fortnight overdue. Typical! The night before he arrived I think I drank a bottle of gin and had umpteen hot baths, but still nothing happened. Then, all of a sudden, he was ready.

"I could see the nurse holding Michael upside down and slapping him. 'He's not breathing,' she said in a panic, 'there's nothing happening'. So the doctor, who had also arrived, took him from her and all of a sudden there was a great big gulp and Michael started breathing.

"We'd thought he was dead at first, that he hadn't survived a very difficult birth, though I was past caring by then! But thankfully he obviously did survive.

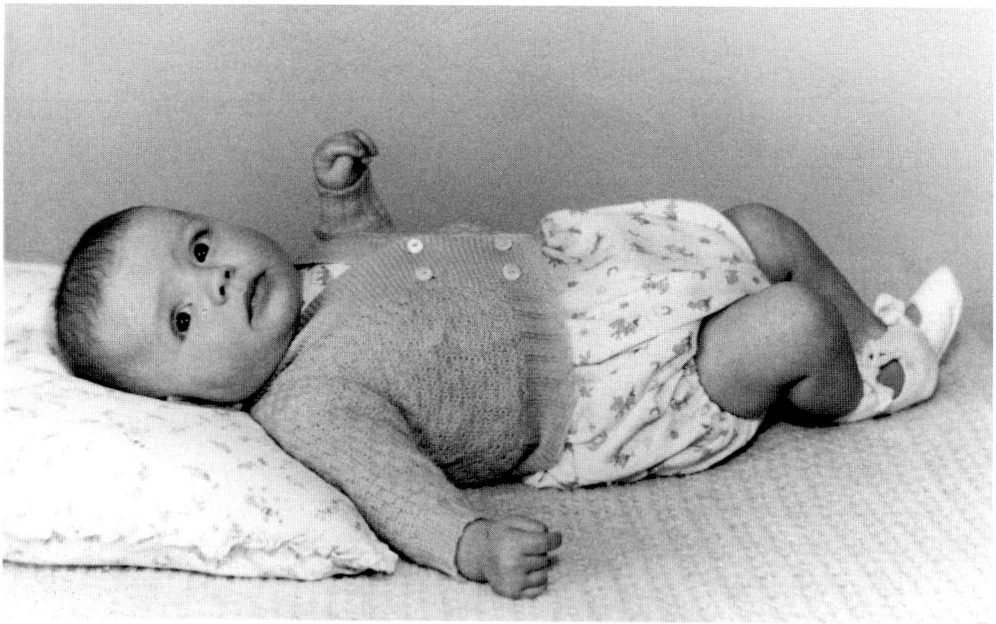

Not a lay-down engine, but a lay-down baby! Michael, at six months, gets ready to roar.

He was 6lbs 7oz at birth."

Born in Cambridge in March 1938, Val did secretarial work after leaving school. Andy, who is three years older than her, established himself as an international scrambles star, racing mainly on the continent where he won almost 200 meetings in Europe throughout the 60s and 70s.

Explaining how she met the tall, slim lad who became her husband, Val says: "I had a boyfriend who did scrambling and it was through him that I got to know Andy – we all used to meet up at weekend meetings in the Cambridge area. My only brother, Ian Mustill, didn't compete at scrambling but he had a road bike, so bikes have always been part of my family."

Michael is the eldest of Val and Andy's three children. Belinda came two years after Mike, while Susan arrived six years behind her big brother. They all used to love their visits to Granny Lee's.

"Gran spoilt us all as kids and I visited her every week," recalls Michael. "Even after I started doing interval rides at King's Lynn, I still spent the night at gran's. When Dad was away racing abroad, Uncle Stephen – dad's brother, who used to work for the Ridgeons timber company in Cambridge – would take me up to Lynn in a Morris Minor pick-up truck. Stephen was still living at his mother's house at the time and he loved his speedway, although he never rode bikes himself.

"Gran really looked after us and I used to love going there. She always gave me a fresh can of condensed milk with my porridge in the morning and, silly as this may sound, I still prefer condensed milk. She looked after us really well."

But when Michael reached the age of nine, his parents feared they would lose him. Recalling this traumatic ordeal, Val says: "One day he'd been riding his little

Proud Mum Valerie with Michael.

Three wheels or two, it'll do.

bike with several other boys over at the pits in Hauxton and when he came home we could see that he'd hurt himself. At first our local doctor thought Michael had simply pulled or torn a stomach muscle but for two days he was walking round all hunched up and in obvious pain. He continually felt sick but couldn't bring anything up. In the end, I took him to A&E at Addenbrookes in Cambridge and they immediately knew he had appendicitis.

"After the first operation they sent Michael home for a few days but he developed a huge abscess on his pelvis. The nurse who had been coming to us to treat his scar had sealed it with something or other but it meant the poison wasn't being released from his body. It had built up until he was in a hell of a mess.

"I rushed him back into Addenbrookes and this time they kept him in. He was admitted to a men's ward and they put him on a drip. It was very serious and there was a period of two or three days when we thought we were going to lose him. They operated on him again but it was touch and go because of the poison caused by the infection.

"The doctors didn't have to prepare us for the worst because Andy and I could see that his life was hanging in the balance, and the men on Michael's ward thought he was a goner.

"He stayed in hospital for two or three weeks and he just wasted to nothing. He was quite a well built little boy – not fat – but he lost a lot of weight as a result of that illness.

"The doctors told us he had peritonitis and that he was lucky to have survived. They said he must have had quite a strong constitution."

Michael doesn't have vivid memories of those worrying days and weeks but he says: "I knew it was touch and go for a while. When the poison from the abscess got into my blood system I had to have two or three blood transfusions.

"The problem was that they had to rush me down to the operating theatre late at night but there was no-one available then who was qualified to perform the op' straight away. The doctor who did it had never done this op' before, so he cocked it up a bit and didn't get all the muck out – on top of the fact that my appendix burst during the actual operation.

"I've always hated hospitals since then and unless I'm on a stretcher you'd have to drag me in screaming. My worst memory of it, though, is when I first went in for the diagnosis. It took about 12 doctors and nurses to hold me down while they put on their rubber gloves for the internal examination. I gave them hell.

"I was quite a plump little kid before I became ill – they called me King Farouk! – but whether what happened to me at the age of eight had any long-term effect on my weight and stature in latter life, I wouldn't know. If you look at Dad, he's tall and skinny like me, so maybe it didn't."

"It was very serious and there was a period of two or three days when we thought we were going to lose him. They operated on him again but it was touch and go because of the poison caused by the infection."

As we chatted at his home while doing one of the interviews for this book, Michael lifted his shirt to reveal a six-inch scar high on his right hip. "An appendix scar should be down here," he said pointing at the legacy of his childhood ordeal, "but because the doctor cut inside me at the wrong place and had to give it the big one, the scar is unnecessarily long. It should have gone by now but it's still visible."

Michael believes it took around 10 weeks before he'd fully recovered and was able to resume lessons at Hauxton Primary School. A knock-on effect of the peritonitis scare was that it caused damage and discolouring of his upper front teeth, which led to a hang-up that would trouble him throughout his adolescent years and onwards into his first few seasons as a much photographed young speedway rider.

Val explained: "Because of the poison that had got into his body and the medication they had to give him to cure the peritonitis, it caused bad rotting of his teeth. He was very outgoing as a kid and seemed to accept how he looked but once he got into speedway the state of his teeth worried him to death. We wanted him to get his teeth done but he wouldn't because he was terrified of dentists.

"But as soon as he was well enough again, all he could think about was getting back on his bike."

By the time the Lees moved from Hauxton to nearby Shepreth in the late 60s, Michael was also very keen on football and would travel down to London with Nicky Billet, his best friend at Shepreth Primary, to watch games. Nick's father, Fred, would take the boys to watch matches, including England Under-21 international matches at Wembley. "I don't know why, but Leeds United was my favourite team and I had the all-white replica kit," says Michael, who played football regularly but was disappointed not to claim the goalkeeper's jersey for the school team.

At the age of 17 poor Nicky Billet was the innocent victim of a very serious accident while riding his motorcycle, when hit by a car on a crossroads. He died from his head injuries years later and Val believes the tragic death of his best friend had a profound effect on her son. She says: "Nicky was brain-dead but they kept him alive in Addenbrookes for up to, I think, eight years before they finally switched off his life support machine. His mum, Jean, lived in hope that Nicky's eyes would reopen and she would go and visit him every day.

"Michael also visited him on a number of occasions and would sit and talk to him. But it broke his heart to see his friend like that. It really did get to him."

It's a long way to Australia.

Recalling Michael's childhood days, Andy says: "He was like will o' the wisp and very energetic. As a child he would sometimes come with me to the continent, mainly France, to watch me ride. Although he was interested in what I was doing, I don't think he was that keen on scrambling – or moto-cross as it's known today. He could probably see how tired I was after racing three hard legs.

Is he rolling?

"He did a bit of schoolboy scrambling and when I was off riding on the continent his mum would drive him to meetings with his bike on the trailer."

Michael confirms: "I was probably about 11 when I entered my first race and to be honest, my machinery – a Suzuki 175cc in a Bantam frame – wasn't competitive. I remember Kelvin Tatum – who I rode against in speedway many years later – also riding in one of my first moto-cross meetings. He was on this totally 'tricked up' thing that his dad had built for him and I think he won every race he was in.

"I felt quite humiliated after that first experience of schoolboy moto-cross and didn't want to do it anymore. Speedway soon became more my cup of tea, although I think Dad was a bit disappointed because he would have liked me to have followed him."

Andy says: "When Michael was about seven-years-old we used to go to France as a family for about a month in a caravan. I'd ride in, say, five meetings during that time but he never showed any interest in moto-cross at all. The only reason he went to the races was because we all did!"

Not that Andy was reluctant to introduce his son to speedway's unique thrills. He says: "I used to enjoy watching it myself because it was so completely different to what I did in moto-cross. I went to Walthamstow, Harringay, Hackney and later King's Lynn. I found it thrilling to watch but at the time I never wanted to be a part of it."

"I felt quite humiliated after that first experience of schoolboy moto-cross and didn't want to do it anymore. Speedway soon became more my cup of tea, although I think Dad was a bit disappointed because he would have liked me to have followed him."

Michael's initiation to speedway came at Long Eaton of all places. It would have been around 1969, when the sport resumed at the Midlands track, and he remembers shinning up an iron girder in the main stand to watch the second division racing from a vantage point above what seemed like a large crowd.

Michael was now hooked on speedway.

"I marked out a track of about 150 yards in the orchard by our house at Shepreth and even built my own 'safety fence' – just so I could crash into it and experience what it really felt like. It was mad!" laughs Michael, who had discovered his own field of dreams.

"The mini track was virtually a circle and, wet or dry, he could slide round it with no trouble at all," says Andy. "I used to say: 'Yeah, that's OK, but can you do so well on a larger track?' I built him a bigger bike – a Triumph Tiger Cub engine in an Elstar frame – and when they cut the corn up at Sheldrick's farm Michael would ride around there. I put four barrels out as corner posts to form quite a big circuit and said to him 'now try that' – and he absolutely flew round there.

"He had incredible balance. If you ask me what Mike's biggest asset was, it was his balance and throttle control. He made his height work for him on a

Fishing with Grandad Claude Mustill on the River Cam at Grantchester Meadow, near Cambridge.

"I virtually left school at the age of 15 without having taken a single exam. The teachers wanted me to go back to sit my final exams but school wasn't in the equation. Speedway was all that interested me."

speedway bike. He was very good at looking for the grip, finding it and moving his body about. He was extremely agile."

"Comparing moto-cross to speedway was like chalk and cheese for me and I took to it like a duck to water. Dad had seen me struggle at moto-cross and he knew this was for me," Michael continued. "The Tiger Cub had been tweaked up a little bit to a higher compression and fitted with a racing cam."

Totally absorbed by motorcycles from a very early age, Michael had his heart set on becoming a speedway rider well before his teens. Nothing else mattered to him. Not girls. And certainly not school.

Val says: "He did take an interest in girls when he was about 13 or 14 and he had quite a few regular girlfriends from the college – I still see some of them! But bikes always came first with Michael. He had quite a few mates round to the house, but they weren't interested in racing motor bikes – only riding ones that got them from A to B."

Michael says: "I wasn't chasing girls or hanging about on street corners up to no good. My whole world revolved around motor bikes and my parents had to accept it, just as the school eventually did."

In his final year at Melbourn Village College, the local comprehensive school, Michael proudly admits he didn't attend lessons on more than five full days. "Yeah, just five ticks on the register – that's all I would have had by then," he says.

He was very clever, though, at deceiving his parents and the school truancy inspectors!

He recalls: "It did get a bit heavy at one stage and the school inspectors would come knocking at our house. I'd hear Mum telling them that, as far as she was concerned, I'd left for school on the bus that morning. What even she didn't know was that I'd let the bus go, hide behind the shelter until the coast was clear and then sneak back into our garage to work on my bike.

"And if she ever did come looking for me in the garage, I had a special little hiding place – in a cupboard beneath the bins!

"I got caught out one day, though, when the workshop door opened unexpectedly and the inspector, who happened to call in on us, saw me."

This is how Michael's mum remembers it: "When the school truant inspector knocked at the door, I said to him: 'I'm sorry, are you sure it's me you want?'. When they confirmed they were calling about Michael Lee, I'd tell them in all innocence: 'But anyhow, he goes to school – I give him a packed lunch every morning'.

"And then the inspector showed me the school attendance register which showed that Michael hadn't in fact attended there for a whole term and a bit. 'Well, what is he doing?' I asked. We sat there talking and the man asked about Michael's interests. 'All there is are his bikes,' I told him. So the chap asked if I'd mind if he had a look at where Michael kept his speedway bikes.

"Of course, when we opened the door of the little workshop, which was like an extension built on the back of our big double garage, there was Michael – working away on his bike. He was wearing overalls, not his school uniform.

"I didn't even know he was in there – the garage was a bit away from the actual house and I had no reason to go inside it because I rarely put my car away.

"He was very crafty. When it was nearly time for the school coach to bring the kids back to our village in the afternoon, he'd put his uniform on again, walk through the field at the back of our house, make his way round to the front of the house and walk down our drive with his school bag – just as if he'd arrived home from school. Then Michael would immediately say: 'I'm just going out into the garage,' and that was it. I never thought anything of it until that truant inspector called round.

"I was a bit angry about him playing truant at first – they were going to take me to court at one stage – but we got over it."

Michael: "Nowadays parents can be sent to prison for not sending their kids to school but back then the school inspectors would listen to your views. One day they asked Mum to go outside so they could have a chat with me. I'm not sure if Rod Yallop, my PE teacher who I got on well with, or someone else at the school had put in a good word for me but in the end the inspector understood what I wanted to do and my obsession with speedway. Rod Yallop even used to come and watch me ride round King's Lynn on a Saturday night, and the school inspectors left me alone after that. They gave up on me."

Where's my bike?

Engage Michael in conversation and you find yourself talking with an intelligent man who has always been good at articulating his forthright views. "There are no flies on Michael," his mother agrees.

He reflects: "My school teachers were disappointed that I didn't make the most of myself academically, because I was quite good at school – certainly in the top bracket at Maths and one or two other subjects. I'm not stupid!

"I was well behaved but in my final year the only lessons I attended were those for woodwork, metalwork and PE, which I enjoyed.

"Sports-wise, I ran cross-country for the school and at district and county level, and did well. Rod Yallop would take three of us up to Royston Heath to train for the cross-country runs. He was tough on us and he'd shout and holler if you didn't conform, but he was a good sportsman.

"Being tall, I was quite good at high-jump. I also turned out for the local village cricket team when they were a man short, but none of those sports were for me.

"I virtually left school at the age of 15 without having taken a single exam. The teachers wanted me to go back to sit my final exams but school wasn't in the equation. Speedway was all that interested me. And they knew it."

Andy Lee says he did try to advise his son about the merits of a sound education, but perhaps with a lack of conviction that was understandable given his own background. "I couldn't condone what Michael did by skipping school but I couldn't condemn it either," smiled Lee senior, who was actually expelled from public school at the age of 15 . . . for repeated truancy!

For Michael, his education was to be found each day in the workshop that he shared with his father at Shepreth. This was his 'classroom'. It's where he first gained a basic knowledge of engines that would continually evolve and serve him so well as a top rider and make him one of the most respected tuners in world speedway today.

Star in the Making

How King's Lynn got their 'carrot' in Orange leathers

Chapter 2

ESSEX-based sports journalist Martin Rogers was asked by King's Lynn Speedway co-promoter Maurice Littlechild to handle the club's administration in 1972, which included things like writing and compiling the programme and getting advertisers. One of the first to take out a full-page ad' was Andy Lee, who owned and ran a thriving motorcycle and accessories shop at 307 Mill Road in Cambridge, where he was well known as a moto-cross star.

Andy Lee Motorcycles Ltd would remain a regular advertiser in the programme for years to come but back in 1972 no-one had heard of his son, who was an enthusiastic supporter of Norfolk's British League team known as the King's Lynn 'Stars'.

Rogers takes up the story of how things evolved: "Michael, who was 13, was developing an interest in speedway and it would have helped as a sweetener for his dad, as a prospective advertiser, that we were prepared to let Michael have after-meeting and interval rides.

"It was very quickly evident he had a lot of talent. He looked good on a bike, quick and confident. In no time at all he became a regular interval attraction.

"Ivan Mauger (and many others) remember seeing this skinny kid do four perfect laps which timekeeper George Chappell routinely clocked at maybe a second or so slower than the top riders had been doing during the match."

Andy recalls Michael's on-track debut appearance at Lynn before he'd bought him his first speedway bike: "The local youth motorcycle club was running a little competition for their youngsters in the interval. We hoped that Michael would be able to join in with them but the club principle said it wasn't possible because he wasn't a member.

"We were so disappointed but they eventually allowed him to join in on condition that he started off a 25-yard handicap. The other youngsters had only gone as far as the third corner on the first lap when Michael went past them all and disappeared into the distance. I thought, 'well, there's a clue here somewhere!'

"At that point Cyril Crane perked up, had a look and said: 'You'd better come along every week and ride in the interval so that we can keep an eye on him.' That's what we did – and Michael went round the Lynn track in incredible times.

"The Lynn management made their minds up very quickly that they thought he had lots of potential but they obviously wanted to see what he was like on a speedway bike."

Michael recalls: "I think I was 14 when we bought my first speedway bike at Hackney – a two-valve Jawa that used to belong to Hawks' No.1 Garry

Middleton. It had blue glitter-guards and I wanted it the moment I saw it.

"When Dad and I arrived at Hackney Stadium they had eight or nine bikes all lined up in a row inside promoter Len Silver's office block at the back of the pits. They were looked after by Terry 'Bert' Busch, the Hackney mechanic, and were probably used by trainees at their Saturday morning training school. I decided straight away which one I wanted. There I was, sat on this bike, 'practicing' on it. My heart was already set on it but Dad told me to hang on because we weren't sure which bike was for sale.

"I think Dad was surprised when Len came out of his room and actually handled the sale himself. Dad had got to know him pretty well from going to watch at Hackney on Friday nights with his mate, Dave Nicholls, before they drove on down to Dover to catch the ferry to France for their moto-cross meetings.

"Len could clearly see what bike I wanted and I'm going 'yes, yes, yes!'. And, lo and behold, that was the one that happened to be for sale! Dad paid something like three or four hundred quid for it and when we got it home I polished it every day for three weeks. It was the same bike I rode when I started at Boston in 1975."

That encounter at Hackney in January 1973 was the first time Michael had met Len Silver but their paths would cross many times in the years that followed. When Lee was trying to rebuild his life in the new millennium, he would have cause to be very grateful to one of the sport's best known promoters for having faith in him when very few others in speedway did.

In the meantime, the teenage Michael continued to impress all onlookers with his weekly interval rides, although he admits there were the occasional setbacks before he mastered the 500cc Jawa.

"Because we bought it during the winter, January I think, the weather was cold and I had to be patient and wait for the ground to thaw before I was able to ride it for the first time at King's Lynn," he recalls. "The track was rock solid but once I got out there I was backing the bike into the corners, just as I had done previously on my Tiger Cub.

"I felt completely at ease and in control but the people watching told me to calm down and I soon realised why. The sun came out and the surface became a bit tacky. I went out once and the bike lurched forward a couple of times, although I managed to control it.

"Then, as a guide to see how well I was really doing, instead of going round on my own they put me out with Steve Taylor – I later rode with him in the Mildenhall training track team before he went on to ride for Peterborough in the National League. Not only was I on the pace, I was leading him down the back straight but I didn't shut off going into the third corner. The track had gone to pulp, it was as grippy as hell, and I just didn't turn.

"I went straight on into the fence. That was it . . . new diamond and new forks bent and a right bollocking from Dad! 'That's why we kept telling you to take it

Abrasive Aussie Garry Middleton put Michael in his place during a training school at Cradley.

"It was very quickly evident he had a lot of talent. He looked good on a bike, quick and confident. In no time at all he became a regular interval attraction."

a bit easier,' they all said when I hobbled back to the pits."

Michael remembers his first close encounter with Garry Middleton whose Jawa machine Michael rode when the Australian international ran a midweek winter training school at Cradley Heath.

"I went there as part of the deal we did when we bought the bike from Len," he explained. "I wasn't old enough to actually take part in the training school – you had to be 16 – but Len thought it would be a good idea to go along there anyway and receive some pointers from Garry.

"I left my brain in the toolbox again and went at it – full gas. He was straight on my case, saying he wanted me to learn the 'proper way', so he placed bollards on different parts of the track and I had to either go inside or outside them according to his instructions.

"Later, he took the bollards away and sent me out on my own again to see

'L' of a prospect. Michael had to fit learner plates to his 50cc road bike – even though he was blasting round King's Lynn and other tracks on a 500cc Jawa.

what I had learnt. I only went and got my bloody footrest stuck in the safety fence halfway down the straight, didn't I? I was doing a Superman impersonation through the air – but without the bike! I wasn't badly hurt, just bruised up, but my pride had been dented.

"Garry laid into me big-time, like I couldn't believe, and he scared me a bit. 'I didn't mean to crash!' I told him, thinking 'that's another set of forks to replace'."

Middleton was a loud, brash Aussie and never shy of venting his views. In 1971 he brought Wimbledon's prestige Internationale meeting to an abrupt haul when he phoned the referee from the pits and falsely accused Ivan Mauger of using the banned nitro fuel additive.

A self-proclaimed 'champion' who never did deliver on his bold promises to reach the top in speedway, he had regular run-ins with rivals and referees, so berating a kid who hadn't heeded his words of wisdom would have come easy to him.

"I was running around like a lunatic, working my nuts off from six in the morning until twenty past eight, when I had to catch the bus to school. Sometimes I'd be chasing the bus up the road with newspapers still stuffed in my hand – well, on the days when I bothered to go to school that is!"

"He really bollocked me and said that I wouldn't be going anywhere until I started listening to him," says Michael. "It was good advice, though, because the next time I rode, I didn't go flat out and remembered what Garry had told me. The bike didn't get bent again and I had it for a long while."

Ironically, a few years later, the same Garry Middleton was dropped from the King's Lynn team in which Michael Lee, his one-time rookie pupil, was the 16-year-old rising star.

Martin Rogers, who quit journalism to become general manager at Lynn in 1973, continues to recall the emergence of the club's finest ever young discovery: "During the next two or three years the relationship with the Lees developed. Michael was a pleasant, polite boy. His parents, Andy and Val, were extremely nice people and they appreciated the encouragement they were getting to steer Michael towards a speedway future."

"The deal with King's Lynn," said Michael, "is that they would look after me and I could practice there as often as I wanted to and go round in the interval free of charge. We were all quite happy with that arrangement.

"There were no flies on Cyril Crane and Martin Rogers and, ideally, they wanted my name on a contact there and then, although you couldn't sign a legally binding

"Give us your autograph, Tiddler!". Ian Turner shows the spectacular style that made him such a big favourite with Michael and other Lynn fans.

"I'd hang over the pit fence and bug the same riders for their autographs every week. I must have got Tiddler Turner's signature 200 times!"

BSPA contract until you were 16. It was a long time for me to wait."

Until that momentous day dawned, he would continue to hone his riding skills by practicing at every opportunity. He had a one-track mind – King's Lynn.

"I remember as a 14-year-old kid supporting the likes of Bettsy, Howard Cole, Simmo and Ian Turner," says Michael. "Simmo was always Mr Smooth and Bettsy was, of course, the big crowd favourite but the one I enjoyed watching the most was 'Tiddler' Turner – he wasn't a No.1 but he was tiny and spectacular and always hanging off the bike.

"I'd hang over the pit fence and bug the same riders for their autographs every week. I must have got Tiddler Turner's signature 200 times! Then, suddenly, I'm up there doing my interval rides and it did cross my mind on a few occasions, 'I wonder if they recognise me as the brat who always wanted their autographs?'

"I remember Bettsy coming over to me and I was so much in shock that I almost tried to hide behind my bike. I was ever such a shy kid. One of his comments was: 'We're going to have to be looking out for you in a few years time' and I thought: 'Bloody hell! Is he saying what I think he's saying?'

King's Lynn's 1974 team that Michael rubbed shoulders with in the Saddlebow Road pits. Back row, left to right: Alan Littlechild (team manager), Eddie Reeves, Bob Humphreys and Barry Crowson. Front: Ray Bales, Malcolm Simmons, Terry Betts and Ian Turner.

"I also bought individual rosettes and photos of the riders. I was just obsessed by King's Lynn."

A decent looking set of leathers was also high on his agenda.

Now while his father did a lot to help launch his son's career and guide him through the best part of it, there were some things that Michael had to do for himself. Like a morning paper round to enable him to save up enough cash to buy his own first custom-made leathers.

His first pair was a very basic orange outfit that had been hanging off the shelf in Andy Lee's shop for some time before Michael put them to good use in his earliest junior riding days. "I think they were a pair of Lewis Leathers and I looked like a carrot in them – but they had sat on the shelf in Dad's shop and no-one was going to buy them!" he said. They would do for now but Michael had his sights set on a more tasteful design ahead of his long-awaited league racing bow.

"Dad had paid for everything to date but to earn the money I needed to buy the leathers I really wanted I did a paper round, or rather FOUR rounds in two villages! I'd do two rounds in the morning and two more in the evening. And they were big villages, so I was running around like a lunatic, working my nuts off from six in the morning until twenty past eight, when I had to catch the bus to school. Sometimes I'd be chasing the bus up the road with newspapers still stuffed in my hand – well, on the days when I bothered to go to school that is!

"I was fortunate that the man who owned the village newsagents, David Gray, was also a good friend of the family. He'd been up to see me ride round at Lynn a few times, so he knew why I was doing the paper rounds and what I was saving up for. Most kids wouldn't have got much more than £3 per paper round but because David knew me well, he paid me £20 a week for my four rounds.

"Dad was friendly with Jimmy Aird, a guy he used to ride against in motocross and who was by now running TT Leathers, a company in County Durham who at that time had a good reputation as one of the leading manufacturers of motorcycle leathers. As time passed and the day when I would be old enough to make my official speedway debut approached, I wrote off to TT Leathers asking how to go about ordering my own set from them.

"Jimmy Aird wrote me a nice, polite letter back, saying how he knew of me through Dad and so on. Also enclosed was a blank picture showing the front and back of a pair of leathers which I had to colour in to indicate how I wanted them to be made up, along with my size.

"While I gave a lot of thought to the design, I continued to save for another two weeks and in the end I had about £500, which I kept tucked away under my bed.

"I wanted a flash set of leathers, with different coloured bands and stars – the lot. Mum was adamant that they wouldn't be able to meet my design specifications but I kept telling her they would – and I tell you what, they bloody well did too! I sent my order off and three weeks later I received a parcel in the post."

The first proper pair of brightly coloured Lee leathers were made in green and orange with red, white and blue bands on the arms, waist and legs, plus black stars, and the name of his first main sponsor 'Andy Lee Motorcycles' stitched into the lower half. On the chest were the words 'MIKE' and 'JAWA'.

"I wore them around the house for a week to 'break' then in. No joking, I had them on every day," continued Michael. "They fitted me perfectly and felt great – but there was no bill with them. Dad phoned Jimmy asking how much we had to pay. With everything I had on them, we reckoned they should have cost £700 but Jimmy did us a big favour and charged only £300. I spent the £200 I had left over on a brand new pair of personalised mudguards for my bike.

"But I'll never forget the help I received from TT Leathers and Jimmy Aird's kind gesture that helped me to get started."

Take Off!

The kid's flying at Mildenhall

Chapter 3

THE winter of 1974-75 saw one of the most intensive winter training programmes yet conducted throughout the UK. Trainees (and their fathers-cum chauffeurs) ignored new Labour Chancellor Denis Healey's controversial 25 per cent VAT hike on petrol prices and travelled the length and breadth of the country to fuel their dreams with endless laps.

Michael didn't have to venture far from home for the Sunday morning sessions at Mildenhall, where brothers Bernie and Barry Klatt had built a trim 300-yard track on Suffolk farmland owned by Terry Waters. The tranquility of the fens was only interrupted by the roar of Jawas and the rumbling engines of the United States Air Force planes screaming out as they flew hundreds of feet above the track at West Row Stadium on their way to and from USAF Mildenhall. But the 'take-off' stirring most interest in these remote parts of the Suffolk countryside was the eagerly anticipated launch of Michael Lee's career.

He quickly established himself as the one to watch in the Fen Tigers team that contested unofficial training track challenge matches against similar amateur sides from Stoke, Crewe and the Kent-based Iwade Colts, who were run from an old gun site on the Isle of Sheppey by Hackney star Barry Thomas and his brother Ivor.

The gangly style was distinctive even then.

First speedway portrait – Michael launches his track career with the Mildenhall training track team.

FOURTEEN SPEEDWAY STAR, November 2, 1974

FEN TIGERS ARE READY

MILDENHALL IS SOMETHING new on the speedway training scheme. Formulated by Bernie Klatt with the able assistance of younger brother Barry — they both admit to having been frustrated trainees themselves — the Fen Tigers are now operating from their second circuit.

"Our gaining access to the first field upset our farmer/landlord a bit," says Bernie, "but things are much better now."

Farmer Terry Waters provided the present site in April, 1973.

Now, Mildenhall boasts a 300-yards ircuit, constructed on a 1,000-ton chalk ase, with a red shale surface and a pukka wooden safety fence gradually replacing the original straw bales.

"When finished, and subject to County Council approval, we would like to apply for an official Training Track Licence from the Speedway Control Board and one day, perhaps, make a bid for full League status," adds Bernie.

The Klatts were originally attracted to speedway when King's Lynn opened in 1965. They'd both visited Norwich previously, but King's Lynn became a egular haunt, the "bug" bit and with school friend Ian Turner and other local Mildenhall hopefuls they set about establishing themselves in the sport.

Turner was the only one to make the rade, although now the Mildenhall ... is lookin... several of their ... kin...

THE TRAINING SCENE No. 1 — MILDENHALL

by Dave Stevens

No machines are yet available for hire but fuel and oil can be purchased. Trainees must have all their own equipment and for the present make their own insurance arrangements which, Bernie stresses, is compulsory.

"There are several good policies available," he says, "and as well as protecting the rider they are of benefit to his fellow trainees too."

Sessions are held each Sunday from around 11.30 am until dusk at £2.25. More detailed information is available from Bernie Klatt, at 102 Church Road, West Row, near Mildenhall Suffolk, telephone Isleham 475.

From the A11, one should turn north at Barton Mills roundabout and head towards Mildenhall where a quick left and then a right turn leads to West Row. Left at Morley's Garage and right into The Green will reveal the track about ...miles on ...

Michael Lee — King's Lynn's schoolboy prospect.

His first appearance in *Speedway Star*.

"The tranquility of the fens was only interrupted by the roar of Jawas and the rumbling engines of the United States Air Force planes screaming out as they flew hundreds of feet above the track at West Row Stadium on their way to and from USAF Mildenhall."

In an era when there were many more enthusiastic young prospects keen to take up the sport and the opportunities for them to practice and learn were considerably greater than they are today, there were also training facilities available at many other venues: King's Lynn, Boston, Belle Vue, Hackney, Coventry, Ellesmere Port, Eastbourne, Weymouth, Workington, plus Coatbridge and Paisley in Scotland.

England were worthy World Team champions and the sport – if not the economy – was thriving, thanks largely to regular television coverage on ITV and through the popular national red-top dailies. Even some of the winter training matches would attract hundreds of curious spectators eager to catch a glimpse of the future.

The King's Lynn 'Starlets' of 1974. Max Brown, Michael, Richard Davey, Brian Paddington, David Gagen (on bike), Andy Sims and Kelvin Mullarkey.

On parade and itching to show what he could do.

Through its regular 'Training Scene' column, *Speedway Star* followed the progress of Lee closely that winter and no-one who braved the chill winds blowing across the open fields surrounding Mildenhall Speedway were disappointed by what they saw. The lanky kid with the matchstick arms and legs didn't look much like your typical sportsman, but the near six-footer had developed his own unique style and was clearly going places in speedway.

Bernie Klatt said at the time: "Michael has more silverware on his sideboard before turning professional than many riders will ever win."

Apart from the thrill of winning races, Michael also loved the camaraderie fostered by these fiercely contested junior fixtures.

Lee signs

KING'S LYNN'S first capture in 1975, 16-year-old Michael Lee, signs on the dotted line watched by Stars general manager Martin Rogers and his father Andy (right).

Michael who leaves school at Easter, practised hard for two years in anticipation of the day when he was old enough to engage in official competition.

Already his times at Saddlebow Road compare favourably with those of accomplished professionals and he will probably be loaned out to a New National League track for additional experience.

Got him! A happy Martin Rogers and Andy Lee oversee Michael signing his first King's Lynn contract at the age of 16.

"I certainly didn't want Michael signing for Boston because it would have given them the opportunity to influence his future in a way which wouldn't necessarily have been all for his best interests, and King's Lynn could easily have ended up being charged a fee to sign a rider they had cultivated!"

One weekend in January, he headed north for matches at Stoke and Crewe in the van with his father but after top-scoring in both matches he returned to Suffolk with his team-mates. They all travelled together in an articulated lorry supplied by haulage contractor Brian Taylor-Balls (Tigers' regular timekeeper), while Bernie Klatt's father Theo paid all fuel bills.

Regulars alongside Michael in the Mildenhall team that winter included Kevin Jolly, Paul Clipstone, Paul Gilbert, Graham Kerry, Fred Mills, Paul Davey and Steve Taylor. With Ipswich's Mick Hines and team manager Ron Bagley supervising some of the sessions, it was no surprise that Jolly, a 16-year-old schoolboy grass-tracker, ended up at his local senior team, who then loaned him to Mildenhall for the Tigers' first season of official New National League racing in 1975.

Mildenhall would love to have included Lee in their NNL team, too, but the hottest property in East Anglian speedway circles had already given a verbal promise to begin his first season of competitive action as a King's Lynn rider – initially on loan to their NNL feeder club Boston. Lynn did actually apply to run a second 'Starlets' team in the NNL shortly before the start of the '75 season but when that was turned down by first division track bosses, Lee inevitably joined the Boston Barracudas, where Lynn co-promoter Cyril Crane also held the promoting reins at Lincolnshire's only second division track. It was common in those days for senior league clubs to have a tie-up with a more junior team from the lower division and the Lynn-Boston link dated back to 1970.

Martin Rogers explained why it was King's Lynn that secured the teenager's coveted signature: "When his 16th birthday was approaching I was working all the angles to ensure Michael signed for King's Lynn and that meant snuffing out opposition from another quarter – none other than Lynn's co-promoter Cyril Crane, who wanted him to sign for Boston.

"I'd accepted the general manager's job at Lynn very much because I felt a loyalty to the Littlechilds, especially Violet, Maurice's widow, after Maurice died in July 1972. To be fair to Cyril, he kept the Norfolk Speedways promotion as a 50/50 thing, as it had started out, but because he also had other interests there were occasions when loyalties were put to the test.

"I certainly didn't want Michael signing for Boston because it would have given them the opportunity to influence his future in a way which wouldn't necessarily have been all for his best interests, and King's Lynn could easily have ended up being charged a fee to sign a rider they had cultivated!

"As it happened, Andy was suspicious of Cyril's motives, so he was entirely comfortable about having Michael sign for Lynn with a view to be loaned out to Boston to start his career path, and having second-halves and such other opportunities as presented themselves at Saddlebow Road.

"I went to Cambridge in December 1974 to get Michael's signature on a BSPA contract, and as he was only 16, Andy's signature had to be obtained as well."

You might imagine that a kid as richly talented as Michael would be the subject of a Dutch auction as speedway clubs from all over the land clamoured for his services and word spread fast that here was a brilliant talent with the potential to go all the way to the top. Not so.

Rogers confirmed: "There was not a penny paid for Michael's initial signature, neither asked for nor offered. I 'sold' Michael and, just as importantly, Andy on the merits of him coming to King's Lynn.

"I took along a photographer to record the occasion, and the picture made it into the local papers and speedway publications."

The East Anglian media would soon be hearing a lot more about young Michael Lee.

Like Father, Like Son

Meet Andy Lee

Chapter 4

WHATEVER Michael went on to achieve as a world class rider, he appreciates that much of it would not have been possible without the help and mechanical expertise of his father, who enjoyed a long and successful career as a motorcycle sports star in his own right.

Just how much Andy did to support his son throughout his life, on and off the track, will become evident at various times throughout this book. It hasn't always been easy for Michael's parents – far from it – and Michael knows that at times he has tested their unconditional love and tolerance to the limit.

But before we get too far ahead of ourselves with how Michael's career developed, let's first examine the huge role Andy Lee played in setting him on the path to speedway fame and fortune, their father and son relationship and Andy's own interesting background.

He was born in Sawbridgeworth, Hertfordshire in August 1935. "My family moved to Girton, near Cambridge, when I was too young to remember," he says. "I had no interest in motorcycles until a neighbour from our road took me to a scrambling event when I was probably 12-years-old. It was the most exciting thing I'd ever seen – I liked the smell of the bikes and everything about it. I wanted to ride a motorbike from then on, although it was some time before I was able to do so.

"Eventually, my mother sponsored me for a cheap motorcycle – a Raleigh with a hand-gear change and Blackburn engine. It cost 10 shillings (50p in today's money) and came in pieces in a dustbin. We put it together with the help of some friends, got it running and I rode it around local fields. I just loved motorcycles from then on," says Andy.

But his passion for bikes was certainly not shared by his father Norman, who worked in the civil service as a collector of taxes.

"I bought a bike that was suitable for riding in a scramble but my father was dead against it, which is probably the biggest factor in my motorcycle career. He never liked me messing around on motorcycles, mainly because he spent a lot of money sending me to a posh school, Perse School at Cambridge, and I got expelled because I spent too much time with motor bikes.

"When it came to sports afternoon, I'd just get somebody else to call out my name at register. I was elsewhere, either working on my bike or riding it. I was caught playing truant several times until they expelled me.

"I got slung out at the worst possible time, just before the equivalent of GCSE exams, when I was 15. Dad was dismayed. Unfortunately, we never saw eye to

The classic moto-cross style that earned Andy Lee countless titles and sustained success over more than two decades.

eye on that, right up until the day the poor old boy died. He was always saying that I would never make anything of my life and he could have been right – but he wasn't. Luck took me the right way.

"If I hadn't gone on to ride and work with motor bikes, God only knows how I would have turned out. Because from the age of 13 onwards it's been nothing but motorcycles – be it my own riding career, working at the shops, my interest in road-racing (we sponsored riders when we had the shops), and of course my involvement in speedway with Michael."

Andy explains how the foundations for his mechanical expertise were laid: "I got a job as an instrument maker for one of the departments at the University of Cambridge, where they made telescopes and that's where I learned machine work. I went to night school and passed one of the engineering courses, so I got a bit of knowledge and then I had a lucky break.

"The father of one of the lads I went to school with was a director of a firm called King and Harper, a big company in Cambridge that sold cars, bikes and just about everything. I was showing a little bit of promise in local events and he presented me with a 197cc Francis Barnett competition motorcycle to go scrambling on. That would have been in 1952.

"I made progress in local scrambles, although to be honest I was a bit of a wild, young Herbert. Whether I had that much talent, I don't know, but I certainly had something – a lot of drive, I'd say. I badly wanted to win.

"After I began winning meetings around Cambridge and also further afield, they presented me with good quality bikes such as a BSA Gold Star. When I started to do well in national events, I gained factory works support from BSA and Matchless when I was 18, which was great.

"I went in the forces for three years and, luckily, I was stationed at RAF West Raynham in Norfolk. They were very good about letting me have time off, so I kept racing most weekends, with Harpers continuing to look after my bikes between meetings.

"I was 20 when I came out of the RAF and had my first trip abroad soon after demob. I got a replacement ride at a meeting near Lyon in the South of France – I went with Jack Hubbard, another top rider from the era, and finished second. I thoroughly enjoyed it, plus they paid me quite a lot of money, which I hadn't even expected because I was only covering for an injured rider. I gradually made a name for myself, particularly in France."

Andy rode against all the top scrambles stars of his era. Viewers of BBC TV's Grandstand sports show in the 60s will doubtless recall winter Saturday afternoons spent watching the spectacular muddy exploits of household names such as Jeff Smith, John Banks, Vic Eastwood, Dave Bickers, Chris Horsfield, Derek Rickman, Arthur Lampkin and the tall Arthur Browning (who went on to ride speedway) battling to control their machines as they jumped, twisted and turned their way around each undulating course. There are still old video recordings (commentary by Murray Walker) of Andy riding his Matchless Metisse to be found on the YouTube website, which serve as a wonderful reminder of those evocative, grainy black and white days when scrambling was one of Britain's most popular motorcycle sports followed by a large TV audience.

But it was mainly on the continent, in Belgium, Spain and Switzerland as well as France, where Andy built his towering reputation as one of the best motor-crossers in the business.

"I did come back here to ride in a few British Championships but I'd only do the individual legs, not the whole series," he explained. "And I did a few Grand Prix meetings too. But in those days they didn't pay the riders very well and, to be honest, I was far better off doing my own thing."

He remembers 1965 as his most successful season of racing. "That was my year – you have those when, you don't know why because you're not riding any differently to any other time, but everything just seems to go your way. I had no breakdowns and I think I won 30 out of 32 international races. By then I was riding a Metisse, a beautiful bike specially made by the Rickman brothers.

"My biggest honour was being picked to ride for my country as a privateer. Normally, only factory riders were considered but in 1964 I was chosen as one of five riders to compete for England in the Motocross of Nations, which we won. Although I won some big international races there is nothing bigger than riding for your country."

Andy was still a moto-cross competitor right up until 1980 – the year Michael won the speedway World Championship – at the age of 45 but he never had the urge to try speedway himself and was always content to remain a supporter on the terraces. He has, though, had the occasional spin on Michael's 500cc machines and this intelligent man's thoughts on the sport are always worth hearing.

"I've tried Mike's bikes," he continues. "It amazes me why they need so much power in such a confined area and how they use as much power as they've got. It's trick motorcycling – I soon found that out when I rode the bike. You do the opposite to what you're supposed to do – you come into the corner, flick the back wheel out and accelerate. If you shut the throttle, you go straight, so there's a trick to it.

"I was fine riding around Mildenhall, because it's almost a circle compared to many tracks and I could keep the bike sliding because the track was slick. Then I went to King's Lynn to ride in a charity race in the interval and, of course, you thunder down the straight so fast, there comes a point where you've got to shut the throttle and break it. That was more difficult.

"I couldn't get my head around not having brakes. I was always thinking that if somebody fell off in front of me, I wouldn't be able to lay it down, and it's absolutely essential to be able to do that.

"I was at my best at the start. I wasn't afraid to whack it on and I used to make the gate but then didn't know what to do next!"

The 'new boys' at Boston in 1975.

"When Michael was riding we didn't use other tuners and did everything ourselves, in-house, and we were very self-contained. Therefore we probably had an advantage and a few 'secrets'."

Between weekend meetings on the continent, Andy kept himself very busy running the motorcycle sales business he built up from scratch. "I'd worked as a motorcycle salesman for King and Harper but didn't like the job – I was more interested in the mechanical side," he explains.

"So in about 1960 a friend of mine, Ken Covell, and I found a place in Ely and opened our own shop selling motorcycles and scooters." After Andy and Ken amicably went their separate ways, Lee senior bought two shops.

"I really expanded and things were going very well on and off the bike. I bought a property in Cambridge (307 Mill Road) and we set up as agents for BMW, Suzuki and Yamaha. Then a shop became available at Royston in Herts (4 Kneesworth Street), so I bought that too and we became agents for Honda, Triumph and Yamaha. The only top manufacturer I didn't have an agency tie-up with at the time was Kawasaki. Otherwise, we were selling the lot in a 15-mile radius.

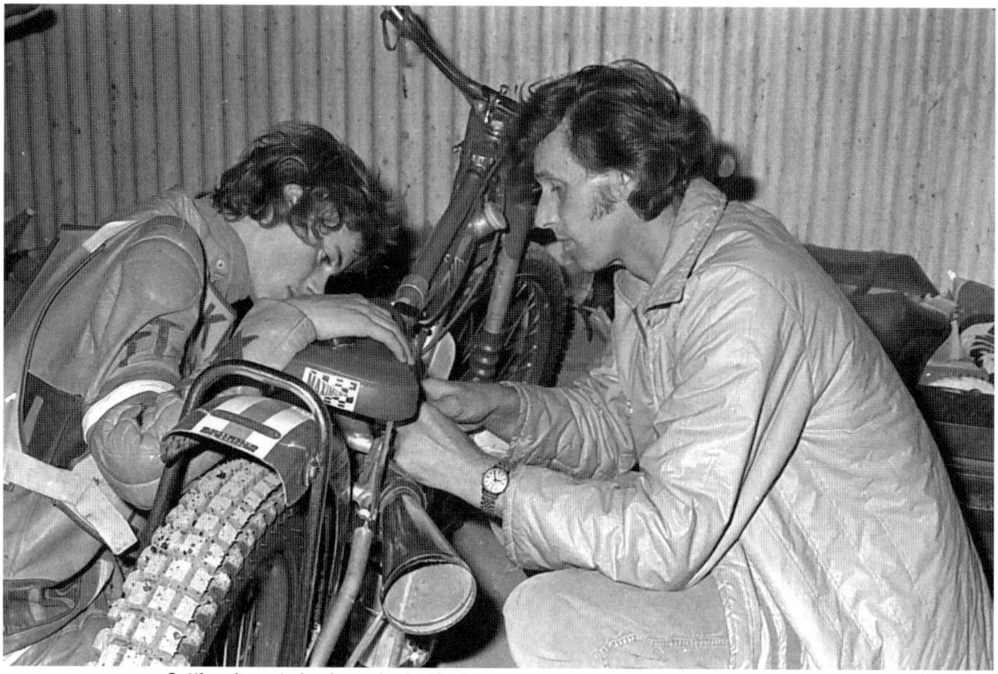

Getting down to business in the Hackney pits in 1975 on one of Michael's first appearances for Lynn.

"We were very enthusiastic dealers and did really well over a period of years. We were into it really deep, investing a lot of money in the business and it really paid off," he says.

Michael also spent some time working in his father's shops but once the speedway bug had bitten and he became obsessed by the dream of becoming a shale star, Lee senior had to divide his time in other areas. It would have been easy for Andy to have put his son in touch with a capable mechanic who could handle the fundamentals and arrange for his engines to be tuned elsewhere.

But the commitment Andy made to Michael just before he was about to launch his speedway career at the age of 16 would not only give him a more than useful head start over his contemporary rivals, but stand him in good stead to this day. Andy was happy to invest his time and effort in Michael from the word go but he also made sure that his attentive son absorbed everything that went on in the workshop.

Andy described Michael as "a natural" in the workshop. "He grasped everything very quickly. We had all that we needed in the workshop, so you could say it was relatively easy to follow what was going on.

"We were buying bikes and doing them up so that Mike understood everything about them. As well as the two-valve Jawa we bought from Len Silver at Hackney we acquired another old one from someone at Mildenhall. We went right through it, even spraying the frame, and I made Mike do everything so that he knew what had to be done to the bike.

"He wanted to do it and I think he knew he had to do it."

Many speedway riders, including some of the all-time greats, had very little

Proud Dad with the 1977 British Champion.

Let's got to work . . . Michael pushing his Weslake into the pits, closely followed by his mentor and mechanical guru.

understanding of how their bikes worked, much less a sound technical knowledge of what went on inside the engine, and all the other little 'tricks' that make the difference between winning and losing. Andy Lee made it his business to ensure Michael understood as much as possible from the earliest age.

"It's very important. When Michael was riding we didn't use other tuners and did everything ourselves, in-house, and we were very self-contained. Therefore we probably had an advantage and a few 'secrets'.

"Michael was totally involved with me at the time in building engines and bikes and what he learned then has never been forgotten. In fact, he's putting it into practice today by doing engines for all types of riders and making a damn good job of it. Technology has obviously advanced a little bit since the days when he was riding but that knowledge is still there.

"When we first came into speedway I always considered us as outsiders and felt a little bit at odds with the sport. We were a unique couple in a way and nobody likes an upstart – and I'm talking about both him and me. But, eventually, I think we were accepted as new boys and got on well with everyone around us."

Andy's ability to 'think outside the box' also benefited Michael from an early stage.

"I thought riders and mechanics were steeped in tradition," he recalls. "I couldn't work out for a while why they were doing certain things, so we went down another path and became a completely self-contained unit.

"For example, I saw other riders' bikes running without air filters and thought: 'That's a lot of good for a bike – all the dust going straight into the carb and the engine!' It was only later that proper air filters came in that protected the engine but we had one fitted to Mike's bikes pretty quickly. We disguised it, but we fitted an air filter and that gave more life to the engine."

Recalling the period when he attended speedway meetings as a spectator, Andy says: "To be honest, I found it a bit weird that some of the riders didn't seem to be particularly mechanically minded, which I was, but they could ride a speedway bike – make no mistake about it."

As early as 1974, when Michael was wowing them every week at the Mildenhall training sessions, people recognised it wasn't only Michael that the opposition were up against. He had a very formidable mechanical guru, too. Fen Tigers' co-promoter Bernie Klatt commented: "I don't think it's generally recognised how good his father Andy is with a speedway engine. I reckon him to be among the best engine tuners in the business."

John Berry, the former England team manager and respected Ipswich promoter, later observed: "With all of that mechanical expertise, experience and talent they made a powerful, if maybe slightly unpredictable, pairing."

Andy and Val Lee divorced many years ago but Val has never underestimated her former husband's role in their son's success. She says: "Andy did an awful lot for Michael and taught him most of what he knows about speedway engines today."

At a shade under 6ft, Michael stands a few inches shorter than Andy but both are slim in build and the similarities are obvious. But do they display many of the same characteristics?

One who believes so is John Berry, who says: "To understand Michael, you have to look to his father. Maybe motorbike riding skills were in the genes? I doubt that. What I suspect is that Michael was raised in a different world to the average kid . . . a world of motorbikes and competition and rubbing shoulders with some of the best motorcyclists in the world.

"Also, Andy's was an off-beat world – a 'Bohemian' life where he would spend a lot of time away on the Continent. Like Michael afterwards, Andy was also well liked by his peers, but was known to have a volatile personality, be something of a rebel and had his own occasional brushes with officialdom."

Val says: "Michael takes after Andy in the sense that he is very independent. Michael rode in a team sport whereas Andy rode as an individual and did his own thing, but I don't think that rubbed off on Michael. He has always liked company and had friends around. People he knew through speedway would stop off at our house and sometimes they would stay overnight."

Pensive faces as Michael and Andy watch practice before the 1979 World Final in Katowice, Poland.

"I got slung out at the worst possible time, just before the equivalent of GCSE exams, when I was 15. Dad was dismayed. Unfortunately, we never saw eye to eye on that, right up until the day the poor old boy died. He was always saying that I would never make anything of my life and he could have been right – but he wasn't. Luck took me the right way."

As in all father-son relationships, there are inevitable ups and downs, especially when those relationships also become a working partnership, partly played out in the public gaze and the pressures of highly competitive motorcycle sport are brought to bear. One of the first things Andy tried to impress upon his son was the value of money.

A principled man from a middle class background, Andy says: "Michael was earning a lot of money from the start and he probably didn't understand the value of money, whereas I did. I started with absolutely nothing, just as he did, and it's so hard to get started."

Berry observed: "Relationships between fathers and sons are often up and down affairs but Andy and Michael always had a far stronger bond than most – except when they were in dispute with each other. Then the relationship would rocket to the other end of the scale."

Andy had a job to recall any specific disagreements between him and Michael that actually occurred at the track during a meeting. But, of course, there were times when words were exchanged.

"He knew he couldn't move me but he had to let off on someone," Andy says with a smile. "Terry Betts, who would be parked up next to us in the pits, used to curl up laughing.

"One day I did something different to the bike during a league match. Michael had won his first race by the length of the straight but he came back in and said to me: 'That's bloody useless, it won't go'.

"And then the tannoy announcer informed everyone that Michael had just broken the track record! I said to him: 'What more do you want?' So he said: 'Well, it still isn't going well'. What can you do?

"The reason why he said the bike wasn't going well enough is because the track was so good and smooth, the bike wasn't breaking traction, so the rider feels as if he's going slow.

"It sounds boring, but I can't remember us having any major bust-ups at a meeting. Sometimes he'd ridden very badly and that would cause friction between us. I could never accept it If I thought he wasn't trying – and neither would his mum. I remember once she went down to the pits at Ipswich to have a word with Michael. He was just messing about and didn't want to race. Kept touching the tapes, you know. So Valerie went after him – ladies were not supposed to go into the pits but she did. She told him: 'If you're going to ride, then race. If not, clear off'.

"I wouldn't get on to him if he was riding badly, because everybody has poor meetings from time to time and you just have to work it out. You can't win 'em all.

"But if I thought he was just buggering about, I'd remind him that everyone around him was putting in a lot of effort and that we weren't there to bugger about. That's when we would have words.

"He'd say: 'The track is shit' and I'd say: 'Yeah, and it's shit for everybody'. It's what I've always said. A lot of the tracks were poor then, and when you see them watering with a garden hose you know it's not going to be much good. And yet there were times when he was ideally suited to go out in the first race because conditions didn't usually worry him."

Val recalls: "They were both quite strong-willed and I just let them get on with it and sort themselves out. They would flare up at each other but I knew they wouldn't fall out for long. It was usually all forgotten in 24 hours."

"On the face of it, until things went wrong, we had an excellent relationship," Andy added.

In 1975, there were no signs of anything going wrong for Michael. He appeared to the world to be destined for greatness...

Very Good Friday

Willie and the Whippersnapper

Chapter 5

ENGLAND captain Ray Wilson had beaten the very best in his illustrious career. In 1971 he made history as the first Englishman to score a maximum in the World Team Cup Final, so the visit of his Leicester Lions team to King's Lynn for the Border Trophy match on March 28, 1975 held no fears for the former British Champion.

His biggest concern on that Good Friday morning was the unseasonal snow blizzards sweeping across the East Midlands and Norfolk that cast serious doubt on whether the meeting would go ahead. It did, but there were some unexpected changes to both teams before a belated start to proceedings.

Two of World Cup Willie's team-mates, Tony Lomas and Norman Storer, never made it along the A47 to Saddlebow Road for the scheduled 11.00am start time and so the visitors had to be loaned a couple of Lynn juniors, 18-year-old Robert Hollingworth and Pete Smith, to make up the numbers.

King's Lynn were due to use the rider replacement facility to cover for the heat leader denied them in the winter Rider Control shake-up but they agreed to forego that and, instead, gave an unexpected debut to their new 16-year-old hopeful Michael Lee. He was programmed to appear only in the second-half event and was surprised to be handed the No.3 racejacket, a role normally filled by an established heat leader and which meant he would be pitted against the opposing No.1 twice under the 13-heat formula.

"Although Ray wasn't happy immediately after I'd beaten him, fair play to him, he came over and shook my hand at the end of the meeting. I think he was stunned. I was too!"

The Lynn faithful had been counting the days until Lee was old enough to make his debut for the Stars and now, quite unexpectedly, his big chance had come. After just one week in the second-half at Saddlebow Road and a few appearances at second division level for Boston, this time it was for real.

How would he handle it? Was he really as good as they said he was? Suddenly, there was a sense of anticipation about the place.

Lee finished a very creditable second to Lions' other England star Dave Jessup in Heat 3 before winning Heat 7 from Frank Auffret and Stars' team-mate Eddie Reeves. Five points from two rides.

It couldn't get any better than this, but for Michael it did.

Leicester and England star Ray Wilson met his match.

In Heat 11 he and Ray Bales lined up against Ray Wilson and Lions' young loanee guest Hollingworth. 'Holly', who had caught the eye along with Michael at Boston in the early weeks of the season, shot in front and the visitors seemed headed for a 5-1 until Lee nipped past the vastly experienced 'Willie' on the inside coming off the second bend.

The crowd erupted.

A new star was born.

"It was like a break in the clouds," reflected Martin Rogers.

The fact that Hollingworth actually won the race is merely incidental to the Michael Lee story. Michael recalls: "It was a horribly cold and frosty morning and the track was a bit dodgy. Some riders were being a bit tentative, not wanting to get too close to anyone in case they lifted or their bike took off. Well, most of them were, but not me. I was definitely on it. I was going for it and telling myself: 'Yeah, I can handle this!'

"It happened on the second bend of the third lap. I'd seen Ray riding in World Finals, so I knew who he was – World Cup Willie and all that. He was comfortably riding the inside line when I suddenly got under him. We were elbow-to-elbow coming off the corner and I wasn't going to back off.

"As soon as it became obvious Michael had the talent and temperament to do well in the top division, we wanted to use any and every opportunity to include him."

"I'd done this sort of thing before as a kid when racing against mates on a pushbike and, to me, this was no different. So I got the throttle full on, almost pushing him out of the way."

A shell-shocked Wilson managed to recover his composure to lead Michael home when they met again in the final heat but Lee's nine points from four rides were the talking point of the match Lynn won by 46-32.

"When you beat someone like him for the first time, then things become clear in your head. It's a case of 'I'm capable of this now' and that's what kicked me off.

"Although Ray wasn't happy immediately after I'd beaten him, fair play to him, he came over and shook my hand at the end of the meeting. I think he was stunned. I was too!" added Michael.

The 1975 King's Lynn side had a slightly Dad's Army look about it. Malcolm Simmons, who had vied with the evergreen Terry Betts for the No.1 status in previous seasons, had left in search of greater recognition at Poole and was not adequately replaced.

Norwich-based Trevor Hedge, who was approaching 32, arrived from Wimbledon in exchange for Barry Crowson, while 45-year-old veteran Olle Nygren was well into his twilight days at the end of a distinguished career. Garry Middleton

Starry-eyed . . . early days at King's Lynn in 1975.

proved an unsatisfactory experiment as Lynn relied on Ian Turner and Ray Bales to support Betts at the top end while continuously plugging gaps with their youngsters on loan to Boston – Gagen, Billy Burton and especially Lee.

"The King's Lynn team in 1975 was in a bit of a state of flux," said Martin Rogers. "Contrary to the youth policy which we were plugging at those times, we signed Nygren to fill one of the spots but clearly he was at the end of his distinguished career.

"As soon as it became obvious Michael had the talent and temperament to do well in the top division, we wanted to use any and every opportunity to include him and David Gagen, who was also on loan to Boston. In those days you could use a number eight to replace an absentee team member and Nygren and Eddie Reeves (29) were both persuaded that their use-by date was up.

"That opened the door to include Michael for most matches as long as there was no clash with Boston's fixtures."

King's Lynn were in need of a new hero. So, too, were the Boston Barracudas.

New National Hero

Impressing Ivan and Briggo

Chapter 6

ANY doubts about Michael's ability to transfer his impressive winter training match form on to the next stage were immediately dispelled on the evening of March 16, as he won his first ever competitive race for Boston and contributed 12 points (from five rides) in their 40-38 KO Cup victory against rivals Peterborough. Rob Hollingworth's maximum was flawless but Lee's dozen, including three wins, confirmed a maturity way beyond his tender 16 years and 94 days.

It was another headline-making debut, albeit overshadowed by his heroics on his senior bow for King's Lynn against Leicester 10 days later, covered in the previous chapter.

But Michael didn't have everything his own way in those early weeks and months of 1975. He recalls an incident that served as a rude awakening.

He says: "Eddie Argall came down with Coatbridge and he took me out on the first bend – big-time. Dad actually went after him but I didn't have a clue what had happened because there were bikes piled on top of me as I tried to catch my breath down by the fence.

"We'd never seen this sort of thing before and I suddenly thought: 'Shit! Does this happen? Did he do it on purpose? I'd better learn quickly!'

"It was at that stage that I realised I couldn't become too friendly with other riders. It stunned me and made me realise I had to watch my backside. The first battering you get in your career is always an eye-opener."

Argall recalls the incident – his first crash since arriving in England for his debut NNL season – quite vividly. Talking today from his home at Hastings Point in New South Wales, he says: "I do remember it quite well. From my point of view, I was leading and riding my own race and the next thing I knew Michael and I tangled and we went down. I didn't know he was there on the outside and thankfully no-one was hurt.

"I was shit-scared laying on the track wondering what the hell had happened, what with Michael's dad trying to kill me along with Cyril Crane and the whole of Boston it seemed. I was stunned, because I was leading and could not understand that I was in the wrong.

"I didn't bother with the usual cold shower you had to put up with at Boston and got the hell out of there. I was stone broke and had no dad to fix and tune my one and only bike. I went back to Halifax at 30-to-40 miles an hour, to help save the fuel needed to get home.

"I was not an aggressive rider, especially for an Aussie, and I'm sure if you speak with some of my past team-mates they would agree.

"Ironically, I wanted to ride for Boston as it was more like a smaller Aussie track and I always went well there. I was going to ask Cyril after the meeting if he would consider me for the following year. Well, that all went out of the window after I tangled with their young star - and what a star Michael turned out to be. Well done to him!"

Happy days . . . the New National League has a new hero.

Although he had viewed many speedway meetings from the terraces long before his son became a rider, Andy Lee admits the inherent dangers of the sport hit home to him once he started watching Michael from the pits.

"I used to really worry for him," Andy says. "The thing that got me about the non-safety aspect of the stadiums was the floodlight pylons. I thought, 'how can they race a motorcycle without brakes, at fast speeds and in such a confined space, with lamp standards just the other side of the fence?' For me, that was horrific and I saw some terrible crashes. It seemed there were no safety regulations at all and it really did concern me. It wasn't how I perceived Michael and his ability, there were other riders involved."

'The Flying Paper Clip' turning it on.

Andy's anxieties were shared by his then wife. Val Lee added: "It used to worry me to death to see him hurtling around the track. Nine times out of 10 I couldn't watch him race for Mildenhall Juniors, Boston or King's Lynn. I'd go out into the car park and walk up and down until I knew the race had finished and I heard the announcer mention Michael's name."

Despite Michael's obvious talent and the fact that he was being widely tipped as a future champion, Val says she never considered her son to be a superstar in the making. "When they were all saying he was going to win this or win that, I didn't take much notice. To me he was just Michael, my son," she says with genuine humility as we chat in the kitchen-diner of her lovely bungalow in the beautiful village of Shepreth.

"In the early days I thought speedway might be a flash in the pan and that he could end up settling down in an engineering job somewhere. Michael was very good at engineering," she added.

While Andy's role in Michael's speedway success story cannot be underestimated, Val also did plenty to help and support their son in a practical way, especially in his early years before he was legally allowed to drive. Even though Andy and Val split up for the first time a couple of years after Michael started his league racing career (they got back together before finally divorcing), both parents remained 100 per cent supportive of him. He couldn't have wished for more support from them.

Val recalls: "I used to take Michael's bike to Boston quite a bit because he wasn't eligible to drive, although he was very naughty on a couple of occasions when, unbeknown to me, he took my car and trailer and drove himself up to Boston before he had a driving licence.

"Andy was usually away racing on the continent, so I'd often drive Michael to meetings. We went to places like Workington, Crayford and quite a few others.

"If Michael had been away riding somewhere in, say, Denmark, I'd sometimes get a phone call from him asking me to drive another bike up to King's Lynn and meet him there. I'd have to organise our two girls and say to them 'I've got to go'. Michael would tell me which bike to bring and where to find the leathers he wanted."

Lee's brilliant form had Barracudas' fans drooling, especially the young females who flocked to the barren wastelands of Lincolnshire to see what all the fuss about. Among them was a local lass called Janet Donaldson, who, along with her sister Carol, was a regular supporter. "Janet and I met at Boston Speedway, in the bar after a meeting," said Michael, recalling the start of a relationship that would last another 25 years.

International honours came Michael's way just two months into his debut season, although scores of eight, two and four points in his first three second division international appearances, against Australasia at Middlesbrough, Peterborough and Workington respectively, would have hurt his pride and strengthened his resolve.

Michael added: "I didn't like being beaten and even if my team had won a match and I'd dropped only one point, I'd still be angry with myself. I worked on the theory that if they could go so fast, then I could go as fast, or even quicker. I wanted to win every race I was in. But if I didn't win, I never made excuses. If I rode like a w*****, I said so."

Michael entered speedway at a time when the sport was in the midst of a mechanical revolution. The tried and trusted two-valve Jawa engine and complete machine that had served riders well since the mid-60s were, almost overnight, about to become obsolete. A couple of Aussies, veteran speedway rider Neil Street and engineer Ivan Tighe, built a four-valve Jawa conversion unit that brought Neil's son-in-law Phil Crump so much instant success throughout 1974 and '75. The astonishing speed and performance of the 'Streetie' forced Jawa to go back to the drawing board to try and produce their own new four-valver that could compete with Crumpie's 'rocket ship' but it didn't happen overnight. Street and Tighe couldn't produce enough of their novel motors quick enough to satisfy demand, while the technical boffins in Czecho didn't come up with their version until the end of 1976. It left the door open for an unlikely new enterprise much closer to home.

In the winter of 1974-75 Weslake, a small family-owned British engineering company in Rye, announced they were about to launch a brand new speedway motor onto the market from their rural base in sleepy Sussex. And after Ipswich and England star John Louis tested it at Hackney one afternoon in December '74, word quickly spread that this was the engine of the future.

Inevitably, there was a price to pay for this giant leap in technological advancement and the 'Wessie' would prove an expensive addition to any rider's workshop. Louis and his fellow England stars Peter Collins and Malcolm Simmons were named as Weslake works riders, which meant free engines and parts, while the rest kept faith with their old Jawas and watched developments from a close distance.

Michael began his first competitive season on the old Garry Middleton two-valver he was so smitten by at Hackney but the Lees obviously kept an eye on the performances of Weslake's big three 'test pilots' and, despite expected teething problems (the conrod on the MK1 version was notoriously vulnerable), it soon became a must-have item of kit for any ambitious young rider, as well as those who were forced to keep up with the Joneses.

Hang the cost, this was the next best thing. And before long, everyone – from superstar to novice – had to have one. Which in itself negated the advantage of extra speed enjoyed by those who took delivery of the earliest production models. Everyone was going a few miles per hour faster but they were all paying quite a lot more cash to do so. It didn't make sense – and there are many who argued then, and still do today, that the governing bodies at the time did the sport a great disservice by not intervening and banning four-valve engines from the start.

The extraordinary part about Michael's switch to Weslake, just a matter of weeks into his first season, was that it was they who approached him, not the other way round.

He recalls: "It was about two months into the season when Weslake appeared from nowhere and said they wanted to back me. It gave me such a boost to know that they must have rated me so highly.

"They were having big problems, though, with lots of conrods breaking and it happened to me, too. I didn't know whether to phone them and tell them their engine was wrecked because I couldn't imagine them giving me another one.

"I finally plucked up the courage to call them and explained what had happened to Michael Daniels, the MD. He just said: 'Get yourselves down here tonight.'

"So Dad and I jumped in the van and headed down to the Weslake factory, which was in the middle of nowhere. As soon as we arrived someone appeared and took the engine from us. We just thought they wanted to analyse what had gone wrong with it and that I'd be going back on to my old two-valve Jawa.

"Then Michael Daniels invited us up to his office – I thought he was going to give me the bill for his blown engine! But, to my surprise, he said he wanted to talk about doing a bit more for me.

"I used to take Michael's bike to Boston quite a bit because he wasn't eligible to drive, although he was very naughty on a couple of occasions when, unbeknown to me, he took my car and trailer and drove himself up to Boston before he had a driving licence."

"Mike took us out for dinner and we'd been down there talking to him for what seemed like hours. After something to eat, we returned to his office in the factory and he made a couple of phone call to the workshop department. Suddenly, a new engine was produced for us to take away.

"And then Michael added: 'Can you come back next week?' We agreed to, not knowing what to expect, but then on our second visit they gave us two more brand new engines to take away.

"Weslake set me up with three sponsored engines – not bad for a 16-year-old rookie who had just started racing. I would never have thought of approaching them about supporting me so early in my career. I'd have thought they'd have laughed at me and said: 'Who the hell do you think you are?'

"I was so fortunate to get that sort of help from them. Well, I suppose I made it happen by what I was doing at the time but I didn't realise it then.

"To me, I was just doing what I wanted to do – racing the bike and winning as often as I could. I was only doing what I expected to do. If I got beaten, I felt almost embarrassed. 'Christ! I can't let that happen!' And that was my attitude

The 1975 Boston Barracudas. Back row, left to right: Robert Hollingworth, Les Glover, Trevor Whiting, Michael and Ted Holding (team manager). Front: Billy Burton and Dave Piddock, with skipper David Gagen (on bike) and the mascot.

to it. It was the fear of being beaten that made me win."

This is a typical example of Michael's natural modesty, an endearing quality he still retains. True, Weslake's assistance came at a good time for him and must have given his confidence a big lift but his precocious talent was obvious to a blind man. Weslake – and Michael – represented the future, so speedway's newest engine manufacturer could have chosen no better young prospect to promote their product.

Mike Lee rosettes sold well at New Hammond Beck Road.

It was obviously a mutually successful alliance because Michael continued to have success on Weslake until the end of 1978, when Jawa came calling. Andy recalls the strengths and weaknesses of the Weslake tie-up: "It was a very, very simple engine to work with – single cylinder, high compression and running on methanol. I'd always ridden four stroke machines, so it was easy for me to adapt to the engines used in speedway, be they Jawa or Weslake.

"Mike Daniels was a wonderful gentleman and he did everything that he said he would do, but they were very erratic with their production. Nearly everything came late or it was incomplete. It was very bitty.

"But they had a very good pushrod engine – light, super for speedway and it proved itself. It had its faults, because if you revved it too hard it popped, or the pushrod jumped out. These were common happenings.

"They couldn't meet the high demand for their engines and parts. Dave Nourish would help you out but the continuation of supplies from Weslake was very poor.

"But we had a good relationship with Ron Valentine, the designer, and they didn't hold anything back. They let us have the blueprints for their cams and everything. They knew we were trying to do a serious job, so why not co-operate with details of all the various cams they made?"

Boosted by this most sought-after backing in his first season of racing (which went unreported at the time), Michael won the annual Lincolnshire Trophy at Boston and then twice defeated Newcastle and NNL top man Joe Owen around New Hammond Beck Road as the Barracudas beat the champions-elect by six points.

His sensational form for both Boston and King's Lynn also earned him an invite as the only NNL rider to compete among a number of senior league stars

Andy Lee stands by as Michael takes advice from David Gagen.

"I didn't like being beaten and even if my team had won a match and I'd dropped only one point, I'd still be angry with myself. I worked on the theory that if they could go so fast, then I could go as fast, or even quicker. I wanted to win every race I was in. But if I didn't win, I never made excuses. If I rode like a w***, I said so."**

in Coventry's annual Brandonapolis classic, where he justified his inclusion with nine points. He later reached the semi-final of Hackney's Champions Chase knockout meeting.

He qualified as Boston's representative for the end-of-season NNL Riders' Championship, the biggest individual night of the year for the second tier boys, and after a nervous start a couple of wins helped him to 10 points for fifth place overall.

Michael crowned his one and only season at Boston by equalling the track record, jointly held by Peter Collins and former 'Cudas favourite Carl Glover in Heat 1 of the home league slaughter of Scunthorpe on September 21 and then set a new best time of 63.6 in Heat 10 on his way to a flawless maximum.

Earlier that week Lee had led Boston's brave, though fruitless, bid for more Inter-League KO Cup glory. The 'Cudas were unable to repeat their historic early season home victory over Hackney when they travelled up to Manchester to face mighty Belle Vue, but they made lots of new friends with their youthful

Michael flanked by Les Glover and Robert Hollingworth.

endeavour. Michael underlined his liking for the wide open spaces of Hyde Road with six points – he even had the temerity to try and split the team-riding Peter Collins-Soren Sjosten pairing in the last race of this semi-final. Reputations never fazed him.

Speedway Star match reporter Frank Maclean remarked that Michael's delaying tactics at the gate reminded Aces' fans of Ivan Mauger. The doyen scribe might have been the first to note Lee's circumspection at the start line but he would by no means be the last!

Four times World Champion Barry Briggs has seen a fair few decent young riders in his time and he is not known for making rash judgements about their ability to go all the way to the top. In his *Speedway Star* column in September 1975, he wrote: "At King's Lynn last year, during one of Wimbledon's visits, I stood on the terracing watching the then 15-year-old Michael Lee riding round on his own. He was too young to race competitively but even so it was easy to see why people thought so highly of him.

"A couple of weeks ago, with a free night, I had to decide between watching Southampton FC or a trip to Weymouth, where Boston, and Lee, were the visitors. I'd heard a lot of stories about Michael's riding this season, in both divisions, and thought it was time I had a look for myself.

"Unfortunately I missed his first race when he did a time of 70.9 . . . three weeks before John Davis, who knows his dad's track well, set a track record of 70.5, so Michael's first-ever ride at the track was fast.

"He's very cool and calm for one so young and seems much more mature than you'd expect for a 16-year-old starting in the game. He's tall and won't want to grown much more, but then his father is built along the same lines and he was an international moto-cross rider.

"Michael has been brought up with motorcycles, and it shows. He is very 'with it' in every way and is certainly as good as any 16-year-old I've ever seen.

"It's been said that he's not a very good starter, but at his age that probably is a good thing. The more he learns about coming from the back the better.

"He looks an easy-going boy, a bit in the Peter Collins mould, always with a smile on his face. Michael's done well for King's Lynn and must have a tremendous future."

A few weeks later Briggo had his work cut out to keep the youngster at bay when Lynn visited Wimbledon. Barry observed: "Apart from his own scoring, he's made the other members of the Lynn team pull their fingers out. Some of the more established riders were possibly not giving 100 per cent but the arrival of Michael on the scene changed all that. Terry Betts admits himself that Michael Lee has made him go all the harder."

Michael ended the 1975 season, his first in the sport, pretty much just as he began it – with victory over England captain and World Finalist Ray Wilson. Reading's guest was twice defeated from the back by Lee as he romped to his first full maximum in Stars' final home league match.

There was another maximum – his eighth of the season for Boston - in his final match for the 'Cudas when Crewe were crushed at New Hammond Beck Road on October 19.

And in a weekend finale flourish came perhaps his most impressive performance of '75, when he grabbed 12 points and fourth place in the international star-studded Pride of the East at King's Lynn. New World Long-track champion, Germany's Egon Muller, was the headline attraction among a galaxy of big names . . . Ivan Mauger, World No.2 Anders Michanek, World No.3 John Louis, Malcolm Simmons, Dave Jessup, Bettsy, the much sought-after Pole Zenon Plech, World Cup hero Martin Ashby, Tommy Jansson and Dave Morton . . . they were all there, and Ipswich's British Champion Louis dominated with a maximum.

But most of the 12,000 crowd bedecked in yellow and green went home that night looking forward to seeing Michael Lee become a full-time British League racer in 1976.

Mauger was in agreement with his fellow Kiwi legend Briggo that Lee was destined for the top. He wrote: "At the end of last season I rode in three or four meetings with Michael and in my view he is better now than Peter Collins was at his age!

"The only advantage Peter had over Michael was better natural balance but in every other facet of the sport I would put the King's Lynn star first.

Showing off the medal he received as Boston's representative in the NNL Riders' Championship at Wimbledon.

"He's fast, he's a good gater, he uses different parts of the track and he doesn't worry about reputations.

"The most impressive thing about his performances was not the amount of points that he scored but the fact that he was recording times equal to any other rider. Usually when lads from the New National League come up they score points but their winning times are a second or so slower than the winning times of established British League riders.

"In Lee's case his times were as fast as, if not faster, than most and he was getting around King's Lynn as quickly as anyone in the world.

"Not having travelled with him, I still don't know too much about the non-riding side of his character. But providing he's got the right off-track mental make-up, he should go to the top of the tree in a couple of seasons."

"Michael has been brought up with motorcycles, and it shows. He is very 'with it' in every way and is certainly as good as any 16-year-old I've ever seen."

When Michael followed his first showing in the prestigious 'Pride' with a maximum to win the Supporters' Trophy in Boston's last meeting the next night, it was the perfect 'goodbye' to fans of the fifth highest placed team in the lower division. With a calculated match average of 9.13 and 347 points from 37 league matches in the second tier, an achievement bettered by only 11 others, and perhaps an even more impressive 7.43 CMA from 27 outings in the top flight, he was clearly ready to commit himself to King's Lynn exclusively the following year.

Andy Lee admits even he was surprised at how well his son had performed in his first season on the shale. He said: "He kept surprising me all the time. For sure, we had some advantages in that we were a motorcycling family and we did all the work ourselves as a self-contained unit.

"Even so, he managed to overcome whatever challenge was put in front of him. Whether he was riding against a top rider or a fellow novice, his only object was to get to the front and that never ceased to amaze me at the time."

What set Michael apart from the rest, in addition to his talent, was his unique riding style. For a tall, thin 'stick insect' of a figure, he didn't look unstylish in the way that most other tall riders invariably do.

John Berry once famously described Lee as 'The Flying Paper Clip', while Randall Butt, former speedway reporter for the *Cambridge Evening News*, said: "Being lean and lanky, Michael hardly looked the part. I remember once describing him as 'like a motorised praying mantis hunting down his victims'. That was what made him stand out from most of the other top riders at the time."

Berry said: "Possibly Peter Collins and Chris Morton apart, the drift had been towards the compact 'jockey' style of riders like Mauger, Jessup, Louis. Even slightly taller riders like Olsen and Simmons had developed much the same upright style.

"Michael blew that theory away, his style was entirely his own. The 'Flying Paper Clip' seemed to have arms and legs of extraordinary length, which most would regard as a handicap. Somehow, he turned them into an advantage by being able to use them to change his centre of gravity as he instinctively moved all over his bike in order to maintain maximum traction.

"This produced a great deal of 'go forward'. Michael's skinny frame – seven stone, soaking wet – meant the bike wasn't carrying excess weight. Andy's engine tuning expertise was able to match the power of the bike to maximise Michael's ability and the combination produced a devastatingly fast rider. Almost as a side product, it also produced a crowd-pleasing spectacle."

Even before the sun had set on the '75 season, the Stars' management made their intentions clear by declaring that Lee had agreed a new "revolutionary 10-year contract" with them. Michael never actually signed a 10-year deal with King's Lynn – he always signed on a standard season-by-season basis – but Martin Rogers insists the story, which the Lees were happy to go along with, was more than just a publicity stunt.

He says it sent out a clear message that King's Lynn would not allow the BSPA's much-maligned Rider Control system, in which riders could be arbitrarily moved around the tracks willy-nilly at the start of each season against their wishes in a forlorn battle to try and balance team strengths, to steal any of their most valued assets.

When experienced *Speedway Star* journalist Eric Linden compiled his annual 'New Year's Honours List' for the British League at the start of 1976, he had no hesitation in naming Lee as his 'Mister Speedway'. Linden said: "We have seen a lot of superb talents come into the sport, but for a first year teenager as good as young Michael I do not know how long back you have to go. Perhaps way back to the debut of a similarly aged New Zealander, roughly a quarter-of-a-century ago, by the name of Ronnie Moore.

"To come into the sport, without a single league match of any kind to his name and, at the age of 16, to end his first season as a heat leader in both leagues; to have scored maximums in both leagues; and generally to have been such a credit to the sport and his tutors as this lad has been, is worthy of the highest honours I can pay him."

‘England’s Greatest Discovery’

Fast-track to stardom

Chapter 7

ON the eve of the 1976 season, Stars’ team manager Alan Littlechild said: “I think we’ve got a boy in a thousand in Michael. He’s the greatest English discovery in years.

“What’s more, by the end of the season, I believe he could be up there along with Peter Collins, John Louis, Dave Jessup and the rest.”

Michael quickly captured the hearts of Lynn’s female followers but that didn’t concern the management who had no reason at that stage to question his dedication to racing.

“Michael is a young man obviously going places in a hurry,” enthused Littlechild, “but the beauty of it is that he remains quiet and unaffected by the waves of publicity and adulation. Mike merely smiles and gets on with the job, an example to any aspiring newcomer with his ultimate dedication to the job in hand, his appearance, the maintenance of his equipment and so on.”

It was his clean-cut image and obvious potential that earned Michael his first major sponsor in Warners Holidays whose gregarious boss, Londoner Danny Leno, took a shine to the Lynn youngster after seeing him in Hackney’s Champions Chase meeting which his company had sponsored at the end of the previous season. “I didn’t know Danny from Adam when he first approached me but I liked him and the Warnersports sponsorship lasted five years. I still have the first set of leathers with their name on them,” said Michael, who also gained the support of one or two other backers eager to be associated with Britain’s biggest rising star.

After passing his driving test at the first attempt in the 1975-76 close season, he received a Ford Capri courtesy of Cambridge car dealers Gilbert Rice. Derek Ireland Trailers of Wisbech provided him with a custom-built three-bike trailer, while Sportac leathers and others also jumped aboard the Lee bandwagon.

‘Big Al’ Littlechild’s belief in Lee’s ability proved to be fully justified. His progress was so rapid that it caught speedway’s highest authority, the FIM, on the hop and made a mockery of their rule which stated that riders had to be 18 to compete in all international meetings inscribed by them.

This had a unique effect on Michael, then 17, in that he needed special dispensation to ride in the prestige annual Spring Classic individual at Wimbledon on April 15 and, laughably, in King’s Lynn’s home match against the touring Poland Test team three days later. Although he scored only four points against the world’s best at Plough Lane, Michael led the way with 11 (paid 12 – dropping his only point to team-mate, new Austrian signing Adi Funk) as the

All set for his first full season in the top flight.

Michael's machinery was always immaculate from day one.

Stars slaughtered the Poles 54-24. Just as well, then, that Speedway Control Board manager Harry Louis and the BSPA's Ron Bott managed to gain clearance for the youngster to ride!

Having an international licence also enabled him to measure himself against a world class line-up in the Embassy Internationale at Wimbledon, a highly prestigious meeting that always attracted a stronger field than the World Final. Malcolm Simmons produced an immaculate 15-point maximum on a rain-soaked track covered in sawdust but the conditions didn't prevent Michael from upstaging a host of big names to grab third place on the rostrum (behind Simmo and Chris Morton) with 11 points. He beat Peter Collins and then rode superbly to defeat Dave Jessup from the back.

Back on home shale, he added the Supporters' Trophy to his collection and retained the Stardust Best Pairs, this time with Adi Funk after having won it with Ray Bales in '75. Only Simmons, enjoying another return visit, stood between

The 1976 King's Lynn Stars. Left to right: Ray Bales, Jan Heningsen, David Gagen, Michael, Adi Funk and Ian Turner. On bike: Terry Betts.

him and victory in the Littlechild Trophy, too.

Simmons and Collins dominated the '76 season between them, appearing almost to take it in turns to win the major meetings on their way to the World Final in Poland, where PC got the better of Simmo to become England's first World Champion since Peter Craven in 1962. As well as proudly providing the world's top two, Englishmen Louis, Morton and Doug Wyer also made it all the way to the final in Katowice.

While the Brits were partying in Poland, Lee was setting a new track record at Saddlebow Road and beating Coventry's Ole Olsen in the process. The following Tuesday, he split new World Champion Collins and Simmons to finish second in the Golden Gauntlets at Leicester.

Michael went into the British Under-21 Championship at Canterbury in September as red-hot favourite to win it and he fully lived up to the hype by winning with a faultless 15.

It's hard to believe now, but England had an embarrassment of riches, most of the talent having emerged from a couple of learning years spent at second division level. Senior internationals Collins, Jessup, Louis, Gordon Kennett, John Davis and Chris and Dave Morton all spent at least two seasons in the lower section before moving up.

What made Michael Lee stand out from the rest is that he'd had just one season in the NNL before rubbing shoulders with, and beating, the world's best.

Danny Leno of Warnersports, Michael's first main commercial sponsor, joins in the celebrations after Lee's victory in the British Under-21 Championship.

"Michael is a young man obviously going places in a hurry but the beauty of it is that he remains quiet and unaffected by the waves of publicity and adulation."

He was being fast-tracked to stardom.

The only reason Michael did not make a full international appearance during that scorching hot summer of '76 was simply due to the fact that England had no home or away Test series. Although stunned by Australia in the World Team Cup involving four-man teams, Len Silver's Lions were otherwise so dominant in world speedway by this stage that with the Swedes, Poles and Russians all in decline and no other country strong enough to put out a seven-man side capable of giving them a decent match, there was no chance to blood promising youngsters such as Michael.

Not that he was able to put his feet up at any time in a hectic first season of top flight racing. At times he was racing four or five nights a week as he became in increasing demand. But he continued to thrive on the pressure and attention his gifted talent brought him.

A 9.43 average (and 10 full maximums) saw him push Terry Betts to within half-a-point per match for the right to be Lynn's No.1. It was a fantastic second season, especially as Michael experienced problems with his Weslakes that

Mixing it with Hull's Frank Auffret and Sheffield's Craig Pendlebury in his first World Championship qualifier at Belle Vue.

"What made Michael stand out from the rest is that he'd had just one season in the NNL before rubbing shoulders with, and beating, the world's best. He was being fast-tracked to stardom."

convinced him to switch to a Neil Street Jawa four-valve conversion in mid-season. The thorny issue of four-valve engines – whether they should be banned and the spiralling costs they inflicted upon riders in pursuit of more speed - became a constant talking point throughout the '76 season.

But Michael was too young and too driven to worry about the politics of the sport back then. He couldn't get enough of racing and there was still his unquenchable thirst to learn and become even better. Most 17-year-olds would have been very content and satisfied with themselves if they had done what Michael Lee did throughout a hectic 1976 but two days after the season ended, he was off on a new adventure.

Watch out, Australia.

New Kid in Town

Aussie highlights

Chapter 8

BY late 1976 Britain started to reel from a new musical movement called punk rock, which briefly became a major cultural phenomenon.

An associated punk subculture emerged, expressing youthful rebellion and characterised by distinctive styles of clothing and adornment and a variety of anti-authoritarian ideologies.

Sound slightly familiar?

OK, so Michael Lee never dressed nor looked like a punk rocker and he was definitely no Johnny Rotten or Sid Vicious, those lovable lads from the Sex Pistols. The rebellious anti-establishment bit and the drugs didn't come until later in Michael's career.

But the boy was changing with the times. He came home from the first of his three winter trips to Australia with a distinctive new look that wasn't immediately recognisable to even his nearest and dearest.

"When I arrived back in England my parents were at the airport to meet me but they didn't even recognise me," he says. "I'd had streaks put in my long hair and after months in the sun and all the salt water, it had bleached and turned proper blond. That was John Davis' influence – as you know, he'd had tints in his hair for some time!

"I was tanned up to the eyeballs and I'd also had my ears pierced while I was out there.

"As I walked through customs I spotted Mum and Dad and they were looking straight through me. I got to within three or four yards of them and it was only at that point when my youngest sister Susan finally recognised me! 'That's him' she went. Mum said that I looked so healthy, 'like a movie star', or words to that effect.

"But no, I've never really been into music – Tom Petty and the Heartbreakers were OK, and I liked a bit of Lionel Richie, but that's going back to the early 80s.

"I certainly wasn't into the punk rock scene, although Susan was into it big-time. She was a full-on punk – all the paint, hair everywhere and bin-liners. Mum and Dad used to get stressed out over the way she went out and I just used to laugh at her, thinking 'she's lost the plot!' But she came through it."

King's Lynn general manager Martin Rogers observed the coming of age of his shining star: "Michael's first big overseas trip to Australia in 1976-77 was a bit of an eye opener. Instead of having Andy at close hand, he was in a different group situation and some of the 'old soldiers' on that tour taught him some new tricks.

"When he got back to the UK sporting a decorative cross emblem in his left ear, and his hair streaked, it was a sign of the youthful push for identity which these

England's touring team to Australia in 1976-77. Alan Wilkinson, Reg Wilson, Nigel Boocock (on bike) and the 'blond bombers' John Davis and Michael.

"When I arrived back in England my parents were at the airport to meet me but they didn't even recognise me. I'd had streaks put in my long hair and after months in the sun and all the salt water, it had bleached and turned proper blond."

days would pass almost un-noticed, but it was considered quite 'out there' in 1977.

"In many other ways, though, he was already growing up fast, had a seemingly unlimited enthusiasm for what he was doing, and rarely, if ever, stepped out of line in any way."

The day after the 1976 British season finished, Lee flew out to Australia to become part of an England squad of five. They were led by veteran tour organiser and former England No.1 Nigel Boocock and also included Alan Wilkinson (Belle Vue), Reg Wilson (Sheffield) and John Davis (Reading). The British Speedway Control Board understandably refused to give the tour official status, so little should be read into the fact that they lost the so-called Test series to the Aussies 4-3.

For the record, the first match was at Perth's Claremont Speedway (won 59-31), followed by three consecutive matches at the Brisbane Exhibition Ground (won 46-44, lost 42-48, won 46-44). The quintet then headed to Sydney where they appeared twice at the Showground (lost 42-48, twice), split by a midweek match at Liverpool (27-63).

In all of these matches, with the exception of Liverpool, the tracks were big, fast and (at the Showground in particular) notoriously narrow, so they would have been unknown territory for Michael.

Even so, 'Wilkie' was the only 'Lion' to outscore Lee, with the teenager recording Test match scores of 10, 14, 10, 3, 14, 6 and 9 (total 66) on the Street-Jawa conversion that was, of course, well suited to the typically huge Australian raceways that made King's Lynn look like a frying pan.

Australia fielded all of its victorious World Team Cup squad – John Boulger, Billy Sanders, Phil Crump and Phil Herne - for the last two matches, which helped to explain Michael's dip in form.

More to the point, it was a great learning experience for England's brightest hope, who celebrated his 18th birthday a month or so into the tour.

Forget the The Pistols, The Clash and The Ramones. To borrow the title line

Foot up and flat out, Michael gets on the gas in Aussie.

Michael, Mitch Shirra and Robbie Blackadder on the 1976-77 tour.

from that eminently more pleasant tune released by The Eagles in December 1976, Michael Lee was very much the 'New Kid in Town.'

"I had a great time in Oz and it was a fantastic experience," he said. "When we turned up for our first meeting at Perth, there was this huge 586-metre track (the largest in the world) and I was like, 'hellfire, how big is this? OK, so where's the track we're going to race on?' I couldn't believe how big the place was."

It didn't faze him, though. Michael capped his first appearance on the then biggest speedway track in the world by setting a new track record and scoring an 18-point maximum at Perth's vast Claremont Park against a Western Australia select side.

"I did a lot of meetings out there but it wasn't just about the racing. It was also about learning to cope on your own and mixing in with the other boys, living out of each other's pockets for three months. I'd always had Dad around and it was time to do my own thing.

"Booey was a fantastic mentor who had everything well organised. Reggie was another 'old stager' but I think they both gave up on trying to be a father-figure to me and John after a while.

"I made a lot of good friends out there. The Australian people were so friendly and hospitable – they couldn't do enough for us and they were so laid back. Then there's the beaches and the weather, so, yeah, I fell in love with the place."

World at His Feet

British champ ruffles feathers

Chapter 9

THE first words Ole Olsen ever spoke to England's brightest young star were concise and to the point. "Michael, what were you f****** doing?"

The Danish three times World Champion, who had smashed the track record in his first race, was being carried through the Ipswich pits on a stretcher at the time, so you can understand why he didn't have the time or inclination for niceties.

He had damaged his hip after being sent sprawling through the collapsible wire mesh safety fence in Heat 13 of the second England v Rest of the World Test at Foxhall Heath in May 1977.

It was the over-zealous Michael Lee who dumped him there.

Michael, who was excluded for his actions, explained: "I took Ole out when the track was as grippy as hell after it had rained all day and some riders weren't keen for the meeting to go ahead.

"He made the gate and went wide going into the third bend. I went under him but found I couldn't turn and I T-boned him about three-quarters of the way round the corner.

"We both cartwheeled into the fence and although I got up and walked away, he looked like he'd broken his collarbone.

"Back in the pits, I had to step back to allow Ole – on the stretcher – and the first aid people to go past. I moved towards him and he almost smiled as he said: 'Michael, what were you f****** doing?'

"I apologised to him because I felt bad – he was the kingpin, along with Ivan and PC and those other boys. I wasn't planning on knocking anybody off but I'd made a mistake. It was a racing accident."

Although neither Olsen nor Lee were fit to race again at Ipswich that night, the Great Dane was back in action for Coventry a few days later, so no harm done.

"I get on well with Ole now," says Michael. "When I visited Denmark I sometimes stayed with him and his wife Ulla."

It wasn't the first time Lee had ruffled feathers in that eagerly-awaited Strongbow-sponsored series between England and the Rest who, as well as Olsen, also included Ivan Mauger, Anders Michanek, Egon Müller, Phil Crump, Billy Sanders. With no other country strong enough to take on a seven-man England team the previous season, the Rest of the World combined their mighty resources.

Anders Michanek, the 1974 World Champion, also had a close encounter with the 18-year-old who had been called up by manager John Berry for his senior international debut at White City on May 11, 1977.

Michael leaves the great Ole Olsen trailing in 1977, but at least he passed him cleanly this time!

"Back in the pits, I had to step back to allow Ole – on the stretcher – and the first aid people to go past. I moved towards him and he almost smiled as he said: 'Michael, what were you f**** doing?'"**

"I remember nudging Mich out of the way down the back straight," says Michael. "There was really no room to pass, so I leaned one elbow against him, pushing him across the track, while my other elbow was running down the safety fence as I went into the lead.

"I won the race and afterwards he said to me: 'You bloody nutter'.

"But, as with Ole, I get on well with Mich. Although he was peed off at being beaten, he soon respected me for being a competent motorcyclist and we shook hands.

"We had some proper hard races, both in England and Sweden, and people warned me: 'Watch Mich – he'll put you in'. But he never did. He was a great guy."

Competent motorcyclist? Another classic Michael understatement of his immense talent at such a young age. He had barely been riding for two years and here he was showing his back wheel to the world's best and demonstrating to his England team-mates, too, that he was well on the way to the very top.

The travelling King's Lynn contingent who went to Coventry to support Michael, Terry Betts and David Gagen at the 1977 British Final.

At White City, Berry paired Michael with Peter Collins and three of their six races produced 5-1 victories. In one race Michael did the old maestro Mauger from the back. Lee scored 11 (paid 12) points – two less than top scorer John Louis – on his full England debut as the Lions swept to a 63-45 victory in West London.

He followed up with scores of three (at Ipswich), top score of 12 (Coventry), eight (Reading) and 10 (Hull). The scheduled sixth Test at Bristol was cancelled due to complaints about the state of the Eastville track, so England missed the chance to level a series that was lost 3-2.

It was a rare blip in an otherwise brilliant season for Lee, who began the The Queen's Silver Jubilee year with full works sponsorship backing from Weslake – a deal, tied in with Gulf Oil, that Andy negotiated while his son was still completing his first tour of Australia.

And they were putting out the bunting in Melbourn all right when Michael came home from Coventry with the coveted British Championship in July. It was his biggest test to date, a night when jangling nerves were stretched to breaking point and a top five place and progress in the World Championship was on the line. Injury wiped out defending champion Malcolm Simmons while John Louis had a rare off night and also failed to qualify. Even the very best have crumbled under such pressure – but Michael sailed through with apparent ease.

After dropping his only point to Bob Kilby in Heat 6, he finished one clear of Reading's Dave Jessup on 14 at the end of a meeting watched by around 15,000 on a Wednesday night at Brandon. A large proportion of them were wearing yellow and green scarves and hats and parading banners bearing the name of their new idol.

Michael gets the wheels of his Weslake in line and for Hackney's Keith White there's no catching him.

"We had some proper hard races, both in England and Sweden, and people warned me: 'Watch Mich – he'll put you in'. But he never did. He was a great guy."

The right side of the law! Cyril Crane and the Stars' fans look much happier than the policeman after Michael's first British title win.

"The atmosphere on British Final night was always electric in those days," says Michael. "I loved Coventry – a proper speedway set-up where everything was done professionally."

After the meeting and Michael had received a million handshakes, he happily stood alongside his even taller father in the pits for the photographs that would appear in *Speedway Star* and *Speedway Mail* the following week. Andy says: "When Michael won his first British title in 1977 I felt very proud. He accepted everything in his stride. Success and winning major titles didn't affect him at all. He was never overawed by any opposition and just enjoyed success, as most people do I guess."

"Victory in the British Final was a sign of Michael's increasing maturity as a rider," added King's Lynn's Martin Rogers, no doubt revelling in the reflected glory Lee's biggest achievement to date brought the Norfolk club that had had so little to celebrate since it gained league status in 1966.

What made Lee's rapid emergence as a world class performer all the more incredible is that, by 1977, he was no longer the young whippersnapper bidding to topple the giants. Well, he was. But he was by now a feared and widely respected opponent in his own right, someone all the others wanted to beat. There was a growing weight on his shoulders but throughout 1977 he simply took everything in his stride. His pursuit of success was relentless.

The top five from Coventry progressed to the penultimate round of the World Championship, the Inter-Continental Final, at White City, where they were joined by Peter Collins. PC had been seeded direct to the London meeting as a reward for winning the world title the previous year.

Collins soon showed he was still the man to beat as he clawed his way from the back time and again to record a blistering maximum. But on a tough afternoon of cut-throat racing, the only other Brit to gain a place among the top seven and qualify for the World Final was Michael, who finished fourth after losing a run-off with Billy Sanders. The others who went through to the final in Gothenburg were Ole Olsen, Ivan Mauger, John Boulger and Finn Thomsen.

In reality this was on a par, or perhaps even a bigger achievement than winning the British title at Coventry. The unlucky John Davis, Dave Jessup, Doug Wyer, Phil Crump and a little known American called Bruce Penhall (three points) all failed to make it through to the Big One in Sweden, where Michael would be the youngest in the 16-man field.

"When he qualified for his first World Final, there was a mood and a sense that anything was possible," recalls Martin Rogers. "In the run-up to Gothenburg, there was an airline dispute and with it the worry that the flights booked might not materialise – so while Andy, and Michael's mechanics, John Coote and Dennis Hicks, went out with the bikes by sea and road, Michael and I flew out of Southend, via Amsterdam. (British Air Ferries, one of Michael's sponsors, were based at Southend in Essex.)

That's our boy – Alan Littlechild (left) and Cyril Crane with the '77 British champ.

"On that flight we were talking about his ambitions, and he said: 'I want to beat Fundin's five world titles'. This, remember, was before Ivan's fifth and then sixth. There was no bravado or big-noting about it. He was genuine in his intent and the belief he might do it.

"When he got fourth – which could so easily have been first – at Ullevi, it merely confirmed how good he was and could become. There was no real sense of disappointment at having missed an opportunity, more pleasure he had done so well on debut."

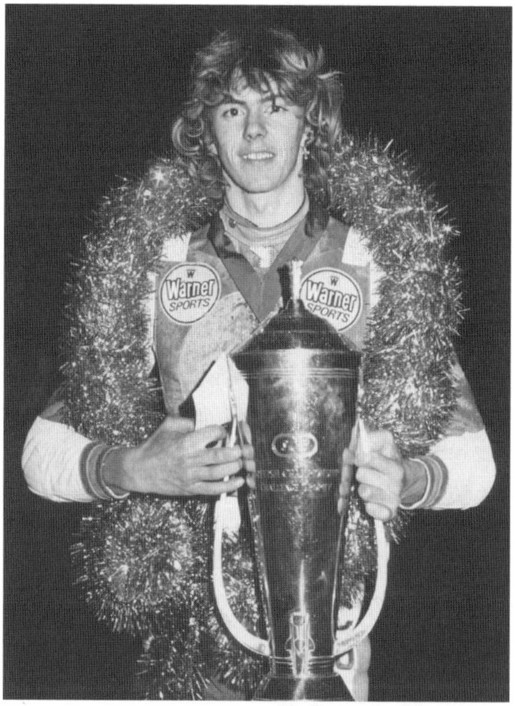

His first major title success.

In conditions more suited to staging the World Speedboat Championships, incessant rain throughout the meeting had turned the Ullevi track into a quagmire by the end. How the meeting was ever completed remains a mystery that has gone down in World Final folklore. They wouldn't start a meeting in similar conditions today and they should never have done so at Gothenburg in 1977.

Michael probing the inside line in this battle with Doug Wyer during the 1977 Inter-Continental Final at White City.

But times and attitudes were different then. Mauger almost picked up his fifth world crown by accident as, one by one, his main rivals ruled themselves out of the reckoning or were dealt a cruel hand of misfortune.

Poor Peter Collins, the big pre-meeting favourite who would have benefited most from a postponement, could barely walk after breaking his left leg in a freak second-half accident at Belle Vue six days earlier and it was an act of supreme courage that earned him second place overall in defence of his title.

The title was finally decided in a bizarre Heat 18 that had to be started FOUR times. The longest race in World Championship history brought together the following (points after four in brackets) in gate order:

Ole Olsen (11), John Boulger (5), Ivan Mauger (11) and Michael Lee (10).

Only the Australian Boulger went into the race knowing he had no chance of becoming 1977 World Champion.

A win, with either Mauger or Olsen second, would have put Michael into a run-off for the crown.

And Lee had certainly earned the right to be there contesting the biggest prize at the end. Storming from-the-back victories over Swedes Tommy Nilsson and Bernt Persson in Heat 8 and Billy Sanders in the very next race, underlined his credentials as a worthy challenger and made a nonsense of worsening track conditions.

Before Heat 15, Michael became embroiled in some starting gate shenanigans with Finn Thomsen – next to him on gate two – which delayed the start. The Dane, who had a reputation as an awkward customer at times,

Michael and Peter Collins, England's only two qualifiers from the Inter-Continental Final, had a great tussle at White City. Michael briefly held the lead in this shot.

Peter Collins goes wheel to wheel on the straight with his great England rival.

After he forces his way past, there's a handshake of respect at the end of another fierce clash of the Lions who were destined for Gothenburg.

Michael posing with a couple of pop stars in Gothenburg.

conducted an animated protest that Michael was encroaching on his grid but it seemed no more than gamesmanship by Thomsen, perhaps looking to do his fellow countryman Olsen a favour by trying to unsettle the English kid.

This unwanted distraction did Lee no favours, because he could do nothing to stop Anders Michanek winning all the way. He had spurned the obvious advantage offered by the inside grid as rain continued to fall, making visibility nigh impossible for those behind.

For the dramatic Heat 18, Lee's outside grid was the least favourable. He knew that anything less than a perfect start and he would be wiped out on the first corner by flying mud.

"On that flight we were talking about his ambitions, and he said: 'I want to beat Fundin's five world titles'. This, remember, was before Ivan's fifth and then sixth. There was no bravado or big-noting about it. He was genuine in his intent and the belief he might do it."

In his haste to make a lightning-fast getaway, Lee stretched the tapes to near breaking point. And then just as he rolled back into position, referee Tore Kittilsen's finger hit the release button, which then caused the tapes to catch on Olsen's helmet as the Dane dropped the clutch and blasted off gate one.

Chaos. Tension.

All four back.

At the second time of asking, Boulger, clearly not content to merely make up the numbers, made it from gate two and all eyes turned to the chasing pack. Olsen was following fast in the Aussie's slipstream as they aquaplaned down the back straight but Boulger was going too fast for the conditions and slid off in turn three. Olsen later received a Unicef fair play award for instinctively laying his bike down to avoid Adelaide's finest, whose reward for his audacity was an exclusion.

So with the party pooper gone, the remaining three are back for the second re-start.

Or is it going to be a one-man 'race'?

Mechanic Dennis Hicks wipes mud from Michael's eyes. His second bike is called for because the throttle on his No.1 Weslake had jammed open after being clogged up by dirt.

Then Lee and his yellow covered helmet re-emerge from the pits and he coasts round to the starting gate. The two-minute buzzer has been sounded. In another minute or so Michael Lee could be contesting a run-off for the world title. Is this real?

He sits. He waits. But there's no sign of either Mauger or Olsen, who are back

England's big two at Ullevi, PC leading Michael in Heat 4.

Michael (outside) has gone past Bernt Persson and is about to go round Tommy Nilsson in Heat 8.

Two views of Michael before he surged under Billy Sanders (11) to win a thrilling Heat 9. Edward Jancarz (6) is third.

in the pits still scraping the mud and water from themselves and their bikes.

Michael's clutch needs adjusting, so, with none of his rivals in sight, he turns away from the tapes for one last tweak.

Now this has been the subject of many 'what if' debates over the years and will no doubt continue to provoke arguments whenever the 1977 World Final crops up in conversation.

What if Michael had remained still at the gate, ready for the race to start, instead of turning away from the tapes as he waited for the two World Final veterans to join him on track?

Would referee Kittilsen have had the balls to exclude both Mauger and Olsen for having exceeded the time allowance . . . and hand the world title to Michael on a plate?

"There's no way he was going to do that," Ivan insisted years later. Mauger knew what every referee had for breakfast and he could count on Tore Kittilsen to ensure a fair three-man battle.

To be fair, a philosophical Lee has no complaints: "I know what people have said about the start of Heat 18 over the years but I was young at the time and you don't think to yourself, 'what if I sit still here – will the ref exclude the other two?'

"I've no argument. It was my first World Final and a big learning curve," said Michael, before acknowledging that Kittilsen acted in the best interests of the sport by allowing all three riders extra time to prepare for their biggest race of the year. "To exclude Ivan and Ole wouldn't have been the right way to decide it," Lee added.

It would have been a ridiculous way to decide any meeting, let alone the World Final, and who would want to win it by default anyway?

When the tapes rose for the third time, there was an inevitability about Mauger speeding clear from gate three and blinding the helpless Olsen and Lee before calmly reeling off four faultless laps. At 37, he was the oldest man to win the title. Ivan was lucky that night but then he always was one to give chance a chance.

But the 18-year-old with 12 points on his World Final debut deserved the highest praise, too. "Lee showed a ability and temperament far beyond his years," wrote *Speedway Star's* Paul Parish.

Despite being beaten from the gate by Olsen in a run-off to decide who would join Mauger and Collins in the medal placings, Lee was still invited to appear in front of the world's photographers along with the top three on the rostrum. "I don't know who told me to go out there for the medal ceremony but it was a very nice gesture and I appreciated it," he said of this unprecedented act of sportsmanship. "I think they must have recognised that I was only a kid and I'd had a good go."

In the final analysis, Michael was unlucky in that he had the worst gate position in his toughest and most important race, when the title itself was on the line. The draw had been unkind to him that night and he couldn't make a decent gate in any of the three attempts to start Heat 18.

Nice and relaxed between races in Gothenburg.

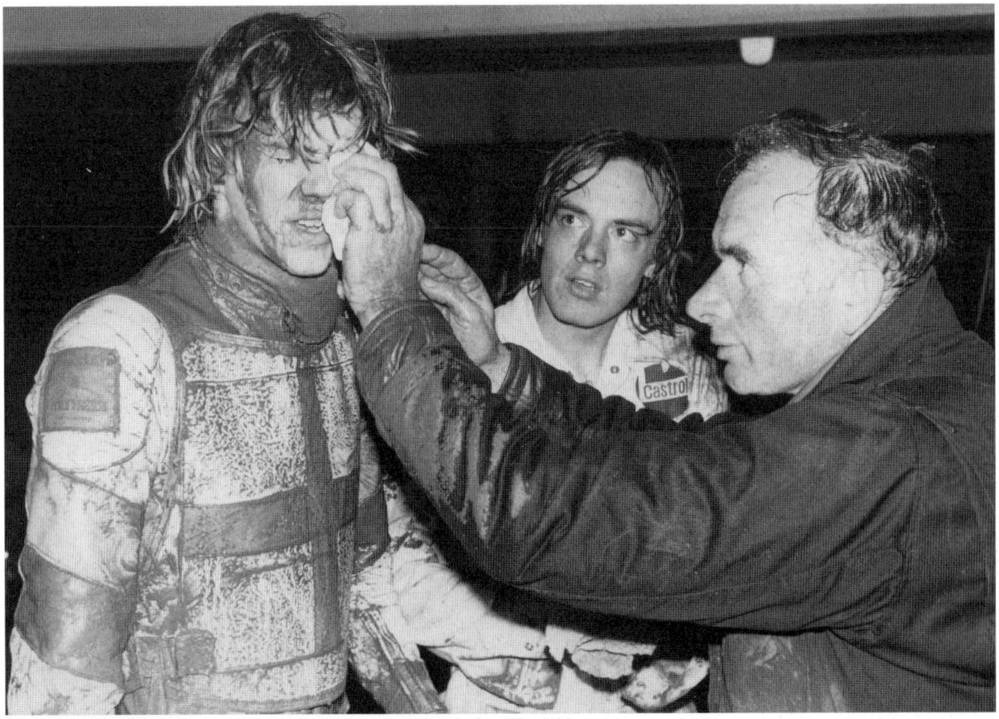

Mechanic Dennis Hicks begins the clean-up operation before Heat 18.

The longest race in World Final history . . . Michael, Ivan Mauger, John Boulger and Ole Olsen looking for dry land in Heat 18.

Fourth place still got Michael on the rostrum in Sweden.

"It was once again Michael's heroics that sparked the wild scenes of delight. He produced a burst of speed to split the Reading pair of Dave Jessup and John Davis on the run in on the last lap of the final heat. Pure drama. Pure joy. Pure Michael Lee."

But Peter Collins, probably the best rider in the world all season, was the unluckiest of all to finish only second. There is no way a fully fit PC would have allowed Olsen to have come storming under him the way he did.

Martin Rogers recalled the aftermath of the '77 World Final: "We flew back on the Saturday morning (Michael, Andy and I) and on the journey up the A10 to the meeting at King's Lynn that night, at his request, detoured into Welwyn Garden City where we found a television store which was showing the final on ITV's World of Sport.

"I think we all watched sensing that this was something special and likely to be the start of something even more special," added Rogers.

There were no signs of mental or physical fatigue as Michael Lee headed up to Saddlebow Road just 24 hours after his first World Final - and won the VW Grand Prix qualifying round with 14 points!

World Champions England after victory at Wroclaw in '77. Team manager John Berry flanked by John Davis and Peter Collins, with Michael, Malcolm Simmons and Dave Jessup in front.

Still no time to rest, though. Sixteen days after Gothenburg Michael won his first World Championship gold medal as a member of England's World Team Cup squad at Wroclaw, Poland, where he scored nine points as Berry's Lions ultimately finished a comfortable 12 points clear of the hosts, with the Czechs and Swedes trailing.

The courageous Collins returned to action with a top-score of 10 but this was a tremendous all round team effort, with Dave Jessup (9), unbeaten reserve John Davis (6) and the injury-troubled Malcolm Simmons (3) also doing their bit. It was Michael's victory in Heat 14 that gave England an unassailable lead. He won it in a new track record of 71.6 – on Simmo's bike!

Given his outstanding success on the international stage all season, it would be easy to overlook what a brilliant campaign Michael also enjoyed on the domestic front. In fact, statistically, it would be his best ever. A final CMA of 10.64 from 36 BL matches that yielded 431 points saw him finish the season top of the league averages, a shade above Exeter's Ivan Mauger who rode in six less matches.

Indeed, it was a measure of the upper strength of top flight racing in Britain at the time that nine riders finished '77 with an average of more than 10 points a match.

For the record, the superstars were:

	M	CMA
Michael Lee (King's Lynn)	**36**	**10.64**
Ivan Mauger (Exeter)	30	10.62
Peter Collins (Belle Vue)	29	10.49
Gordon Kennett (White City)	36	10.41
Billy Sanders (Ipswich)	35	10.39
Anders Michanek (Cradley Hth)	11	10.35
Ole Olsen (Coventry)	32	10.33
Malcolm Simmons (Poole)	26	10.22
Dave Jessup (Reading)	35	10.20

Michael challenges Ivan Mauger in the 1977 Inter-Continental Final. They were the top two in the BL averages that year.

In action for the KO Cup winners at Bristol, where Michael leads Bruce Cribb.

If you include his Speedway Star KO Cup meetings, his figures make equally impressive reading. From an ever-present 44 league and KO Cup matches he scored 519 points (inc bonus) and averaged 10.59, going unbeaten by an opponent in just over a third of those matches (13 full and two paid maximums).

His elevation beyond Terry Betts to become the new No.1 at Lynn meant Michael would contest the British League Riders' Championship at Belle Vue, where he finished third behind the undefeated Ole Olsen and home track favourite Peter Collins.

King's Lynn won the SSKOC for the first time in 1977 and Michael played a big role in delivering the club's first piece of silverware held aloft by Bettsy on the last Wednesday of October. Trailing by eight points to White City after the first leg of the semi-final, shortly after that momentous night in Sweden, Michael clinched a maximum when he and Ian Turner roared to a 4-2 in the last heat of the second leg at Saddlebow Road.

The aggregate win over Reading in the final remains arguably the biggest occasion in the club's history (certainly the best attended) and is still fondly remembered by those in green and gold who were there to see it.

Lee's five-ride maximum in the first leg at Smallmead restricted the Racers to a narrow 40-38 lead. There was a huge crowd – reportedly 10,000 – at Saddlebow Road for the second leg and most of them jumped the fence and danced around afterwards, accompanying the riders on an impromptu parade around the track.

It was once again Michael's heroics that sparked the wild scenes of delight.

He produced a burst of speed to split the Reading pair of Dave Jessup (unbeaten all night, as Lee had been at Reading) and John Davis on the run in on the last lap of the final heat.

Pure drama. Pure joy. Pure Michael Lee.

Even after mechanical gremlins had denied him a win yards from the check flag earlier in the night and being the victim of a ragged start to the vital last heat, Lee recovered his composure and once again produced the goods when the pressure was at its most intense.

Those two priceless points in a dramatic finale to Heat 13 meant King's Lynn won 41-37 on the night and 79-77 on aggregate. It secured Stars' first national trophy and made up for the disappointment of losing the previous year's final to East Anglian rivals Ipswich.

But it almost didn't happen. Lynn were struggling to stay in contention in the first semi-final at White City, which the Rebels won 42-34. Rogers says: "Michael's bike stopped a couple of times and he blew his top and stamped out of the pits on his way to the dressing rooms."

Reports claimed that a clearly irritated Lee brandished a couple of 'Harvey Smith type' gestures at the jeering Wood Lane crowd as he made his way along the centre green towards the dressing rooms at the far end of the famous former Olympic stadium.

Rogers continued: "It took one of my more eloquent speeches and appeals to his better nature before he somewhat sheepishly agreed to come back and continue the meeting, scoring vital points in the later stages that kept the tie alive.

"It was a quick snapshot into the build-up of pressure and expectation which all too soon became a recurring theme."

Not So Good Friday

AWOL for the first time, but British Champion again

Chapter 10

THE 1978 season – British speedway's Golden Jubilee – saw Michael more or less maintain the brilliance he'd shown throughout '77. He became increasingly in demand as a major drawcard – not just throughout England, but across Europe as the sport continued to expand internationally.

He was by now an established England star, an automatic choice, and his performance in the World Final at Gothenburg brought with it even higher expectations as well as lucrative rewards. Michael was under the spotlight much more.

Most of the time he responded magnificently, highlighted by his historic victory in the British Championship in August that brought him a second World Final appearance.

Off the track, he was as well organised as anyone. A new American-style van that not only transported his bikes and other gear to meetings but also provided sleeping accommodation, ensured he was well equipped to meet the demands of an increasingly hectic schedule.

On the technical side, with Andy still running his business and Michael racing all over Europe, they recruited the services of Warrington-based Martin Hignett as a full-time mechanic. Blond and leggy and not too dissimilar to his employer in looks or age, Hignett had been Peter Collins' spanner man the previous year and turned down an offer to work with road-racing star Mick Grant in order to join Lee's support team. Michael recalls paying him a weekly wage of around £180 plus bonuses.

So it came as a disappointing shock to the Lynn management and supporters when their Golden Boy failed to arrive at Ipswich early on in the '78 season. At the time his absence was publicly explained away as a 'car breakdown'.

Martin Rogers recalls: "The first real signs of things fraying began to appear in 1978. We had a Cup Winners' Cup home and away match against Ipswich on Good Friday. Picture the scene: Ipswich, one of the stellar teams, against King's Lynn, flexing their muscles and starting to suggest they could challenge for supremacy in East Anglia. Big interest, big crowds, huge contingents of travelling fans.

"Ipswich came to Lynn in the morning and Michael got a 12-point maximum (Stars' won 45-33) – business as usual. Come the afternoon, thousands decamped down to Foxhall Heath. No sign of Michael, no word of explanation. King's Lynn predictably thumped (51-27).

"From high excitement to a feeling of let-down and huge disappointment, not to mention embarrassment, within a few hours.

"It was, as far as I'm aware, the first time he had missed a meeting, so historically significant from that point of view. With some difficulty we accepted it was an aberration, a never-properly-explained-but-to-be-overlooked drama, we guessed because of some domestic difficulty, maybe over machinery. Even in the best of times Andy and Michael fought and made up on a regular basis and we put it down to one of those occasions.

"It did serve to put us on notice to monitor how Michael was going and this increasingly was a time when everybody wanted a piece of him.

"There were also signs of a bit of rebellion against the established order of things, as either Michael, or maybe Andy, maybe both, could wind themselves up over perceived injustices and short-sighted behaviour from promoters.

With road-racing legend Barry Sheene at the 1978 British Motorcycle Show at Earls Court.

"It was a time when the Master of Speedway series was hoping to establish itself and Michael was one among several riders who were keen to be involved in bigger, better international competition and all that it promised."

'The Masters' was the brainchild of Ole Olsen and his business manager Peter Adams, who championed the idea of the world's top riders being cherry-picked to contest a small series of rounds in which points were accumulated on a grand prix-style basis and the overall winner collected a huge cash prize of £10,000.

Naturally, all the big boys were up for it even though their BL promoters didn't share their enthusiasm for a new competition that could detract from their own product and make unwanted calls upon their most prized riding assets whose wages they were paying on a routine basis. You could understand why a bid to stage one round in England at Coventry – Olsen's home track - was turned down flat.

The 'richest competition in speedway's history' was launched in West Germany in front of around 20,000 fans at Bremen on Sunday, April 23, with three more rounds at Gothenburg (May 23 – yes, it rained) and Vojens (April 30 and August 13), Olsen's purpose-built track in Denmark which he opened in 1975.

Sparring with East Anglian boxing favourite Dave 'Boy' Green in the gym at Cambridge.

Peter Collins scooped the lolly ahead of Olsen, with Michael Lee third overall, but the initial series was badly flawed in that the four nominated local riders were totally outclassed by the 12 superstars and PC had clinched the title before the fourth, and final, round was staged!

The best Lee could manage in the individual rounds was third place in both the opener at Bremen (where a tapes exclusion by ref Tore Kittilsen cost him his chance of claiming second place in a run-off with Olsen) and the first meeting at Vojens.

But a third place finish after four rounds still earned the King's Lynn No.1 around £6,000 – very good money in 1978 and more than enough to satisfy most riders today.

Fast-forward to 1995, when the visionary Olsen finally got his way by securing the necessary financial backing from sponsors and television companies to convince the FIM they should scrap the traditional one-off World Final that had served the sport since 1936 and, instead, decide the World Championship over a full season using the Grand Prix formula. Whether you approve of this system or still hanker for the instant drama of the sudden-death days, you have to admire the dogmatic Olsen for making it happen.

His inaugural Master of Speedway series, though flawed and destined to disappear from the calendar completely after 1980, laid the foundations for what, by 2010, had developed into an 11-round series with each one broadcast

On his way to victory in the 1978 British Final, Michael goes wide of John Louis and is about to pass race leader John Davis.

live on TV across the world. Obviously, Lee was eager to be involved from the start – even though it caused unease among his bosses at King's Lynn.

Martin Rogers recalls King's Lynn's home defeat by lowly Leicester on May 20: "It was Lions' team manager Vic White's 49th birthday and part of the gift came when Michael crashed riding as a tac-sub in Heat 12 and didn't take his scheduled Heat 13 ride (due to a knee injury).

"He was due to ride at Birmingham on the Monday but cried off, choosing instead to go early to Sweden where there was a Master of Speedway round at Ullevi on the Tuesday. I was genuinely concerned he wouldn't come back after that meeting in time to ride at Hull the next night, so I flew to Sweden for the meeting (where he rode in between stints on crutches, a la PC in the '77 World Final) and made sure he was with me on the return flight!

"King's Lynn got whipped at Hull, where most people were reluctant visitors, but Michael got 15 out of 26 and rode like a champion."

British Champion again.

Michael and his 'team' in the pits after he retained the British title. Martin Rogers, Andy Lee, mechanic Martin Hignett and Alan Littlechild complete the happy scene.

Just as he had done in winning his first two rides in Stars' home win over Bristol before having to reluctantly withdraw from the meeting when the pain became too much. Lee had been left battered, bruised and sore after a high speed crash in a long-track meeting at Skovde in Sweden, where he tangled with Hasse Holmqvist and suffered a dislocated shoulder, broken finger and concussion. Onlookers said he was fortunate to have avoided more serious injury.

"It happened in the semi-final and I ended up going over the wooden board fence, clipping my head on it as I went over the top, and landing in the crowd," Michael recalled.

One of the newspaper comments attributed to Michael that summer referred to the BSPA's refusal to stage a round of the Masters of Speedway series. In one national newspaper (in the days when they were actually interested in speedway and gave it prime space) he reportedly branded British promoters "amateurs" and also went on to question the wisdom of combining the British rounds of the World Championship with the Daily Mirror-Volkswagen GP series.

In fact, Olsen and Collins both declared themselves unavailable for the GP final at White City on July 9, months before it was even staged. The Dane, no doubt still miffed by the BSPA over his Masters snub, didn't even contest the qualifying rounds, while PC was fully focused on the World Long-track Championship – and the quarter-final in Germany was scheduled for the same day as the GP final.

Collins added to the British organisers' embarrassment by winning all his three qualifying rounds for the combined World Championship/GPs and would have gone through to the GP final at White City with a maximum 30 premium points.

A more contrite Michael was subsequently quoted in *Speedway Star* as saying that he had been phoned by a journalist with a pre-conceived question and had been misquoted. Michael's words of contrition sounded suspiciously like they had come from the pen of a fire-fighting Martin Rogers, who provided the *Star* – where he'd spent some of the early part of his journalistic career in the 60s – with a weekly editorial update from Saddlebow Road which carried no byline!

Lee says now: "The Masters was a major tournament, so why wasn't a round held in England, which was at the centre of world speedway at the time? As an Englishman who wanted to race in England and do all the big meetings here, it was ludicrous that there wasn't a round staged here.

"Ole didn't try to interfere with the individual World Championship. He was trying to set up another major GP system to run alongside it. So yeah, I was bound to say things that the BSPA might not like to hear – and why not, if I felt strongly enough about something? Speaking my mind got me into trouble at times but sometimes people have to speak out against certain things. To me, 'amateurish' is the term I'd use

Chatting with motorcycling ace Phil Read before the 1978 World Final.

Doing well to hide any nerves on the Wembley parade.

again to describe the promoters' head in the sand attitude to what Ole was trying to do back in '78."

After victory in the Lynn round and second place at Ipswich, Lee also looked to be a strong contender to win the GP final but he only lined up at White City as reserve after withdrawing from his third qualifier at Bristol.

Rogers recalls: "He walked out of a Daily Mirror-Volkswagen Grand Prix round at Bristol complaining about the state of the track, the most high-profile of his transgressions to that point. With the 'help' of Graham Baker, who later ghosted a column for him in *The Mirror*, he made various critical comments which depicted him in a less than good light – as you know, I'd spent years at Lynn cultivating and trying to protect their image and his new-found status as an angry young man was a bit of a distraction."

The controversial Bristol surface – a unique blend of sand and shale – had worried many riders since the sport was introduced to large crowds at Eastville Stadium at the start of 1977. The England v Australasia Test match, scheduled for June of that year, had to be scrapped after Malcolm Simmons and Dave Jessup both refused to appear there. "Bristol was the worst track I'd ever ridden," said Simmo at the end of an illustrious 30-year racing career.

Conditions at Bristol did improve but even in '78 the surface was blamed for too many nasty crashes and even a number of the top riders dreaded going there.

On May 19, 1978 Lee scored four points from his first two rides at Bristol before riding straight through the pits and into the car park, where he loaded up and went home without stopping to inform referee Mel Price. He was immediately fined £25 by the official and his walk-out brought him a further £50 fine by the Speedway Control Board, who also ordered him to pay £40 costs. It wasn't sour grapes at failing to qualify that drove Lee to quit the meeting early – he'd beaten eventual meeting winner Joe Owen in his first ride.

Amid simmering discontent between promoters and some of the elite riders, there was talk in the national and trade press of 'rider power'. Reg Fearman, the then BSPA chairman and boss of Reading, was particularly vocal in his condemnation of those he considered were putting their lucrative continental bookings before British commitments. A steady increase in major British meetings being scheduled for Sunday afternoons, when the top boys could nip off to greener pastures of Europe to earn at least twice as much at a grass-track or long-track event, was also a growing bone of contention around this time and would remain so for years to follow.

"Riders at the top end are only interested in themselves. We may eventually have to tell them to take it or leave it," Fearman told the *Daily Mirror*.

Later, Fearman would have much more to say about the antics of Michael Lee in his last year as a speedway promoter.

To put Collins' £10k Masters windfall into perspective, when his Belle Vue team-mate Chris Morton later won the GP final at White City, he picked up a comparatively meagre £1,250, albeit a large sum by British prize-pot standards.

Not that money was the main motivating factor for Michael. He was very well rewarded but he simply loved winning races and his rivalry with Collins for the right to be acclaimed England's No.1 proved a fascinating sideshow as the '78 season unfolded. We didn't know it at the time but Peter's best years in the World Championship were already behind him, although he still had lots of success ahead of him in the World Team Cup and Pairs. Michael's star was still very much in the ascendancy.

"Our rivalry was a good thing for me and Michael," reflects Peter, "because we both wanted to beat each other even though we had a lot of success riding together for England. Seeing Michael go so well definitely brought out the best in me."

"I became a better starter through practice and trial and error. It's especially hard nowadays. When I rode, tracks were different, the pace was slower and it was possible to manoeuvre myself into position before passing others."

In July '78 Collins beat Lee (2-0 at Lynn and 2-1 at Hyde Road) to retain the Golden Helmet match-race title but it was a different story in mid-August when they met again in the British Final at Coventry, where Collins bowed out of the World Championship in bizarre circumstances.

England's top two met in the second heat, where Michael signalled his intent by roaring past both PC and early pacesetter Dave Jessup to begin the defence of his title in brilliant style. And when Lee overhauled his old mate John Davis to win Heat 7, he was clearly the man to beat. Consecutive victories in his next two races meant he could afford to drop a point to Malcolm Simmons in his last ride and still retain the crown with 14 points.

Simmo, Jessup and Gordon Kennett joined Lee among the four qualifiers who progressed directly to the World Final at Wembley. For Collins, marooned on just six points and plagued by mechanical problems all night, there was only despair. It was subsequently proven that PC's fuel had been affected by traces of sugar, both at Coventry and the next night at Sheffield. It was a pity that the general bitter disappointment that greeted Collins' exit inevitably removed some of the gloss from Michael's second British title success and his historic achievement in becoming the first Englishman to win back-to-back British Championships.

In the build-up to the World Final at Wembley in September there was speculation in the press about a 'special' Weslake that Andy had tuned especially for Michael, who was making his debut under the Twin Towers.

He certainly started with a flourish, winning Heat 2 in a new track record time and, after a poor second ride when he missed the gate badly and went far too

Although he gated ahead of Ila Teromaa and Jerzy Rembas, Michael couldn't stop Ole Olsen from going on to win the world title.

wide on the first turn, he hauled himself back into contention by winning his third race in another new record time (67.1).

Defeat by champion-to-be Olsen in Heat 16 finally ended his title dream, so he went into the penultimate heat knowing a win would guarantee him the silver medal and two points a run-off for bronze. Instead, he finished a disconsolate last behind surprise packet Kennett (who separated Olsen and Scott Autrey on the rostrum), Jessup and Anders Michanek.

It had been an inconsistent night but then, as Michael points out, Wembley could trouble even the best.

Michael says: "It was very disappointing to score only nine points but Wembley was a strange place for me – and it had nothing to do with the atmosphere or the size of the crowd (86,500, just short of the 92,000 capacity).

"It wasn't a racer's track and it helped to make the gate there, because it had no banking and it was a job to go round people. I wasn't such a good starter earlier on in my career – I liked to hang off the back and get it on, but that didn't work at Wembley.

"I became a better starter through practice and trial and error. It's especially hard nowadays. When I rode, tracks were different, the pace was slower and it was possible to manoeuvre myself into position before passing others."

Michael had told readers of *Speedway Star's* World Final preview issue of his relief that he would be excused having to ride in King's Lynn's match at Swindon two days before the World Final so that he could fully prepare for Wembley without the untimely distraction of an inconsequential league match. But he did

Olsen and Jiri Stancl go clear of Michael in the 1978 World Team Cup Final at Landshut.

appear at the Wiltshire track, having to rush straight there from the official Wembley practice which, as usual, was held on the Thursday afternoon prior to Saturday's final.

Martin Rogers recalls the friction this caused: "Michael had a bit of a huff at Swindon a couple of days before Wembley – he didn't want to ride and when we twisted his arm he really didn't appear to be bothered and got four points. No doubt he or Andy, or both, thought he should have been excused the meeting as the final was so close. But the world, and domestic speedway, didn't stop because of the World Final and it wasn't as if a trip to Blunsdon was unduly taxing," said Rogers.

Michael rounded off the international year with five points from three rides in the World Team Cup Final at Landshut. Named at reserve for England's five-man squad, he came into the meeting as early as Heat 5 when, as a replacement for Dave Jessup, he passed all three opponents – Poland's Jerzy Rembas, Czech Jiri Stancl and young Dane Hans Nielsen. It was no mean achievement because there was little overtaking all night on this large and typically flat German track. And it was the only point the match-winning Nielsen dropped in his sensational 11 points haul that saw Denmark crowned world team champions for the first time.

On the home front, 1978 was another impressive year even if there were too many second places in individual meetings for Michael's liking. A CMA of 10.39 meant he was the fourth highest ranked rider in the British League – only Malcolm Simmons (Poole, 10.78), World Champion Ole Olsen (Coventry, 10.71) and Scott Autrey (Exeter, 10.59) did better than the Lynn teenager, who scored more points (382) than any of the leading trio.

Smile Please!

No more photo paranoia

Chapter 11

WHEN Michael Lee triumphantly held the British Championship trophy aloft for the second time in a year in 1978, his gleaming, ear-to-ear grin revealed a new self-assurance to match his natural riding talent.

The reason for his new-found 'ring of confidence'?

He'd finally had his teeth fixed.

And it was all thanks to John Berry, the then Ipswich promoter and England team boss who had given Michael his senior England debut the previous season.

Berry recalled: "Even though he had so much ability and even though he had more public adoration than he could handle, Michael had very little respect in himself. A classic example of this was his teeth.

"They were in a terrible state, all brown and green mottled. I pestered him to do something about them because it spoiled his whole looks, which were otherwise good, but he told me he had a phobia about dentists.

"Eventually, I organised for my own dentist, who was also a friend, to come to a speedway meeting at Ipswich when Michael was taking part. I called Michael into the office after the meeting. The dentist had a quick look and agreed that the only hope was to crown the front six teeth.

"The deal was, he would do it under full anaesthetic so Michael wouldn't know what was going on.

"They were in a terrible state, all brown and green mottled. I pestered him to do something about them because it spoiled his whole looks, which were otherwise good, but he told me he had a phobia about dentists."

"So we arranged a time when we could do the work whilst the dental surgery was closed. Michael arrived and was immediately put to sleep. The dentist then prepared the front teeth for crowns and tidied up the back ones. I watched whilst all this was happening. I then took the lad back to my house and he had a sleep whilst the crowns (not temps, but the finished articles) were made in a couple of hours by a dental technician who had agreed to assist and had been standing by.

"Finally, I took Michael back to the surgery and he had the crowns fitted. They looked tremendous and it made a huge difference to his appearance."

Michael explained: "John Berry is a good person who helped me a hell of a lot, although I wasn't particularly grateful to him after he'd tricked me into getting my teeth fixed. The peritonitis I had when I was nine caused bad scaling of my teeth but I was always too shit-scared of the dentist to have them fixed.

"I was so embarrassed about how I looked that when I first started in speedway, I kept my lips sealed whenever photographers came near me. It was a major hang-up. I was paranoid about it.

"Then I was at Ipswich one night when John made an excuse for me to meet a couple of his friends, one – John Fraser - who happened to be a dentist. JB had already primed him and it was arranged for me to go to his surgery in hospital the next morning to have some x-rays taken. I actually stayed the night at John's place – and I admit,

A pose for the teenyboppers, but no sign of a smile.

"I was so embarrassed about how I looked that when I first started in speedway, I kept my lips sealed whenever photographers came near me. It was a major hang-up. I was paranoid about it."

I thought about legging it because I was so petrified of going to the dentist!

"But I respected JB and went through with it. Before I knew it, I was in the surgery and had been knocked out by anaesthetic before his dentist had my mouth open wide and was capping my teeth.

"The work on my teeth was done at a special price, which I happily paid for, and once the swelling went down and I could smile, I went: 'Good man – yeah – that's so much better.'

"At least I looked good in my World Final pictures!"

Val Lee added: "Michael's teeth looked lovely after John Berry organised for him to have them done and it made a big difference to him, it gave him more self-confidence.

Even Mum couldn't make him smile this time!

"That was until Michael managed to remove all the caps when he went over the handlebars and hit his mouth! I think he had them replaced and it happened again."

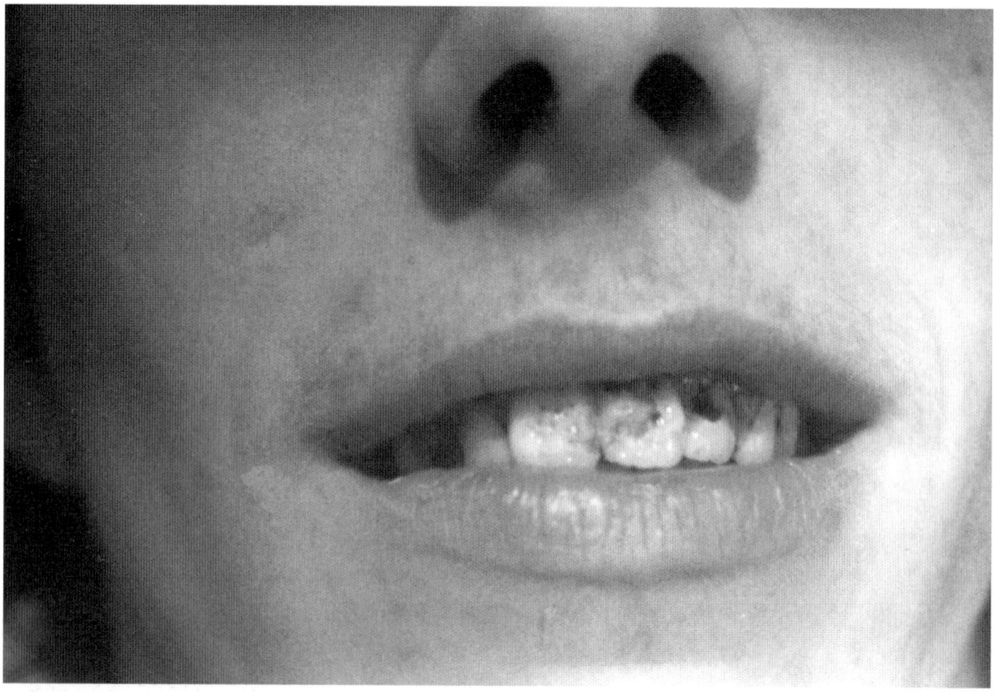

Before and after . . . how Michael gained the new ring of confidence after being almost forced into the dentist's chair.

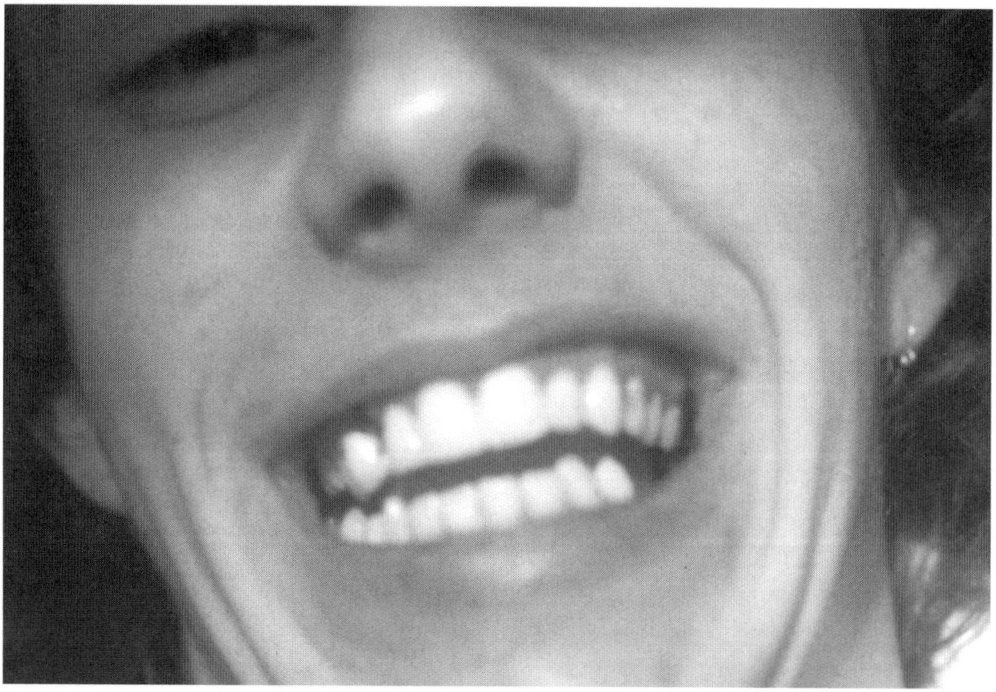

Big Bang in Australia

Who are you calling a cheat?

Chapter 12

MICHAEL Lee was so good and so fast throughout the British Lions' tour of Australia in the winter of 1978-79 that at least one well-known local speedway official suspected him of gaining a big advantage over his opponents by cheating.

Lee won the opening meeting of the tour at Perth, the annual King of Claremont Trophy, with an 18-point maximum and returned to the massive Claremont track a week later to romp to another unbeaten six-ride maximum as the Lions won the first Test match by an emphatic 30-point margin.

He was untouchable on the raceway that measured 620 yards in length, 45ft wide on the straights and 65ft wide on the bends - and where riders were said to enter the bends at speeds approaching 90mph.

It was after the Test, watch by a reported 18,000 crowd, that retired Perth speedway legend Chum Taylor, by then the meeting referee at Claremont, demanded Lee strip down his Weslake engine for an internal examination by the local machine examiner.

Was Lee's stunning form too good to be true? Was he really running an illegal or oversized engine at a huge track where speed counted for everything? There have been occasional instances of riders being suspected of using 'big' engines over the years – they resurfaced again in the GP in 2009 – but these were usually no more than rumours and none have ever been proven.

Chum Taylor, the former Australian Test captain, wanted to find out for certain about Lee.

Recalling his eventful second visit to Australia, Michael says: "I'd beaten the Perth track record twice, so they're thinking: 'We're going to check this kid's engine'.

"They said: 'We know what a 600(cc) goes like and we reckon you're on one'. So I asked: 'Well, how do you know what a 600 goes like, then?'

"I've never ridden a 'biggie' and no matter what people think or say, I never have. There were many rumours that I was supposed to be on a 'big' engine and running nitro, but it never happened. Dad was always straight down the line with my engines.

"We knew that a few people were running big engines here and there but our philosophy was that it would do me no good in the long run.

"So there I was at Claremont being accused of being on a big one. A cheat! I had to strip down the engine to prove my innocence.

"Now they obviously thought that Chum, who knew quite a bit about engines, would take the engine from me and strip it down himself. He clearly wanted to

Michael blowing away the opposition at Perth . . . and riding into a storm about his engine in December 1978.

have a good look at whatever was inside my engine but the Aussies were quite shocked by what I had to say to them.

"The first thing I made clear to them is that no-one else would be pulling down my engine in the pits. And their response was: 'Oh no, you don't have to do it'.

"But I came straight back at them: 'Oh no, you are not going to do it,' I said. 'I can do it – I've worked on engines for quite a while'. "They were stunned. I told them: 'I'll strip down the engine and rebuild it myself'.

"The first thing I insisted on was somewhere clean and tidy to do it – certainly not in the pits, where dirt and dust can easily get into the engine and mess it up."

So Michael wheeled his Weslake flying machine into promoter Con Migro's office, where he ordered everybody out apart from Migro, Lions' unofficial 'minder' Nigel Boocock and Taylor, who were welcome to stay to oversee the youngster clear his name.

LION'S 'SUPER' BIKE CLEARED

By PHILLIP CHRISTENSEN

ENGLISH speedway hero Michael Lee has had his motorcycle cleared by West Australian machine examiners.

The 20-year-old Lee has demoralised the opposition in the Lions first two outings in Perth.

He remains unbeaten after taking the Governor's Cup a fortnight ago and then top-scoring in the first Test last Friday night.

Lee twice broke the Claremont track record in leading the visitors to a 69-39 Test annihilation.

His form was such that the steward of the meeting decided to check the engine size of Lee's machine.

But he declared the bike was legal in every respect.

Lee is on his third trip to Australia and the seasoning he has received during the Australian summers has helped rank him in the top five riders in the world.

Meanwhile the Australian side has been disrupted by the withdrawal of former national champion John Boulger.

Airey will evaluate the prospects of three riders including Brisbane's Steve Koppe before deciding on a replacement.

The full squad will assemble in Sydney tomorrow before flying to Adelaide for the second Test on Friday night and the third at Liverpool on Saturday night.

How the Aussie press announced the innocent verdict.

"We got the measuring tools out," continued Michael, "but all Chum really wanted to know was what cam I was using."

The cam used in their engines and, more important, what tuners and riders do to them to make the engine go faster and perform better, have always been one of the most closely guarded secrets of the game.

Sensing an ulterior motive for wanting to look inside his motor in Perth, Michael says: "No way was I doing that. 'There's no need to take the cam out to check the cubic capacity of an engine,' I told Chum.

"He knew I was right and just said 'OK' as we got on with measuring my engine. Sure enough, it measured 492cc – under the 500cc limit."

Lee had the last laugh, though. He said: "After putting the engine back together, I thought 'I'll give you some work to do now' – and I dumped oil on the floor of Con's office! It was childish behaviour but I was still spewing with anger about what they had forced me to do to clear my name and prove I wasn't a cheat."

Reflecting on the behind the scenes drama more than 31 years later, Chum Taylor said: "I was the steward (referee) at the time – I'd given up racing. I noted on Michael's first run at Claremont he was winning his races by a good 50 metres. Don Hall was an experienced machine examiner with all the right equipment, so during the week I'd arranged to have Lee's Weslake measured right after the Test.

"I've never ridden a 'biggie' and no matter what people think or say, I never have. There were many rumours that I was supposed to be on a 'big' engine and running nitro, but it never happened. Dad was always straight down the line with my engines."

"But it was spot on," Taylor confirmed.

In 2010, Con Migro said: "He (Taylor) didn't stop picking on Michael. He even had the cheek to ask him if he could show him how he tuned his carbies.

"It left oil on my office floor and it was very embarrassing," said Migro, who later described this touring Lions squad as "the best prepared and most professional Pommie side to come here in years."

Migro remembers the first time he saw Lee in action on the 1976-77 tour: "The first time Michael rode for me was when he was 16. Wow! What an awesome racer," added the long-time Perth promoter who took over the reins from the legendary Aub Lawson.

Looking back now at the furore surrounding the allegations against him in Perth in November '78, Michael says: "I was disappointed they didn't take my word for it. They were a bit shit-faced about it and in the end I was smug, to put it mildly.

The powerful British Lions that roared in 1978-79. Left to right: Alan Grahame, Steve Bastable, Phil Collins, Doug Wyer (on bike), Michael, Gordon Kennett, Phil Mountford (team manager) and Nigel Boocock.

"After putting the engine back together, I thought 'I'll give you some work to do now' – and I dumped oil on the floor of Con's office! It was childish behaviour but I was still spewing with anger about what they had forced me to do to clear my name and prove I wasn't a cheat."

"But it all ended amicably and afterwards Chum was always very apologetic to me about the incident. His son Glyn was working for the Taylor-Yamaha garage at the time and they gave me a road bike to run around on while we were in Perth. I've always got on OK with the Taylors since then."

England took one of their strongest ever sides to Australia for the 1978-79 tour that was officially sanctioned by the English Control Board. Michael formed a potent heat leader trio with Doug Wyer and World No.2 Gordon Kennett and with Alan Grahame, Steve Bastable, Phil Collins and veteran Nigel Boocock as reserve, team manager Phil Mountford's squad had no weak links. Lee's mechanic Martin Hignett also joined the party and was on call to help all the visiting riders.

England won the Test series 7-0 while Lee was also the overall top scorer. His blistering form in Perth was followed by 17 out of 18 in front of 12,000 fans at the soon-to-close Rowley Park (Adelaide), 12 at Liverpool (where he stopped twice while leading), eight at Newcastle, 15 in Sydney and then dual scores of 14 in Brisbane (total 98).

He also top-scored in other matches at Rockhampton, at Pioneer Park in Ayr and scored double figures again in the final tour match at Avalon.

Although outstanding on the track, away from the race meetings Michael has always been sociable and well liked by his peers. Phil Collins, the youngest tour member and about to start his first full season in the BL with Cradley Heath, remembers a boozy night out in Adelaide when the amber nectar took its toll on Michael.

"We'd ridden at Rowley Park," says Phil, "and had a bit of a drinking session afterwards before returning to our room. There was Michael, Steve Bastable, Alan Grahame and me sharing one room when Mike suddenly needed to go for a pee. All our suitcases were on the floor in a line – we hadn't even unpacked – when Michael lifted the lid of Alan's case as if it was a toilet seat and, with one arm lent against a wall, proceeded to piss on Al's clothes! My Cradley team-mate was half asleep at the time and barely aware of what Mike had done – but he had to spend the next afternoon in the laundry!

"Mike was a good lad on tour and would always mix in well with everyone," said Phil.

"When I saw inside the engine I knew that it would never have lasted a three-month tour. Everything had been lightened. The con-rod was very thin and had holes drilled in it and it had snapped just below where the piston connects. It looked to me like it had been built for a World Final, not a three-month tour of Australia."

The Weslake that has caused such a row in Perth would also prove a talking point among Michael's English team-mates after it blew in Heat 2 of the third Test at Liverpool, New South Wales.

Doug Wyer, a Sheffield legend, 1976 World Finalist and experienced skipper of the Lions on the '78-'79 tour, admits his respect for the double British Champion only increased after witnessing his skills both on and off the track.

Doug, who is some 11 years older than Lee, says: "Michael was more than just a great speedway rider. I raced against him many times and, as all riders do, we study each other and try to find the other riders' strengths and weaknesses.

"It was on this tour Down Under when I first realised that there was more to Michael than I'd first thought. We were a strong team and won the first Test at Perth comfortably.

"The Aussies were keen to have a look inside Michael's engine but then I remember that also happening to me one year when I bought a Swedish ERM engine from Ivan Mauger and broke the track record at Claremont.

Michael and Aussie Glenn McDonald during the stormy Test at Newcastle.

"I must give Michael credit. He worked on it in my garage for 48 hours solid and had it ready for the press day at the Showground on the Thursday. It went like an absolute jet."

"I noticed, as did everyone there, just how fast Michael's bike was and how well he was riding. But at Liverpool his Weslake engine let go in a big way and was wrecked beyond repair.

"When I saw inside the engine I knew that it would never have lasted a three-month tour. Everything had been lightened. The con-rod was very thin and had holes drilled in it and it had snapped just below where the piston connects. It looked to me like it had been built for a World Final, not a three-month tour of Australia."

Tour organiser Nigel Boocock confirmed: "The con-rod in Michael's Weslake was as thin as a razor."

Wyer continued: "Seeing Michael's engine reminded me of a conversation I had with Ole Olsen at Reading a couple of days after he won the World Championship at Wembley and his engine had just blown up. I said: 'That's a shame, Ole'. And he replied: 'Don't worry, it's done its job. It was built to do six races – five and a possible run off – and I've just done three races here tonight which were a bonus'.

"A week after Michael's Weslake blew up we were in Adelaide and wondering what Michael was going to ride. Well, I don't know who organised the deal but an old friend of mine, Brian Fraser, who was the Jawa importer, came to his rescue with a new engine.

"Now everyone who races speedway knows that a Jawa and a Weslake have very different characteristics, which is why riders have two or three bikes that all have the same type of engine.

"We all thought that Michael would struggle to go as well on the Jawa as he had done on his super-tuned Weslake, and so it proved. He did ride well but the engine needed setting up for him and I wondered who would be able to do that for him in Australia.

"Another week later, we were in Sydney. We stayed at Nigel Boocock's place in Maroubra, where we all used his workshop. After a couple of phone calls home to his dad, Michael pulled the standard Jawa engine down and rebuilt it. He was still very young at the time but he did it alone at night with no help from anyone. He probably put the engine together while we were all boogying the night away in some club up Kings Cross!

"I was surprised that a kid of his age could strip down and rebuild a different type of engine to the one he'd been used to, let alone make it go fast, but that's just what he did."

Booey said: "I must give Michael credit. He worked on it in my garage for 48 hours solid and had it ready for the press day at the Showground on the Thursday. It went like an absolute jet."

Wyer agreed that the Jawa Michael re-assembled in Booey's workshop was as quick as any Weslake on that tour. "I borrowed it from Michael a couple of times and it was as fast as anything around. I think it was the start of his changeover from Weslake to Jawa.

"This is why Michael had the success he did – he learned his trade while he was still young and that's why he became speedway World Champion and World Long-track Champion, winning many other titles along the way.

"I'm sure his father should take a lot of the credit for helping him get to the very top in such a short time. He gave him a short cut to success in a mechanical sense.

"None of my family was interested in speedway or had any experience of riding motor bikes, so when I came into the sport I had to learn it all for myself, and that applied to many other riders too.

"Not only did Andy do so much good for Michael as his tuner, but also for providing bikes and all the equipment that he needed, driving him to meetings when he was not old enough to drive himself, and for just being there with good advice. That must have been a big help to Michael in the early days.

"After the 1979-80 Aussie season, when I was a resident rider in Adelaide and raced Brian Fraser's Jawas, I actually paid Andy to tune of those engines for me. Brian sponsored me with two new bikes and had them sent to me in the UK, and I immediately thought of Andy. After a few weeks Andy said: 'I have been watching your scores and you don't seem to going very well', so I told him that the bike didn't seem fast enough for me.

"I know that some engines go better than others and Andy said that he had done his best with the engine and, fair play to him, he gave me all my money back. Andy is a smashing bloke.

"I suppose there was a lot of stuff that Michael and Andy did to Mike's engines that will never be known to anyone other than them. I went to five or six tuners in my time and when you changed to another one they have to get to know and trust you, in case you just take the engine home and strip it down to see exactly what they have done to it.

"To his credit, Michael must have been a quick learner. Then along with his riding ability, he became the top class racer that we can all remember so well."

It wasn't only Michael's outstanding points scoring performances and his engines that provoked reaction on that second trip Down Under. His antics at the starting line also caused a furore. In fact, during the fourth Test at Newcastle, NSW, Nigel Boocock and Australian team manager Jim Airey came to blows over him!

After The Lions' third Test victory at Liverpool, The Australian tabloid *Sun-Herald* newspaper wrote about Lee "hanging back and then charging as the tapes lifted." They reported how, at one point, Airey actually ran onto the track at Liverpool and "gesticulated towards Lee."

At Newcastle, Airey protested vehemently to the referee about Lee's starting line antics. Michael was excluded from Heat 17 when the green light did not go on and he remained at the gate. This, after Gordon Kennett (twice) and Wyer had both been excluded for tapes offences earlier in the evening.

Things soon escalated when Nigel Boocock came to the tapes as Lee's intended replacement. Boocock said: "We're good friends now but Jim grabbed hold of my handlebars and tried to move me and my machine off the track."

Boocock, with his helmet still on, and Airey, were involved in an unsightly brawl beside the starting gate. Booey described the head-butt he gave to Airey that night as the "Newcastle Nod".

Australian Journalist Steve Magro added: "Michael was observed by many to not be still at the tapes and frequently had rollers. This had been commonplace over the years, such was the standard of Australian refereeing. Some Lions - and Aussies - were guilty of rolling, but in Michael it seemed more obvious. Whatever the case, he was certainly the main culprit for moving at the start at Liverpool, Newcastle and the Showground."

Michael's start-line antics and his almost perpetual battle with referees would ultimately play a key role in his demise in speedway.

All Change

Bye, bye Bettsy

Chapter 13

A WORKS sponsorship deal, the club captaincy, robbed of the chance to win his first World Championship gold medal, two major international titles to his name, at loggerheads with his King's Lynn bosses, a transfer request turned down, more fines and a couple of walk-outs. Oh yes, and a rostrum place in the World Final.

It's fair to say that 1979 was no run of the mill season for Michael Lee.

The biggest thing to happen to King's Lynn in the winter of 1978-79 was the Terry Betts saga. He had been – and remains – Mr King's Lynn Speedway since the track opened on an open licence basis in 1965 but at the end of '78 he told the fans he "probably wouldn't be back next year."

In the event the Lynn management decided, after the lessons of 1974-75, when Simmo went to Poole and getting someone else in was less than successful, to accept that Betts would be retiring and planned for '79 without him.

Martin Rogers says: "Replacing Bettsy was going to be immensely difficult and with nagging doubts about Michael's continuing contribution also in mind, it needed someone of special stature to come in. Dave Jessup, who had just had his famous Wembley near-miss, was keen to come, Bettsy's long-time sponsor Peter Thurlow was eager to help make it happen, so DJ was signed from Reading in a big money deal."

The all-time leading scorer in the Norfolk club's history with 6,799.5 points from 658 matches, including 105 maximums, Betts later claimed that he would happily have stayed with the Stars. In 2008 he told *Backtrack* magazine: "Martin offered me a part-time rider/coach role but I told him what to do with it and said I'd pack up.

"I don't think Cyril Crane and Violet Littlechild knew too much about it at first – but then Violet went ballistic when she found out I wasn't in the team. Having said that, they were both there for the press conference when Jessup signed. It wasn't the way I wanted to finish at Lynn and I was disappointed with Martin."

As it transpired, Betts admits he received an irresistible offer from Reading to prolong his career by one year before retiring on the eve of the 1980 season. Even though Terry was still averaging a shade over eight points a match at the end of '78, there is no doubt which of the teams emerged best from the controversial deal. There is a 10-year age gap between the blond bombshell (who was 35 at the time) and Jessup, who cost Lynn a then club record £18,000, and by then their respective career paths were clearly going in opposite directions.

The biggest transfer deal of that winter also had implications for Michael Lee.

Words of wisdom from the master, Michael listens to Terry Betts.

Rogers explained: "Part of the thinking in signing Jessup was that the presence of another world-class rider, and a consistent and dependable one at that, would help 'keep Michael honest', so to speak. The two of them were chalk and cheese personality-wise, but it was some spearhead. They had rivalry but not as far as I am aware any real issues – though the rival sets of camp followers mostly had a fair bit of hostility towards each other.

"Michael was appointed captain, another gesture towards his status and invitation to do things properly and assume greater responsibility and maturity. But as his escalating representative commitments caused him to miss a few matches, it caused a few ripples here and there."

Michael says he was sorry to see Betts left out of the equation at Lynn as the '79 season dawned. The club's elder statesman had been an inspirational skipper since Lee burst onto the scene early in 1975 and throughout their four years together at the top of the Stars' scorechart, Michael had only total respect for the man he succeeded as No.1 – and that is still true today.

He says: "Terry was great. I was pitted next to him and I couldn't have wished to have a better person alongside me.

"He was a bit of a cynic and a mickey-taker but he kept my feet on the ground. He also inspired me and gave me a lot of confidence. I think we fed off one another. I was the young whippersnapper pushing Bettsy a bit harder towards the end of his career - and he brought out the best in me too.

"Bettsy was a major influence on my career while we were together at Lynn and I still get on great with him today."

Terry came from a completely different era to Michael, although he'd been a bit of a rebel and so-called 'wild boy' himself in his early days, but he had no problem in accepting the challenge of Stars' new young gun.

Betts says: "I never had the same sort of rivalry with Michael that I'd had with Simmo. You could see right from the start that he was a special young talent and I wanted to encourage him all I could. Well, no bugger helped me when I started riding.

"Did he listen to advice? Yes, he did. The trouble was, he listened to too many people!" laughed Bettsy.

It was Betts who helped trigger Michael's switch from Weslake to Jawa machinery. "I had no doubts about switching when the chance arose in '79, because I'd tried Terry's Jawa the previous season. One night at Lynn I won both my second-half heat and the final on a bike borrowed from Bettsy, so I knew what it could do once we added a few little 'trick' bits to it."

Michael went into the '79 race term as a fully works-sponsored rider for Jawa – the engine Ole Olsen had used to win the previous year's World Final and the motor that impressed Lee so much during the latter part of his second Australian tour. While Michael was still Down Under, Andy Lee handled the negotiations with Jawa's senior management at the factory in Divisov, near Prague, Czechoslovakia.

"In fact, I had to countersign Michael's contract with them because, according to Czech law, he wasn't old enough," said Andy, who found himself back in the thick of things at the major meetings following main mechanic Martin Hignett's amicable departure from the Lee camp to pursue other business interests in the software industry.

Michael says he was sorry to lose Hignett. "Martin was a good mechanic and we both worked very hard in the year we spent together. He was a very talented mechanic and would do everything on my bikes except the clutch, which I always liked to set up and maintain myself.

"He was with me in Oz the previous winter and he liked it so much out there that I think he went back to live in Australia for a couple of years before returning to the north of England to run his own successful business."

Andy Lee also recognised Hignett's qualities and says: "I got on fine with all of Mike's mechanics. Dennis Hicks and John Coote were probably with him for the longest period. "They were both good characters. Dennis wouldn't say boo to a goose but he was so faithful to Michael. When Mike was riding in an important meeting Dennis would never, ever leave his bikes unattended because he didn't want people tampering with them.

"He was absolutely wonderful. He did the refuelling and other odd jobs in the pits on race night but that was it.

"John did much the same as Dennis but he did a lot of travelling and would occasionally take Michael and/or his bikes to continental meetings.

"But they never got involved on the technical side or attempted to do any running repairs. If anything went wrong with the bike, it was just loaded onto the trailer and they would simply get another one out. I'd be left to sort out the wreckage once Michael got home!

"Against my better judgement, I recommended Steve Burgess to Michael. I say that because Steve worked for me at the shop for four years, which meant I lost a good and very reliable mechanic. He worked for Mike for some while and was there on the night he won the World Final."

Dave Jessup arrived in 1979 for a club record £18,000 fee.

Michael says: "Steve worked for me for about two years and he was a good man. He ended up racing cars successfully and I was pleasantly surprised to find out that he became World Hotrod Champion in 2003.

"My other full-time mechanic before my career went pear-shaped was Dave Monroe. He'd previously worked in New Zealand for the Kawasaki road-racing team before moving to Oz to work for Honda. I just bumped into him in a bike shop one day – I was working on my bike out the back – and he seemed intrigued by speedway. I invited him over and he worked full-time for me for a year after Steve left.

"My full-time mechanics would work with me in the workshop at home – you can't do everything yourself – but I still wanted Dennis Hicks to stay involved and be part of the team because he'd been there from the very beginning. While he did the basic, mundane jobs in the pits, it eased a bit of the pressure on my full-time mechanic at the time."

Michael always smiles when recalling the loyal dedication of Hicks, now 79 but part and parcel of the King's Lynn scene since a ploughed field in Saddlebow Road was transformed into a speedway stadium by Maurice Littlechild and Cyril Crane in the mid-60s. He has known Lee since he first started doing his interval rides at Lynn. Before then he worked as a part-time mechanic for Stars' Clive Featherby and Bob Humphreys.

"I remember when Michael first started to ride round at Lynn," says Dennis. "One week his mother would bring him and the next week he'd come with his father, so they asked me if I'd keep an eye on Michael.

"When Bettsy and Simmo first saw him ride as a young kid, I think it was

Simmo who turned to Terry and said: 'One of us will probably have to go to make way for this boy'."

"Dennis has been at Lynn since the year dot and he still works there now, checking the riders' pit passes!" laughs Mike, who has never forgotten the commitment he had from the fresh-faced 'old boy' who is such a familiar figure at the speedway.

"Dennis was great for me and very reliable," says Michael. "No matter where I was riding, he'd always be at the meeting very early. We'd arrive and see him eating sandwiches in his little Mini parked up in a corner of the car park. He'd go straight from work to every meeting, no matter where it was in the country, and never be late.

"Dennis never asked for a penny – you couldn't give him money, so we just bought him something nice at the end of the season as a thank you gesture. I'd try and get him to stop off for something to eat with us on the way home from meetings but he wouldn't. He was just a true country boy who worked on the land in agricultural engineering.

"He'd never been out of the country until we took him to Gothenburg for the 1977 World Final. We couldn't send Dennis out as our driver with the bikes because he wasn't a van man – he drove a Mini! – so John Coote, a big, old boy who used to mechanic for Bettsy, did all the driving. He used to work on the fairground – not as a traveller but being a true Romany type, he was used to long journeys.

"Dennis had to obtain a passport especially for the trip and we booked the mechanics into the Ramada Hotel with Dad and myself. We were chatting away over our evening meal one night and there was a carafe of wine on the table. Dad was geeing Dennis up, saying: 'Go on, have some wine'. Dennis wasn't a wine drinker at all but he probably felt obliged to join in.

"Instead of pouring the wine from the carafe into a glass, he picked up the carafe and said: 'OK, Andy, is this one mine?' The carafe wasn't more than half full but there was no way he was going to be able to drink it without spilling some. My piss-taking old man was sitting there laughing his head off as the wine went all over Dennis!

"Dennis wasn't too keen on the Swedish meatballs, though. 'It's not like what we eat back home,' he'd say. I don't think he's been out of England again since the 1980 World Final!"

Back in '79, Michael reasoned that the "niggly" problems he'd experienced with the Weslake engine would be eliminated by switching to Jawa, who, unlike the relatively small British company, manufactured a complete bike with a long and proud history of sustained success in speedway and all other forms of tracksport. Not only did they ensure he was fully equipped for another hectic season in speedway, the Czechs were also fully behind his plans to pursue success on the lucrative continental long-track scene, where the big bucks were to be made.

It marked the start of Michael's long association with Jawa that, on and off, has endured to this day. "It was a massive thing for me to gain the backing of Jawa at that stage of my career," he says.

"Only two others had full works support from them at the time and they were Mauger and Olsen, so I felt honoured to be asked to join them. It was a deal I couldn't refuse.

"Weslake had been giving me free motors and frames, although their frames were perhaps not developed enough at the time.

"Money wasn't really involved in my deal with Jawa, just bonuses. It was mainly all products. But when I say products, it was immense. I had three complete speedway bikes, two long-track machines, two spare engines and more than enough kit to see me through an entire season.

With one of his new sponsored Jawa machines in '79.

"And it wasn't like I had to go and get all this stuff from them or phone them up to order it. You went to their factory in Czecho in February with a low-loader and filled it up! There were literally 50 pistons, 25 con-rods – everything I needed.

"For me, Jawa has always been the speedway engine, an international brand synonymous with our sport. Although they have since changed their name to JRM, which is one of the engines I tune now, Jawa has been a major part of speedway since as far back as I can remember.

"You can go right back to the mid-60s, when the ESO was first around and before the complete machine from Czechoslovakia simply became known as Jawa. It may be JRM now but it's still Jawa to me.

"Before Jawa was taken over by the Czech 'government', it used to be run as a family concern. Masek, who made a speedway engine a few years back and which I was involved with a little bit, is a member of the family that made the early ESOs. Some time back, Masek decided he wanted to make a speedway engine to rival Jawa. Unfortunately it didn't work out for him but you still see the odd Masek motor around.

"My contract with Jawa at the start of '79 changed everything for me. It made me more professional," added Michael.

As with Weslake, Andy Lee had no difficulty extracting track record-breaking performances from the Czech engine. He said: "At first I was a bit worried about making the switch but I knew how comprehensive Mauger and Olsen's contracts were, so we had to be on a winner with Jawa.

"They were absolutely brilliant to deal with, although I had a feeling they needed us, in the West, and that included Ivan and Ole, as much as we needed them. Things happened very slowly between East and West in those days, so all they could do was provide us with all the gear and let us get on with it, which is what happened.

"When they outlined the contract to Mike, there was a feeling that, OK, they might not be quite as competitive as Weslake and we would have to do bits ourselves, but all the various parts were always readily available on the shelf and we were never going to want for any spares – and that's the way it turned out. The back-up service from the factory was excellent.

"He was a bit of a cynic and a mickey-taker but he kept my feet on the ground. He also inspired me and gave me a lot of confidence."

"I went to Czecho with Michael many times to collect gear or to do something at the factory. I loved Czecho and the people at Jawa. I got on ever so well with 'Stan' (we never knew his real name), the works mechanic, because we were both practical people and had a very good mutual respect. He showed me his way of truing a flywheel and I said: 'Christ! You can't do it like that', but he said 'we always do it this way!' They hit them with hammers but I didn't do that!

"Then you had Jaroslav Cervinca, Jawa's chief designer, and I got on ever so well with him too. Michael told me he met him again at the recent (2010) Grand Prix in Prague.

"Needless to say, we did all sorts of things to the engine – some improved it, some didn't. The biggest thing we did was make a centre port cylinder head for the carb. The original was positioned on the side of the engine, so in a rash moment we decide to change it. I sawed the back off it, welded a centre block on and made up a stub. I started working on it on a Wednesday afternoon and Mike rode it at King's Lynn on the Saturday. It was absolutely marvellous.

"With the carburettor in the middle and the frame either side, you didn't have the filters sticking out of the side, which all standard Jawas had. I think it was the only one that had ever been done at the time. It gave him a beautiful downdraft."

As we chatted in the garage at his home in the delightful village of Hinton in Cambridgeshire, Andy rummaged through an old wooden box and pulled out what he informed me was a Jawa timing case, which once fitted on the side of one of Mike's old motors. "Feel the weight of that," Andy said, handing me a lump of almost heart-shaped metal that surprisingly weighed much less than I

Forget luxury transporters and motorhomes, transit vans were the accepted mode of transport for the stars of the late 70s.

thought it would at first sight. "That one is made of magnesium, which is about three times lighter than the standard aluminium timing cases that were fitted to the bog standard engines, but only the works sponsored riders had the ones made of magnesium," he emphasised.

Despite failing to score for England against Denmark in the first floodlight international at Vojens and then managing just four as the Lions were dumped out of the World Team Cup by New Zealand and the USA in the qualifier at Reading two days later, victory in the Embassy Internationale at Wimbledon on Spring Bank Holiday Monday earned Lee his first ever call-up for the World Pairs. As well as collecting the £1,000 winner's cheque at Wimbledon, it was also a chance for him to show off his growing list of sponsors to a national TV audience as the BBC broadcast rare coverage of the annual Plough Lane classic.

John Berry initially brought Lee in to partner Gordon Kennett as a replacement for national skipper Malcolm Simmons, who stood down because he was still struggling to get to grips with the new Godden machine that had been launched at the start of the year. Poole No.1 Simmo and Eastbourne star Kennett had won the World Pairs title in Poland the previous year, so England were bidding for a record fourth consecutive victory in the FIM World Championship event ranked third highest behind the individual and team titles.

But before Lee and Kennett began the defence of the Pairs in their semi-final in Germany, Michael nipped off to Sweden to win the opening round of the Master of Speedway series at Kumla, where he pocketed a £3,000 cheque after defeating American Bruce Penhall in a run-off. Series co-organiser Ole Olsen – the only rider to beat Lee in the Internationale – was well down the field on six points and decided after the meeting to take a short break from racing after declaring himself on the brink of exhaustion.

It's worth pausing here a moment to consider what a typical summer routine was like for the superstars of the late 70s and early 80s.

Unlike a number of today's top riders who race for clubs in the leading leagues of Poland, Sweden and Britain, in addition to contesting the Grand Prix rounds, the elite group in 1979 confined their league activity to the UK, where the only professional league existed back then. But with the FIM seemingly hell bent on filling every available Sunday with international meetings (in both speedway and long-track), and Ole Olsen's Masters still attracting the big names with its unrivalled prize money, the heroes of some 30 years ago faced a gruelling and relentless schedule if they wanted every slice of the action.

Another significant difference between then and now is that riders didn't have several mechanics and a raft of bikes dotted all over Europe. In Michael's case, his King's Lynn-based mechanic John Coote would clock up thousands of miles in a matter of weeks, driving his bikes to meetings in countries such as Sweden, Germany and Denmark, while the ever reliable Dennis Hicks would always be on hand to cover the domestic commitments.

Although the riders had the luxury of being able to fly to their overseas engagements, they often found themselves racing three or four times a week in England, which meant long hours up and down the motorways. With 18 teams meeting home and away in the British League and every track hosting at least one (and in some cases two, three or even four) individual meetings a season, not to mention the Knockout Cup, the Inter-League KO Cup and lesser fixture-fillers like challenge matches and three and four-team tournaments, there was no respite for the major crowd-pullers such as Lee. Even with mechanics to drive the riders everywhere (in transit vans or Citroen Safaris with the bikes wedged in the back), it was very tough on men and machines and you shudder to think what the superstars of 2010 would make of it.

In '79, the best England riders were also involved in Test matches – remember them? – against Australasia (five matches) as well as trips to Poland (two matches) and Denmark (one), plus a challenge that pitted the British Lions touring side against England's World Team Cup squad. Lee rode in all but one of those nine international meetings, having chosen to spend the previous British close season racing in Australia.

His mammoth '79 summer schedule would have been even more demanding had the planned four-match England v Denmark home Test series not been cancelled at the last minute after the BSPA rejected the Danish motor federation's financial demands.

For Michael, the endless slog was exacerbated by the fact that he, along with his father, prepared and maintained all his own engines. When things occasionally went wrong with them, the Lees would burn the midnight oil to put things right.

The full King's Lynn first team and junior squad with their promoters and management at the start of the '79 season. Back row, standing left to right: Alan Littlechild, Bent Rasmussen, Andy Margarson, David Gagen, Craig Featherby, Richard Hellsen, Derek Harrison, Pete Smith, Peter Wordingham, Phil Vance and Martin Rogers. Front: Dave Jessup, Violet Littlechild, the new skipper, Cyril Crane and Ian Turner.

That, of course, was their choice but it added to the burden on young Michael's shoulders. Peter Collins had Dave Nourish in Leicestershire to tend to his motors, while Bruce Penhall had the renowned Midlands-based tuner Eddie Bull to tune and take care of his. Lee was always very much hands-on.

In his current role as engine tuner for British Grand Prix rider Tai Woffinden, Michael knows only too well the demands today's stars (and their tuners) have to contend with – but they are comparatively light to what the superstars of his era accepted as the norm.

He recalls: "You had to be totally organised, with a full stable of bikes here and make sure they got to wherever you were going abroad. It was tough and exhausting and by the end of the season you'd had enough. We worked it out once that in one season I was riding, on average, five nights a week EVERY week of the season.

"The Grand Prix stars all seem to think they've got it tough now but they have two bikes sat in Sweden, two more in Poland, bikes in England, plus those they put aside for the GPs. I'm not saying it's not tough now, because there is a lot of pressure on them, but it was just as hard, if not harder, back then due to the organisation factor.

"Now there are low budget airlines, Ryanair and EasyJet, operating cheap flights to Poland and Sweden every week, whereas we had to organise our own private aircraft to get us to overseas meetings. The likes of myself, PC and Penhall would all meet up at, say, Luton Airport after racing here on a Saturday night and fly off in a twin-engine Cessna leaving at four o'clock in the morning. The six of us would pay a fee to a company to fly us out to Germany or wherever.

"On top of that, you had to arrange for all the equipment to be transported out there. Sometimes we'd double up, so that mine and PC's or Bruce's bikes would go off in one van driven by one of our mechanics, or I'd send my van from the South and PC would send his from where he was based in the North. We didn't have a string of mechanics everywhere to do everything for us.

"The clubs would organise a police escort to get us from the airport to the track in plenty of time. It was usually all very efficient.

"I used to eat, breathe and sleep speedway. If I wasn't physically riding or travelling to meetings, I'd be in the workshop or organising the logistics of each foreign trip. OK, I had Dad to help me in the workshop but it was still a major job. And people kind of forget about that side of it."

With so many domestic and international meetings to cram in between March and October, there was always the risk that bad weather would cause problems somewhere down the line. Sooner or later, something would have to give - and it did, with Michael Lee at the eye of the storm.

After Lee (13 points) and Kennett (seven) had looked less than impressive in grabbing the third qualifying place behind Australia and Finland in the World Pairs semi-final at Landshut, Simmons was recalled to partner Michael in the final scheduled for Vojens on Friday, June 22.

Except that it rained heavily, as it had a habit of doing on big occasions at Denmark's premier track, and the meeting was postponed until lunch-time the next day.

The overnight delay did Lee and Simmons no harm as they combined to register three maximum 5-1 heat advantages in the first half of the meeting and then came from the back to beat Denmark, the pre-meeting favourites, 4-2.

It is part of World Pairs folklore that the English duo were controversially denied a run-off for the title after Edward Jancarz clearly snatched second place on the line when Poland met Denmark in the decisive final heat.

But instead of confirming the evidence of most people's eyes and declaring the race a 4-2 in favour of Denmark, which would have left them tied with England, referee Tore Kittilsen awarded a match-winning 5-1 to the lucky Danes.

Had the Norwegian official been influenced by the fact that Ole Olsen raised the arm of his partner Nielsen to signal their victory before the result of the race had been announced?

Did he hear the roar of the 20,000 Danish crowd after Olsen's clever ploy and fail to see beyond a popular home triumph?

Michael offers no argument now about the outcome but John Berry and Malcolm Simmons remain utterly convinced that England were robbed.

"It was the biggest con in speedway," says Simmo in that typical no-nonsense way he gets straight to the core of every controversy.

Having reflected on the last race drama for more than 30 years, Berry is still equally adamant that his boys were cheated out of a run-off for the title. He says: "I could see a tight finish coming, so, being on the centre green, I positioned myself level with the start/finish line.

"Sure enough, Eddie slipped alongside Hans on the run-in to the flag, heading him certainly by a full wheel on the line.

"I filled in my programme and rushed to the pits in order to sort out the race-off for the title. It was some little time before I realised the result had been announced as Eddie coming third."

Berry's protest to the Norwegian official came to nothing. He recalls: "When I gently pointed out to Kittilsen that Jancarz finished half-a-bike in front of Hans, he said he left the decision as to the way the riders crossed the line to the timekeeper – the DANISH timekeeper, who knew a second place for Nielsen would hand the title to Denmark for the first time in their history.

"There was a TV monitor in the ref's box. I begged Kittilsen to check the finish himself on the replay. He told me he was not allowed. Olsen was already a powerful figure in FIM circles and I'm sure this was not lost on the referee."

Simmons added: "If the referee had awarded second place to Jancarz, as he should have done, I'm convinced Michael would have beaten Olsen in the run-off."

Lee finished what would be his only World Pairs Final on 15 points, with Simmons on nine. But having beaten the Danes from the back when they met in their toughest race, it was one that got away in the most contentious circumstances.

"I'd argue about certain things but not decisions like that, although it did look as if we should have had a run-off with the Danes," says Michael, who expressed surprised at being called up by Berry.

"I went better in the first half of the meeting and Michael was superior to me in the second half," added Simmo. "It was only after we got home that I discovered a crack in my frame, which slowed me down."

Michael was unhappy with Simmons over comments he made about him in his book published in 2006, but he has never had any complaints about his former England team-mate's riding capabilities. He added: "It was a pleasure to ride with Simmo. He was a smart motorcyclist, very clever, and if he was on the pace, as he was then, anyone could have ridden with him. I could ride where I wanted to at Vojens and didn't have to worry about what he was doing."

Vojens '79 represented a watershed in the sport's history. After Olsen's Wembley victory and Denmark's surprise success in the team cup at the end of 1978, the Danes now held all three World Championship titles for the first time.

What happened immediately after that extended wet weekend also soured Michael's relations with Martin Rogers.

This Jawa needs more top end speed!

Among the Stars at Lynn in 1976.

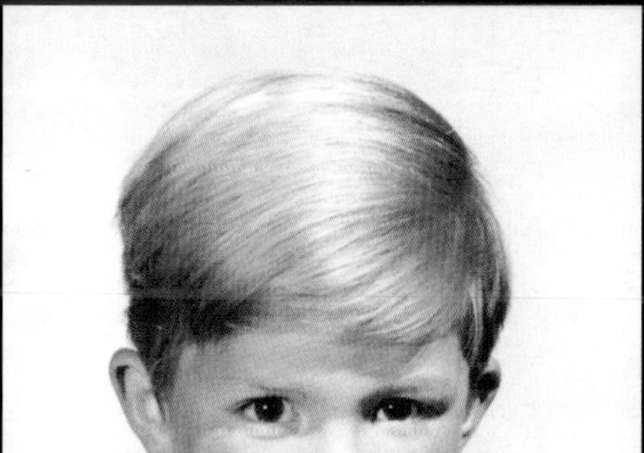

First school photo, at Hauxton Primary.

You're not getting a smile out of me!

The 1977 KO Cup winners. Back row: David Gagen, Carl Glover, Richard Hellsen and Billy Spiers. Front: Michael, Terry Betts and Ian Turner.

The Stars of 1980. Cyril Crane, Mel Taylor, Bent Rasmussen, Michael, Richard Hellsen, Chris Turner, Pete Smith, Dave Jessup and Alan Littlechild.

A great example of how quickly Michael got his wheels in line on the exits from the corners, as he leads Ole Olsen in the 1977 Inter-Continental Final at White City.

All smiles from the 1978 British Champion.

In the leathers and on the Jawa bike used to win the world title.

1980 World Champion . . . and how the press acclaimed his emphatic victory in Gothenburg. Michael has even signed the author's programme!

Action In Speedway

DAILY EXPRESS

Dream win for our youngest-ever champ

IT'S SKY HIGH LEE!

DETAILS

How they finished

PHILIP RISING IN GOTHENBURG

MICHAEL LEE put English speedway back on top of the world in Gothenburg last night.

The 21-year-old King's Lynn captain scored 14 points to become England's youngest-ever world champion.

Lee, only the third English winner in 19 years, shrugged off a first-race defeat to finish two points ahead of King's Lynn team-mate Dave Jessup and Australian Billy Sanders.

Mirror Sport

Saturday, September 6, 1980 No. 23,816
Telephone: (STD code 01) — 353 0246

WORLD SPEEDWAY TITLE THRILLER

OUR MAN'S A WINNER!

MICHAEL LEE became the youngest Englishman to be crowned king of the speedway world on an East Anglian glory night here at the Ullevi Stadium.

Daily Mirror columnist Lee, the 21-year-old King's Lynn superstar, piled up a magnificent 14 pts from five rides to emerge as the first Englishman to win the championship since 1976.

From GRAHAM BAKER in Gothenburg

His team-mate Dave Jessup finished second on 12 points after a run-off with Billy Sanders of Ipswich.

It was the realisation of a dream for Lee, from Royston, Herts, who used to play truant from school to practise speedway.

The title will open the door to potential earnings of more than £120,000 in the next year — and will confirm Lee as one of the most exciting talents in British sport.

Lee to give the clear impression that he could well grab the title. But Jessup dropped a point in each of his next three races.

Lee had made a last-minute decision

On the way to the grand slam of 1980, Michael leading American Scott Autrey in the World Team Cup Final at Wroclaw.

England's triumphant World Cup winners. Ian Thomas, John Davis, Michael, Peter Collins, Chris Morton, Dave Jessup and Eric Boocock.

On top of the world again, Michael after winning the 1981 World Long-track Final.

Back on the speedway, British Final action from Coventry.

Feel the power. Michael opens the gas at Scheessel, Germany to lead Georg Gilgenreiner and Steve Bastable (far right) in the 1981 World Long-track semi-final.

An England Test recall in 1983, this time against the USA at Sheffield.

A fine shot of Michael, on his Weslake 'gold top', leading Erik Gundersen in the 1983 World Final at Norden.

Michael Lee

Classic first bend action from the 1982 World Team Cup qualifier at King's Lynn. Michael gets across from the outside gate to nip across Billy Sanders (Australia), with Dennis Sigalos (USA) and Mitch Shirra (New Zealand) squeezed out.

Michael Lee

A study in poise and beauty . . . a perfectly balanced Michael finds the dirt to leave his big rival Bruce Penhall trailing during the 1982 World Team Cup round at King's Lynn

Michael Lee

Golden Boy! Well, not quite, but he did get his hands on the Golden Helmet again during his time with Poole

As this fine action study shows, Michael had moved on to GM machinery at Poole in 1983.

Fading star . . . Michael at the start of 1991, his final season of racing, with Lynn team-mate Henrik Gustafsson.

With Nicky, his soul-mate and the woman who turned his life around.

In the garden at Worlington with some of Nicky's finest floral decorations.

Peterborough's Technical Advisor at Panthers' practice/press day in March 2010.

Ipswich skipper Danny King (above) and Wolverhampton's Grand Prix star Tai Woffinden (below) - two of England's brightest prospects who have had good reason to appreciate Michael's mechanical expertise and guidance in recent years.

Where's Michael

A fine mess, then Rogers and out

Chapter 14

THE Inter-League Four Team Championship was destined never to live up to the high expectations many senior BSPA members had for it when the competition was first devised and added to the domestic race calendar in the summer of 1979. In fact, after a second staging in 1980, it was chopped from the calendar and never staged again.

The inaugural finals day at Sheffield in '79 always will be remembered more for those who were not there rather than the eight teams that were (OK, so hands up all of you who remember Hull winning the trophy on a damp and miserable Sunday afternoon in South Yorkshire?).

King's Lynn's former general manager Martin Rogers will always remember it, though – for all the wrong reasons.

He recalls: "The big blow-up came when Michael went to ride in the World Pairs Final in Vojens, scheduled for a Friday night. Lynn were at Ipswich the night before, with the return fixture on the Saturday. The Pairs was rained-off and rearranged for the Saturday, so Michael was missing for the two standout matches of the BL season.

"That couldn't be helped but on the Sunday he was due to lead King's Lynn at Sheffield in the Inter-League Four Team Championship. We had a seat for him on a private plane which came back from Denmark to Norwich on the Saturday night but he decided he wanted to stay on and have a good time with the boys. "

The outcome was that King's Lynn went to the meeting without him, narrowly losing out to eventual winners Hull in the first semi-final which began at midday. Ironically, it was largely through Lee's efforts that the Stars had scraped into the final as the highest scoring runners-up after a series of qualifying rounds.

But Rogers still insists: "It was more than 'just a 4TT', it was a major event – the BL promoters recognised how successful the concept had been at NL level and wanted to emulate it," he said. "And King's Lynn, not least in the shape of a general manager-cum-BSPA management committee member who had worked hard to promote it and elevate it in the public's mind, were let down.

"I told Cyril Crane and Alan Littlechild the club should not let the slight pass – the club was paying Michael quite handsomely by this time to be their standard bearer and leader and his no-show was effectively sticking up his fingers at his employers and the fans, hundreds of whom were also let down.

"I said that it was pointless issuing a token fine to someone who was regularly and routinely earning big money, so a figure of £1,000 was set. Michael's response was to say that he wanted a transfer."

Michael looks for the grip out wide of Malcolm Simmons and Larry Ross as he charges after team-mate and rival Dave Jessup during the 1979 Commonwealth Final at White City.

"I said that it was pointless issuing a token fine to someone who was regularly and routinely earning big money, so a figure of £1,000 was set. Michael's response was to say that he wanted a transfer."

It should be mentioned that Lee was not the only rider due to be at Sheffield's Owlerton Stadium on the morning of Sunday, June 24 who didn't turn up for the marathon 48-heat meeting. His Lynn team-mate Ian Turner, celebrating his testimonial season, also gave Owlerton a miss. He was fined £250 by the club for reportedly going on a family holiday to . . . Hunstanton!

More significantly, the new World Pairs champions, Olsen (Coventry) and Nielsen (Wolverhampton), along with Bruce Penhall (Cradley Heath) and Ivan Mauger (Hull), also failed to make it back from Denmark. But as Rogers pointed out at the time, Hackney's Polish star Zenon Plech and a number of British press men did make the effort and succeeded in getting from Denmark to Sheffield.

"It was some time before ruffled feathers were smoothed over and it put a strain on my relationship with Michael," says Rogers, whose days at Saddlebow Road were by then numbered.

He continued: "Over the next few months it became clear Cyril and Alan would do anything to accommodate Michael at any price despite my conviction that even the superstars – particularly the superstars – have to toe the line if it

Another major title along the 1979 World Championship trail, this time victory in the Inter-Continental Final after a run-off against Peter Collins (left), with third place man Finn Thomsen alongside them.

is in the interests of the club. And the disharmony caused when someone is allowed to go their own way while other team members are expected to be well-disciplined was something to be avoided."

Michael continued to make very strong progress towards his third individual World Final. A few days before the Pairs final, he broke the Coventry track record at the start of his bid to win a record third straight British Championship (passing Lynn team-mate Dave Jessup in the process) but this time had to settle for second place after dropping his only point to maximum man Peter Collins.

And with the Sheffield furore still bubbling, Lee bounced back in style to win consecutive rounds of the World Championship – the Commonwealth and Inter-Continental Finals – at White City. The rift between rider and management widened the night before the Commonwealth Final on July 1 when the Stars' skipper failed to appear for Lynn's home ILKOC match against Sheffield.

He claimed he was suffering from tonsillitis – one or two others who travelled on the boat back from Denmark, including Phil Crump, displayed similar symptoms - but his offer to produce a doctor's certificate was rejected by the King's Lynn promotion. Ian Turner also missed another couple of meetings in protest against the fine Lynn tried to impose on him, which ended his long unbroken appearance record in the green and gold.

The next afternoon, Lee rubbed Lynn noses in it by winning the next round of the World Championship on a bumpy West London track – even though he'd forgotten his riding boots and had to borrow a pair from other riders and was

Michael and Andy (in his 'I Like Mike The Bike' t-shirt) looking relaxed in the Katowice pits during World Final practice.

seen walking around the pits between races in his socks. Ironically, at the start of the year Michael lent his name to a new product called the Michael Lee Rekord Boot, for which his father had the UK distribution rights!

After beating Birmingham's Australian star Billy Sanders in a run-off for the title, he spoke to the press about his determination to leave King's Lynn over their attempt to impose the £1,000 fine recommended by Martin Rogers.

But it never came to that. Despite Rogers' protests that the club's No.1 should be made an example of, he lacked the necessary support of his co-boss Cyril Crane, who settled for the slap on the wrist approach. No wonder Rogers felt increasingly undermined.

Michael's relationship with the Stars' hierarchy became further strained after an incident at Reading on July 30, when the visitors were beaten 46-32. With Lynn six points down with three heats remaining, he was brought in as a replacement for Ian Turner.

But when Lee pushed hard against the tapes, referee Martin Palmer judged that he had gone too far across the line and so excluded him. Michael couldn't believe it and for a while refused to leave the track. He did eventually leave, but not before he drove right through the tapes.

According to *Speedway Star*, he headed straight for the dressing room and then left for home, leaving King's Lynn officials angry.

Referee Palmer fined Michael £50 for 'failing to acknowledge authority' and reported the England star to the SCB for leaving the meeting without permission.

Two views of how Michael spoilt Ivan Mauger's maximum in the 1979 World Final.

One that got away . . . Michael misses the start and can do nothing to catch Dave Jessup and Kelly Moran.

Comparing Lee to George Best for the first time, the *Star* wrote: "The 20-year-old lanky lad from East Anglia is undoubtedly one of the most exciting riders in the world. Lee looks set to become World Champion one day.

"But at the moment his progress to the very top appears to have hit trouble, and that's sad, not only for him, but for his club and his hundreds of followers."

But at this still relatively early stage of his career Michael had the uncanny ability to simply shrug off such moments of indiscipline and carry on regardless. He could turn on form like a tap and successfully did it time and again at various stages of his career.

Six days after his Reading walk-out he returned to White City, where track conditions had improved significantly, and added the Inter-Continental title to his growing list of achievements. He'd much rather have had a hat-trick of British titles but the Commonwealth and Inter-Continental victories were evidence that his wrangles with Lynn and the flare-up at Smallmead had in no way threatened to derail his main aim of winning the World Championship in Poland.

Victory over arch rival Collins in the run-off to decide the Inter-Continental struck another timely psychological blow. It was Michael's second win over PC that afternoon, having earlier burst past first Sweden's Jan Andersson and then the Belle Vue kingpin to win a breathtaking Heat 13 by inches on the line.

It was a moment of pure class, Michael at his brilliant best, and perhaps helps to explain why so many people were always prepared to give him the benefit of the doubt and forgive his occasional transgressions. For sure, he was a flawed genius. But a genius all the same.

At least he made it onto the rostrum in Poland by passing old mate Billy Sanders, with Ole Olsen and Kelly Moran behind in the run-off.

"It was a moment of pure class, Michael at his brilliant best, and perhaps helps to explain why so many people were always prepared to give him the benefit of the doubt and forgive his occasional transgressions. For sure, he was a flawed genius. But a genius all the same."

A heavy fall in the first race of the second Master of Speedway round at Bremen ruined his chances of winning the '79 series, which Bruce Penhall claimed with second place behind fellow American Scott Autrey in the final round at Vojens. Michael had to settle for fourth place overall, behind Penhall, PC and the in-form Autrey, but it was still more cash in the bank.

But all the money in the world can't buy the world title. No-one (except probably those riders involved) can readily remember now who won any of the Master of Speedway series but World Championship glory transcends cash. It's what all the top riders strive for most and the dedication and skill needed to achieve it is what separates the greats from the rest. A decent slice of good fortune helps, too.

When the World Final came round on September 2, Lee travelled to Katowice as Coral's joint 3-1 favourite alongside his big rival Peter Collins and Ole Olsen.

On that sunny Sunday afternoon in front of nearly 100,000 fans in the Slaski Stadium, Lee did better than his two co-favourites but not well enough to

Michael collects the bronze medal alongside champion Ivan Mauger and his wife Raye Mauger, Mr and Mrs Zenon Plech, plus fourth place getter Kelly Moran.

"As Ivan was nearly 40, somebody asked him who was going to take over at the top, and he replied: 'Who else is there but Michael Lee?'"

prevent the old stager Ivan Mauger from sneaking his record-breaking sixth title as each of his rivals fell by the wayside.

Despite making a good start in Heat 2, Michael couldn't keep local hero Zenon Plech at bay and that early dropped point ultimately cost him the silver medal, which went instead to the Hackney star.

Wins over Collins and Mauger respectively in his second and third rides gave Michael a share of the lead with Ivan and Ole at the interval stage, before it all went badly wrong for both Lee and Olsen in their fourth outing, Heat 15. Jessup and Kelly Moran did Mauger a big favour by filling the first two places this time and when Ivan won Heat 17 from his former protégé Olsen, the Kiwi maestro had clinched his sixth title an incredible 32 days short of his 40th birthday.

At least Lee finished his third World Final with a flourish, winning Heat 20 followed by the four-man run-off against Moran, Billy Sanders and Olsen to claim the bronze medal.

He says: "It was the first time I'd fancied my chances of winning the final. I felt settled on Jawa and had good equipment but when I finished last in heat 15 . . .

"I can't remember exactly why that happened but it was probably the pressure that got to me. I must have missed the gate and fought my tits off but still ran a last. And when you throw a last, you know it's over."

The slick, dry and dusty conditions did him no favours either. This was the dirt-less Katowice 'motorway' – not the grippy surface that Collins revelled in to win races from miles back in that epic final of 1976.

"It was as slick as hell and really difficult to pass," Michael recalls. "If you got in front you could make good ground and pull away from people. But it was hard once you were behind. Katowice was a typical Polish track – big and slick.

"It didn't come off for me that year but I learned a lot from the experience. I learned that no matter how good you are week in, week out in domestic racing, to put it all together in a one-off World Final was what it's all about. Winning is the only thing that matters.

"At least I'd made it onto the rostrum properly in third place, after just missing out at Gothenburg in '77."

Michael's time would come and he'd be among the fancied contenders again in 1980. That wasn't just the widespread view of supporters and pundits, the newly-crowned World Champion was convinced of it too.

Randall Butt covered most of Michael's major World Championship meetings between 1977 and 1980, at home and abroad, for the Cambridge Evening News. He recalls: "I remember being in Ivan Mauger's company in our hotel in Katowice after the final, in which of course Michael was the only rider to beat the great man. As Ivan was nearly 40, somebody asked him who was going to take over at the top, and he replied: 'Who else is there but Michael Lee?'"

Events at Saddlebow Road had taken their toll on Martin Rogers, who would no longer be around at Lynn to watch his schoolboy prodigy's inexorable rise to the top. Explaining the background to his first departure from King's Lynn, Rogers says: "I was having increasing 'philosophical' differences, especially with Cyril. He and Alan never warmed to DJ as they had to Bettsy, and some of that rubbed off on me because they blamed me for being instrumental in getting Jessup there – and they missed Terry. He had been an enormous and almost entirely beneficial presence around the club for 13 years, so he was always going to be a hard act to replace personality-wise.

"The reality was, though, that even if his latest (winter of '78) retirement talk had been bluff, the team needed something more for '79 and it was unlikely King's Lynn ever could have accommodated Lee, Jessup AND Betts (especially with a new maximum points limit of 50 introduced at the start of the year). "

"But the spillover from that was another factor and although I was in the middle of a three-year agreement with the club, I was unhappy with the tensions and I think they were not too distressed when I resigned in December '79.

"I mention this not to make it all about me, but because I do feel the club's ability to keep Michael in any kind of check diminished after I went. The whole justification for having someone to manage the club for several years was that it meant Cyril, Violet and Alan didn't have to do much more than carry on with their lives and businesses during the week and then turn up for payday at Saddlebow Road on the weekend. It worked successfully, and mostly profitably, for a long time and part of its success was the image the Stars built up of being a well-run, professional outfit.

"Having a top man whose commitment to the club was being compromised by his increasing international stature was a challenge which was only going to become more difficult.

"Michael became increasingly difficult to handle and was involved in a number of incidents and situations which had a negative effect. The odd no-show became rather more of a frequent occurrence and speedway fans hate that. So too, of course, do promoters, sponsors and the like.

"But I think Norfolk Speedways allowed themselves to continue to pander to Michael and tolerate his indiscretions in 1980, '81 and '82 because they felt he was so important to them. He was the cash cow, the super drawcard," admits Rogers who, with his wife Lin, left at the end of 1979 to become the new promoter of British League rivals Leicester.

The facts, however, underline just how important and quickly Lee became to King's Lynn Speedway. For all the disputes over Sheffield and his increasing brushes with authority, Michael remained a colossus at Saddlebow Road in 1979. His BL average may have dipped slightly to 10.29, but only three riders – Scott Autrey, Ivan Mauger and Phil Crump – did better, statistically, for their clubs.

Fourth place was the Stars' best finish to a campaign in six years, so the expensive signing of Jessup had also benefited the club in terms of its improved status and fan appeal. In subsequent years, though, Cyril Crane pointed out that the 1979 season had resulted in a £29,800 loss for the promotion. It depends how you measure success.

Whether they could really afford their two world class stars or not, in Lee and Jessup King's Lynn possessed arguably the most potent spearhead in British speedway, with both England regulars capable of going all the way in the World Championship. But that wasn't necessarily a good thing for their club either.

Jawa or Weslake?

The big final dilemma

Chapter 15

THE year ended with a dream come true . . . but 1980 began like Michael Lee's worst nightmare.

Instead of preparing for another all-out assault on the World Championship, he was laid up in hospital with a broken back.

And the crazy thing is, the injury that nearly wrecked his title chances happened in a meaningless off-season meeting in mid-January that was never meant to be taken seriously.

"It was supposed to be a bit of fun but my natural racing instincts took over again and I pushed it too far. Being on the bike was never just 'fun' to me – I always wanted to win," says Michael, who underlined the point by managing to incur a tapes exclusion!

He had, though, adapted well to the tricky synthetic latex surface before crashing during the first ever indoor speedway meeting held at Birmingham's National Exhibition Centre.

It looked a fairly innocuous spill as he clipped the fence on the home straight of the 150-yard track while chasing indoor specialist Jan Andersson in a match-race.

He was stretchered off and taken to hospital, where it was confirmed that he'd suffered his most serious injuries to date – two fractured and compressed vertebrae.

Recalling the accident at the NEC that threatened his 1980 title aspirations, Michael says: "At one stage it didn't even look as if I'd be able to ride at all that season. As I lay there in hospital, I thought my season was gone. I was devastated.

"Then, suddenly, there was a bit of hope, although the doctors told me there was no way I was going to ride for probably six months. So we were looking at July. I would have missed everything by then – I wouldn't have been able to make the World Final.

"My only hope was to be riding again at the beginning of April, before the World Championship qualifiers got underway," added Michael's, who became a father for the first time on February 9 when his partner Janet gave birth to their son Jody.

But Michael made it back in the saddle even quicker than that, defying medical opinion and advice to take his place in the prestige, televised Daily Express Spring Classic, won by John Davis at Wimbledon on March 20.

His premature comeback even caused Cyril Crane some self-inflicted embarrassment. He had assumed his skipper wouldn't be fit to ride in the club's opening meeting of the season and so never booked him to appear in the Supporters' Trophy event, which went ahead without him! A paid maximum against

Hackney a week later confirmed Lee was more or less back in the usual routine.

As well as vying for the No.1 spot at King's Lynn, Lee and Dave Jessup also went head-to-head throughout the '80 season in their pursuit of the biggest prize.

"I managed to scrape through the qualifiers," continued Michael, whose British semi-final round took him to Sheffield, where nine points was just enough to secure one of a top eight qualifying place.

But he had only six to his name going into his last ride and really needed the win he easily collected from Heat 19 at the expense of his club-mate Jessup. DJ admitted recently that he was quite content for that to be the only point he dropped in winning the meeting – but how that favour to a team-mate in need would come back to bite him on the backside later in the year.

"It was supposed to be a bit of fun but my natural racing instincts took over again and I pushed it too far. Being on the bike was never just 'fun' to me – I always wanted to win."

Jessup's domination of the '80 season began with him winning the Embassy Internationale and continued throughout the summer. The diminutive racer was by far England's best rider in their 3-1 Test series defeat by the USA and by breaking the track record in successive home meetings at Lynn he proved that his works sponsored Weslake was as fast as anything around. A maximum and victory (with Peter Collins) in the World Pairs at Krsko in Yugoslavia brought him another gold medal to add to the four he'd previously won as a member of the Lions' World Team Cup squad.

But it was Jessup's outstanding performances in the World Championship rounds that made the pundits believe that it would be his year.

He clinched his first British Championship by beating Lee in the final heat to complete a perfect maximum – the only point Michael dropped at Coventry. And DJ was calling the tune again in the Commonwealth Final at Wimbledon, where 14 points earned him another main title and Lee scampered through the qualifier on nine points.

It reflected well on King's Lynn Speedway that Lee and Jessup were in constant demand for their country. On the other hand, the Stars' management complained that they were regularly deprived of their top two riders for their Saturday night home meetings far too often than was good for business. Team manager Alan Littlechild said: "I'm sick to the teeth at constantly not being able to track my top riders. I know that England is important but Cyril Crane and myself get our living from King's Lynn. We've got our crowd to think about."

The candid Crane talked openly of cutting back on the number of meetings he would stage in the future, warning that he may not run at all on the weekends when Lee and Jessup were unavailable for club duty. Even though King's Lynn was still then one of the best supported tracks in the country, relying on a solid hardcore support from the market town population of around 30,000, he rightly recognised that supporters were being much more selective in the meetings they attended.

With Martin Rogers, the master of spin, having taken his typically more considered and diplomatic approach to Leicester, the controversial Crane often found himself in the spotlight from 1980 onwards and he was never short of a quote or three for grateful local hacks looking to a splash headline. Whether you agreed with his regular and increasingly outlandish outbursts or not, Crane was usually 'good copy' (well, the printable stuff was!) and banner headlines that screamed 'disgusting', 'fumes' and 'hits out' became commonplace in the two weekly trade publications as well as the local *Lynn News* and *Advertiser*.

Funnily enough, many of the most scathing comments that tripped so easily from the lips of the irascible Crane were aimed at his own riders! He never pulled punches, although he landed a few.

Like most promoters of the regular Saturday tracks, of which there were still six operating in the 17-strong British League in 1980, Crane hated the proliferation of FIM meetings held on Sundays – except the ones staged on English tracks which the BSPA happily promoted on behalf of the sport's international governing body and earned a share of profits from.

But the clash of domestic and international dates was just one of many problems UK track bosses had to grapple with amid dire warnings from numerous respected journalists and others within the game that British speedway urgently needed to clean up its act if it was to halt the decline in attendances at a growing number of venues. Constant infighting among promoters, rows over the 50-point limit, an over-reliance on poor imported foreign riders and rules being routinely bent and manipulated all brought discredit to the domestic race scene at the start of a difficult decade in which the nation as a whole entered a new period of recession.

Riders who failed to appear, as advertised, was another recurring headache for track bosses and fans alike. Michael Lee was usually cast as the villain, although he claimed a "mix up" over his booking for the Berger GP round at Reading caused him to miss the Smallmead meeting. He was reportedly "unwell" when Martin Rogers received a phone call at 4pm to say that his former No.1 wouldn't be coming to the Elf Golden Gauntlets, which was due to start at Leicester just three-and-a-half hours later.

Rogers recalls how he viewed events from the opposite end of the A47: "When Lin and I went to Leicester to take on our first promoting gig in 1980 we were, of course, keen to see how King's Lynn would fare, especially in areas of image, organisation, etc, which were so important in the club's rise through the 70s from country cousins to being widely acknowledged as one of the most professional, best-run and best-presented teams/clubs in the BL.

Michael was one of the stars of the first indoor meeting held at Birmingham in January 1980, as this shot of him leading John Davis and Steen Mastrup shows.

It all went horribly wrong when Michael crashed ......

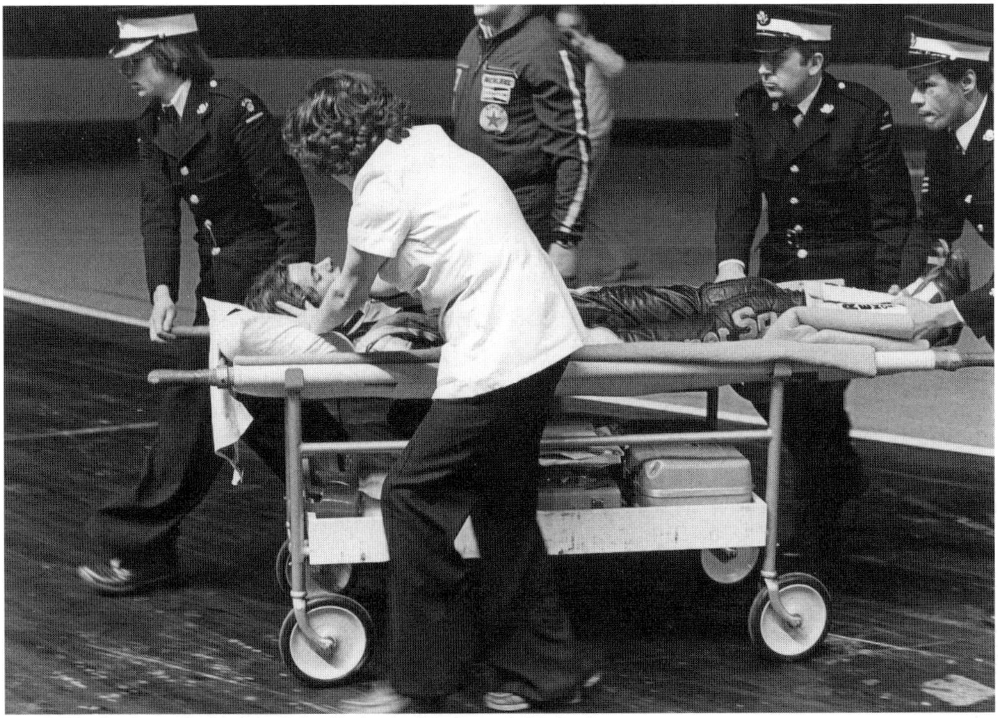

. . . . and had to be rushed to hospital suffering broken bones in his back.

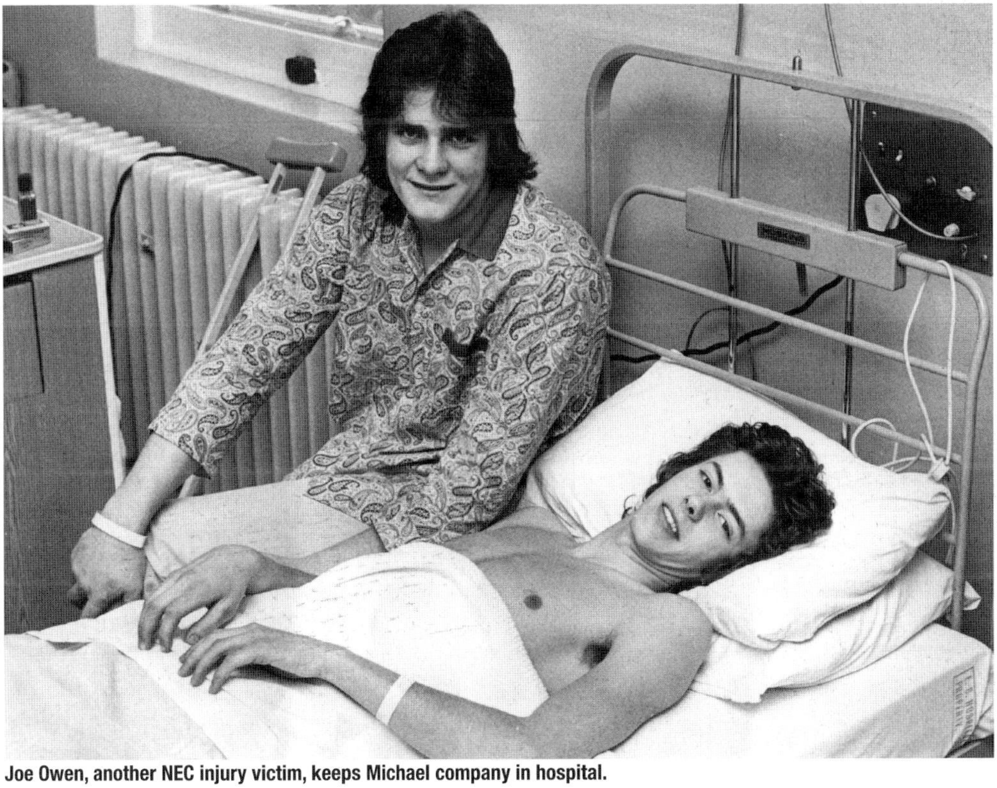

Joe Owen, another NEC injury victim, keeps Michael company in hospital.

"And of course we had more than a passing interest in how Michael would go. It gave us no pleasure when, during that 1980 season, he had a few brushes with authority although being at a distance now, we hadn't a full picture of how he was beginning to play up. "

Back on the World Championship trail, nine points was ample to see both Lee and Jessup cruise through the potentially hazardous Inter-Continental Final at White City. Chris Morton claimed the biggest title of his career by beating Bruce Penhall in a run-off but, unfortunately for the spectacular Mort, most of the post-meeting talk was about the shock elimination of two of the six non-qualifiers, Ole Olsen and reigning World Champion Ivan Mauger – the first time the Kiwi giant had failed to reach the World Final in 15 years.

"Michael had a contract with Jawa and there he was using Weslakes. The people at the Jawa factory were just putting up with it, hoping it would come right."

With the 'old guard' gone and Peter Collins a slightly fading force at the very highest level, the stage was set for one of the new wave of international superstars to grasp the sport's richest prize. Jessup wasn't exactly young but he was enjoying a new lease of life, while the charismatic Penhall and the ever-consistent Lee were being widely tipped as the men to beat in the World Final at Gothenburg.

But Michael faced a huge dilemma in the build-up to the big night. Just three weeks before the World Final he won the Berger Grand Prix Final in appalling conditions at Wimbledon with 14 points . . . on a Weslake.

He explained: "Jawa had brought out their double overhead twin-cam engine and there were doubts about how good it really was or would be. Mauger and Olsen both had problems with it. We all tried to have an input, including Dad, but we were struggling to get consistently good results with that engine."

In the first half of the season Michael had been plagued by mechanical problems. "So I went out and bought a Weslake about a month before the World Final – which was probably a big mistake," he admits. "Weslake got a sniff of this. They obviously wanted me back on Wessies because if I gave up my Jawa contract and had a good World Final using their engine, what better advert could there be for their product?

"I went to Gothenburg with a big decision to make – whether to stick with Jawa, and the people who were backing me, or go back to Weslake. In fact, I took two complete Jawa bikes and a Weslake with me to Sweden and at first we didn't have a clue which bike we were going to use.

"I'd ridden the Weslake a few times in league racing in the preceding weeks and it had gone really well. I was actually fastest on the Weslake in practice at

Gothenburg and I would have used it in the meeting, too, but for one thing. I was still a Jawa works rider and the look on the faces of the Jawa people as I came into the pits with the Wessie – not a look of anger but one of disappointment – convinced me to ride their machine on the night.

"When they saw me with a Weslake they could have collected everything up off me and took it away, because the deal was you only rode Jawa machinery, nothing else, and they fully expected that commitment from their riders."

Andy Lee remembers "a very difficult situation." He says: "Michael had a contract with Jawa and there he was using Weslakes. The people at the Jawa factory were just putting up with it, hoping it would come right."

Despite reports to the contrary, there was no serious threat of Jawa taking legal action against Michael for using a Weslake.

"I couldn't get to Gothenburg until after practice," Andy continued. "Mike phoned me afterwards and said: 'I've practiced on both. The Jawa was good but I really thought the Weslake was quicker'. But all the people from the Jawa factory were there watching and Michael said they looked absolutely crestfallen.

"I asked him what he thought he was going to do and he said: 'I think I'll use the Jawa'. I agreed with his choice and told him I thought he was making the best decision overall for his career."

"Most people had nothing – and I mean nothing. Getting up to go to work each morning was the highlight of their day. And remember, they worked for naff-all."

The promoters who felt let down by Michael from time to time have had their say in this book but it would be wrong to brand him an inconsiderate person with a heart of stone. His thoughts on how he arrived at his decision to choose Jawa over Weslake at Gothenburg in '80 provide a revealing insight into his character.

He continues: "The Czech people had looked after me so well – just as they did all their works riders. They were suppressed in an East European country and you really felt for them. Going back to the Communist days, it wasn't easy for them out there. They didn't want sympathy but you felt so sympathetic towards them because of the way they lived in those days of communism.

"Compared to them, we in Britain don't know what a hard life really is. When they were ruled by a communist regime, as it was when I first went to Poland in the 70s, it was unbelievably tough. You know, we had a bloody easy life over here compared to what I saw for myself in Czechoslovakia, Poland and other countries like that in the late 70s and 80s. Most people had nothing – and I mean nothing. Getting up to go to work each morning was the highlight of their day. And remember, they worked for naff-all.

"But the Jawa boys loved their jobs. It felt special for them to work at the Jawa factory and they felt a little more privileged than their fellow countrymen when they managed to go over to the West go out to World Finals in Western Europe.

"From Stan, the factory mechanic, to the top man at the company, they were very genuine people who couldn't do enough for me. I just couldn't let them down. We'd spent hours in their workshop with Stan showing us different tricks and telling us the things they had done and how they went about it, which helped Dad too. Their influenced me and my future results in speedway.

"In almost two years, we'd done so much with them and been to the factory many times. We knew everyone there very well and enjoyed a very good relationship with all of them. And because they just wanted what was best for me, so I wanted to do my best for them.

"So after practice I had a big dilemma. I was going faster on the Weslake but didn't know what to do for the best. We'd prepared everything ready for the final ourselves. When it came down to it and we walked into the pits in Gothenburg, I still hadn't made up my mind what to do.

"The Jawa representatives came over and asked what I was going to ride in the final - and that's when I decided. You could see that their chins were on the ground. They thought I was going to choose Weslake – apart from myself, I think the only others using a Jawa in the final were the three Czech riders (Jiri Stancl, Petr Ondrasik and Ales Dryml). Everyone else was on Weslake.

"Anyway, I chose Jawa - and won it! The smiles on the faces of the Jawa people at the end of that final made it all worthwhile," added Michael.

Penhall and the Red Mist

How the world title was won

Chapter 16

THE first gripping lap of Heat 5 – that's when Michael Lee became a man so possessed that he knew nothing would stop him from going on to win the 1980 World Final.

And he says he has Bruce Penhall to thank for giving him the extra spark he needed to go all out for victory after finishing second in his first race.

Not that Cradley Heath's American favourite intended to do one of his main rivals any 'favours' in Sweden.

Lee and Penhall were good mates, and remain so to this day, but it was something 'naughty' the American superstar did at the end of the back straight when they met in Gothenburg on the night of Friday, September 5 that inspired Michael to achieve the ultimate success.

Lee explains: "On the first lap of my second race Penhall threw an 'S-bend' on me down the straight, as we came off the second corner by the pits. I was coming up the inside and had the run on him, but he turned left on me.

"Now until that moment I didn't know if I could have done that to him had our positions been reversed – even in a World Final. We were good friends.

"I was very surprised by what he did, because I wasn't one for throwing S-bends down the straight. When I see people do that, I think it's pretty nasty and unnecessary. You can push people wide, you can close the gap . . . but I was always one to leave people enough room to get themselves out of trouble, even though they might have lost 15 yards in the process. I was never one for taking them all the way over the top. Anyway, Penhall did that to me and if I'd have lost it there I would have hurt myself.

"I saw red and it took me a lap-and-a-half to catch him. I came under him, pointed at him and took his left leg away. On my DVD you can see him hanging down off the bike as I go past him. I did that purely in response to what he'd done to me earlier in the race.

"From that moment, mate, I was on a mission," added Michael.

Dethroned champ Ivan Mauger said before the final that only Penhall could realistically stop Jessup, Lee or Peter Collins from taking over his crown. Chris Morton and John Davis completed the English quintet – the largest representation by any country – but they were not regarded as genuine title contenders and so it proved.

In his pre-meeting analysis of all 16 finalists, Mauger said of Lee's chances: "It depends on what he has to ride on the night. He has been going well on Weslake, which may have him confused. Gothenburg's long straights will suit

SKANTIC TV
SEIKO

A panoramic view of Ullevi Stadium. It's Heat 5 and Bruce Penhall makes the early running, with Michael, Billy Sanders and Jan Andersson in hot pursuit.

the Jawa's top end speed but the fairly tight corners don't help its handling qualities. But he has always been one of my favourites."

And Mauger added: "I trust the new World Champion will carry the burden that goes with it and be a good ambassador for the sport. In that respect I strongly believe that either Collins or Penhall would make the best champion."

He reasoned that with No.10 in the riding order, Jessup had the "perfect draw", including the inside gate in his opening race against his big two biggest English rivals. And when he met Penhall in his final race, Mauger pointed out, DJ would be going off the outside grid, where there was likely to be more grip.

"DJ and Bruce were the biggest favourites that year," recalls Michael, "and yeah, there was a bit of rivalry between me and Dave even though we were team-mates at King's Lynn. I went into the final wanting to beat everyone but I knew that if Dave won it, the limelight at Lynn would be on him instead of me. So the thought of that spurred me on, too."

With no threat of a repeat of the bad weather that had marred the previous two World Finals at Gothenburg, in 1974 and '77, a crowd of around 30,000 settled down to watch Michael Lee bid for speedway immortality.

Race-by-race, this is how he did it . . .

HEAT 3

It looked like Jessup – an 11/4 shot with Corals - was going to prove the bookies right when he flew from the gate and quickly forged an unassailable lead in Heat 3, the race involving the three main British challengers and Finland's Kai Niemi. PC, who was sandwiched between DJ and Michael (gate three) on the start-line, led the chase and held second place until the third turn of the fourth lap when Lee forced his way through an inviting gap on the inside to snatch two priceless points.

HEAT 5

Facing three opponents who had each won their opening rides, Michael (gate four) bounced back from a tough first lap. Billy Sanders couldn't make the inside gate pay and was soon passed by Lee, who then set off in pursuit of Penhall. After initially being thwarted, he forced the American wide on the second bend of the third lap to win in convincing style. Already, it was obvious that there would be precious little passing on a rock hard track that offered nothing for those who liked to chase the dirt out wide. The ultra-slick conditions suited the Weslake from the start but Lee demonstrated in each of his first two rides that his Jawa had more than enough speed after the first 30 yards. Local favourite Jan Andersson's last place ultimately cost him a rostrum position.

HEAT 11

Michael's easiest race on paper proved to be just that. After initially bending the tapes, he led all the way from gate two to the flag, with Ales Dryml, Finn Thomsen and Petr Ondrasik all peering into the distance to try and catch a glimpse of Lee's back wheel.

HEAT 16

Another sharp start by Lee (gate one), who showed the back of his No.9 Union Jack racejacket and black/green/yellow leathers to Hans Nielsen, Egon Müller and Jiri Stancl before the German retired.

HEAT 18

With three second places having severely damaged Jessup's title hopes following his early win, victory in Heat 17 meant DJ had finished another frustrating night on 12 points. As he lined up in gate one with John Davis, Chris Morton and Poland's Zenon Plech (on a duff engine) for company, Michael knew that two points would be enough to clinch the world title. None of his three opponents had any hope of finishing on the rostrum, so Michael had no-one to fear. Only an unthinkable machine failure could stop him from completing the job.

Davis led from the tapes and briefly put up some resistance when Michael challenged him on the back straight on the third lap. But when JD left a generous gap on the inside as they entered the first bend on the last lap, Lee seized the opening and eased clear down the pits-side straight.

It was typical of the natural racer in him not to accept a cosy second place, and to instead go flat out for the win that put the seal on a thoroughly deserved victory. "I thought to hell with it, let's win it in style," he told reporters afterwards.

John Davis insisted to me a few years ago that he was not riding to England 'team orders' and didn't deliberately allow Michael, a good friend, to come past in their final race. Maybe the flamboyant natural showman in JD couldn't resist taking the lead, as if to prove a point, before graciously stepping aside for his mate as they entered the final lap? Whatever, Michael's clash with his two fellow Englishmen, Davis and Chris Morton, in Heat 18 provoked some angst in the pits just moments before the race.

England co-manager Eric Boocock seemed to contradict Davis, though, when he revealed: "Michael's World Final triumph was another glorious night for British speedway, although one Englishman who wasn't smiling too much was Don Godden. Ian Thomas and I had a furious row with him because Michael was riding Jawa while John Davis was on a Godden. John was going very well but it was obvious that, when they met late in the meeting, the one who had fewer points was going to help the other one out.

"I told them not to mess it up for each other and pointed out to John that, if Michael was in front, he shouldn¹t try to pass him or they could both end up losing out.

"Don didn't like that. He argued that, as John was an Englishman with an English engine, he shouldn't take any notice. My point was that we wanted an English World Champion – and it didn't matter if John was on a lawnmower! As it turned out, Michael beat John but he was given a much harder race than expected."

Davis, who shared fifth place with Penhall in the final reckoning, says:

Move over, Bruce! An angry Michael powers underneath Penhall to take the lead in Heat 5.

"I was very surprised by what he did, because I wasn't one for throwing S-bends down the straight. When I see people do that, I think it's pretty nasty and unnecessary."

"I definitely wasn't riding under instructions from the England management or anybody else and I made that clear to Don Godden afterwards.

"My bike slowed because three of the five engine bolts had broken, causing the carb to flood. That's why my engine spluttered.

"It wasn't a gift win for Michael – but I'll tell you this, there's no way I would've done anything to stop him winning the title. If I'd looked round and seen him in third or last place behind Mort and/or Zenon, I would've pulled straight onto the grass and let him have the points he needed to clinch the championship.

"Michael and I were good mates, we roomed together on England's foreign trips, so there's no way I would have got in his way if he'd been desperate for points in our last ride."

What happened on the final lap of Heat 18 proved irrelevant anyway, since Michael needed only a second place to wrap up the title. Lee punched the air with delight as he crossed the line before receiving the customary bumps from his pit crew and numerous riders, including meeting reserve Ole Olsen and a sporting Dave Jessup.

Ole Olsen keeps his Jawa colleague informed from the Ullevi pits.

Olsen hadn't scored enough points in the penultimate round at White City to qualify among the starting 16 but he still did a useful job for Lee on final night – maintaining a filled-in programme and keeping in close contact with his Jawa stable-mate. "He's part of this success," acknowledged a grateful Lee, by now the finished article as opposed to the rookie international whose youthful exuberance had sent Olsen through the Ipswich safety fence in 1977. It was noticeable that the Great Dane paid much more attention to Lee in the Gothenburg pits than he did his fellow countrymen, Hans Nielsen and Finn Thomsen, who scored seven points each. Clearly, loyalties among the riders of 'Team Jawa' transcended nationalities.

Jessup had put Lee and the rest in the shade for most of the season, and did so again when he and Michael met in Heat 3. But when it really mattered, when the pressure was piled on, DJ again came up a little short. He'd been unlucky with mechanical gremlins at Wembley in 1978 and Ullevi two years later would prove to be his closest shot at the title. After finishing two points behind Lee, Jessup beat Sanders in a run-off to complete a memorable King's Lynn one-two.

By contrast, Michael had timed his run to perfection, finding top form at just the right stage of the year to become only the fourth Englishman (after Tommy Price, Peter Craven and Peter Collins) to win the World Championship since it began in 1936.

Typical of the horrendous schedule the superstars of the day had to cope with, Michael had little chance to let his hair down in the hours that immediately

A fast start sees him take an early lead in Heat 16 from Egon Müller and Jiri Stancl.

followed his greatest speedway triumph.

Lee says: "The thing I remember most is seeing a drunken Zenon Plech staggering across the dual carriageway outside where the after-meeting reception was held. 'You a werry good wider, Michael', he slurred and I said to him: 'And you are very pissed, Zenon!' I tell you, cars were swerving all over the road to avoid him!

"There wasn't time to really appreciate what had happened and take it all in on that Friday because I had to get back to ride at King's Lynn the next night. We were booked onto a flight that left Gothenburg for Heathrow at 8.30 the next morning.

"But I did go and have a word with Mr Penhall later on that night during the FIM reception. He was very down because he really thought he was going to win. His mentor 'Spike', the dude with the handlebar moustache who wore a big Yankee hat, told me I was wasting my time because he reckoned Bruce was 'too pissed off to talk to anybody'.

"I ignored him, though, and went to Bruce's hotel room, where we did have a little chat about what had happened earlier. He knew what he'd done, and I told him he'd brought it on himself, but he still wouldn't come out of his room.

"I told him that if he hadn't thrown that S-bend on me, I probably wouldn't have gone on to win the final.

"And then, after a while, he just smiled at me. He didn't apologise – you don't apologise for things that happen in racing – but he knew exactly what he'd done

England conference before the decisive Heat 19 involving managers Ian Thomas and Eric Boocock, with Michael and Chris Morton.

"After a while, he just smiled at me. He didn't apologise – you don't apologise for things that happen in racing - but he knew exactly what he'd done in our race. And he knew how much it had cost him."

in our race. And he knew how much it had cost him. After what happened early on in that race, I was gonna have him no matter what . . . even if I came down myself!"

Their long-term friendship wasn't damaged by the events of Gothenburg, though.

"Bruce was one of my best mates in speedway – I used to go over to his place and he'd come to mine," continued Michael.

"It's hard to say that you're good mates with someone when there is so much fierce competition between you and I tried not to get too close to anyone, which is what Dad bred into me.

"But Bruce and I had full respect for one another on the track. The reason I saw red in the '80 World Final was because I didn't have respect for anybody who would throw an S-bend on me along the straight.

"What happened between us on the track in Sweden that night didn't affect our friendship, though, because he never threw another S-bend on me again!

"Don't get me wrong, I could be as dirty as anyone if I had to be. But I

John Davis and Zenon Plech lead Michael to the first bend in Heat 18 (above) and then the soon-to-be-crowned champ puts the pressure on JD (below).

wouldn't do it unnecessarily and I wouldn't do it unless provoked."

Despite that flashpoint in the '80 final, Lee and Penhall – the American being the elder by 19 months – retain a mutual respect that endures to this day.

Michael says: "There was never any doubt in my mind that Bruce would win a World Final. He was a tremendous motorcyclist in every way, a true character, and he deserved to win it in 1981 and '82."

In February 2004, when Bruce briefly returned to England for a Q&A forum at Telford, Michael was surprised to hear the Californian tell a packed audience that Lee, above all others, was the one rider he feared throughout his five seasons (1978-82) of racing in the British League.

Michael has never been one to go in search of plaudits but, standing almost unnoticed near the back of the main hall in the Telford Moat House Hotel that night, he was genuinely moved when Bruce paid him this huge compliment. After the show ended, these two great former rivals shook hands and the mutual respect they shared throughout their careers (Ullevi not withstanding) was once again there for all to see. Their physical looks had altered significantly in the passage of time – Bruce's famous blond locks were by now short and dark while Michael also had his hair neat and short and both men wore glasses – but their respect for one another remained undiminished.

"I was in my hotel room feeling sorry for myself. I heard a knock at the door and it was Michael. He had a few words of comfort for me that I'll never forget. He said: 'Mate, your time will come sooner than you think . . . now quit whining and let's party!'"

In 2009, Penhall reaffirmed his admiration for Lee via his column for the retro *Backtrack* magazine. Our American contributor's email read: "I have gone on record several times when asked to name my most feared opponent, and without question it was 'Mike the Bike'. There wasn't a race when I faced Michael that I knew he couldn't pass me at any given time – even when he wasn't at his best.

"I don't know what it was but I can honestly say that we brought out the best in each other. It didn't matter if it was at Cradley, King's Lynn or in an international meeting somewhere, it was always going to be a battle. We always rode very hard – and maybe not so fair – against each other from time to time but I can say there was always a ton of respect for each other.

"I will never forget the 1980 World Final. I'd made a good start in my race against Michael but I knew that he would be there in no time at all. I pulled it down on him very hard and it wasn't a lap later that he came hard underneath me. Michael's pass was very fair – hard but fair. Remember, this was a World

Championship and time for the weak at heart to stay at home!

"I remember after the final when I felt as dejected as they come for not winning that night," continued Bruce, who had earlier felt the pressure of the occasion as an American CBS film crew tracked his every movement on and off the track. "I was in my hotel room feeling sorry for myself. I heard a knock at the door and it was Michael. He had a few words of comfort for me that I'll never forget. He said: 'Mate, your time will come sooner than you think . . . now quit whining and let's party!'

Ole Olsen, Andy Lee and Dennis Hicks congratulate their man.

"Michael, along with PC and myself, spent many a Sunday together on the continent, racing either on speedway or long-track, and because all three of us rode for Saturday tracks in England we were always jamming to catch flights and racing to get home for Monday meetings, or recuperating from a busy week. Back in those days we were riding a good 150 days/nights of the year.

"But Mike the Bike was truly one of my favourites from my time in speedway."

September 5, 1980 was a memorable night for all of the Lee family. While Andy was working away in the pits throughout the meeting, alongside Dennis Hicks and Steve Burgess in their matching royal blue overalls and white baseball caps bearing the NGK logo, Valerie was sat high up in the stands cheering her son to his greatest triumph.

She recalls: "I was sat next to Danny Leno (Warner Sports), Michael's Janet and one or two others. We were way up near the top of the stadium, overlooking the pits opposite the start. I just didn't dream that he would win it.

"Towards the end of the meeting when Michael had just one race left, Danny and I were gripping each other so tightly that I had bruises on my upper arms. It was so exciting. We were shouting and jumping up and down. Danny lit up a cigarette and although I don't smoke, I asked him for one. I needed it to calm my nerves!

"At first, I couldn't get down to the pits to congratulate Michael. We were jammed in our seats because the supporters at the end of our row wouldn't let us past until they had finished marking their programmes! I shall never forget one English woman saying: 'We know your son's just won it but we want to fill in our programmes'.

"Eventually we were able to make our way down to the pits. I gave Michael a hug and a kiss and he said: 'That's enough of that, mum!'."

Val gave an insight into Michael's personality when she added: "He didn't like a fuss and he was never one for public shows of affection. Right from a young child, he didn't like to be kissed and cuddled by his mum or anybody else.

"If something upset him or he'd hurt himself, he would always go and hide. He would never let you see him cry or show his emotions.

"He is a soft-hearted person, so when any of our animals died – we've always kept dogs and cats – that would always upset him more than anything."

Andy says: "I was a bag of nerves before the final, more so than Michael. I knew it was possible for him to win but you never know if it's probable. Of course, he won it fair and square in the end and we were obviously all delighted for him.

"Valerie and I flew back to Luton that night and we were on the plane when the captain of the Swedish airline announced Michael's victory over the tannoy. Then cabin staff brought us a glass of champagne each, which was really wonderful. It was probably at that moment when it sunk in that our son had become World Champion."

Val said: "There were lots of speedway supporters on the plane with us. It took a while to sink in but when they announced it, I thought 'that's my Michael'. Before then I'd never really thought about him winning the World Championship. I accepted that he rode speedway and, being a mum, my main hope was that he would go through his career injury-free."

Back to Andy: "To be truthful, I wasn't surprised that he won the title as soon as he did. I knew he had the ability and the machinery to do it and it was down to him on the night. He just badly wanted to win and when he did it, I felt proud and relieved."

"Dad deserved a lot of credit for his work on my engines," says Michael. "He was doing a lot with my motors by that stage and that was probably the beginning of the engine revolution that has now gone absolutely crazy.

"There were Mauger and Olsen who'd been riding their long-stroke Jawas from the factory. They had their trick equipment and we had ours – and we were using things they weren't, which probably confused them a bit.

"Jawa gave me a lot but we weren't relying on the Jawa factory to look after us – we did our own thing. Dad had some special cams made, having re-designed the profile of the cams, which made my bike pull so well off the corners in Gothenburg that year. It was only the second time we'd tried them, so to use them in the World Final was a gamble."

Andy gave more of a technical insight into what went in to Michael's victory. "I designed a cam and had it made by a car company – it's the one Mike used at Gothenburg and I still have it in my garage as a souvenir," he said, pulling that

A toast to the champion. Belinda, Susan and Val with Michael the day after the final.

Michael has always appreciated the backing he received from Jawa.

very camshaft out of a box he keeps in a tin in his garage. I asked him to try and explain to laymen like you and me exactly what effect a 'special cam' would have on the engine.

"The cam opens the valves and that's the secret to the engine. Michael is now absolutely ace at making his own cams. It's like a spindle with lobes on and you get them ground to your own requirements. How you grind them determines how the valves will open, which is your timing, so you can have an intake of fuel a little earlier, or the exhaust opens a fraction earlier and gets rid of stuff – all very technical. If you get it right, the bike goes faster. But if you get it wrong . . .

"It's often said that the boys at the factory should know what is required when they make these parts but occasionally you have to tune for your own rider. For Gothenburg, we knew what the track was going to be like, with its very long straights, because he'd ridden there in the 1977 World Final and again in a Master of Speedway round.

"We wanted a little more drive out of the corners and I worked around this. In my head I knew what we wanted but it's difficult to explain. I didn't want to knock off speed at the end of the straight but I wanted more drive from the engine, so I had a special exhaust cam made to my own spec – and it worked.

"It made Mike's bike drive better out of the corner and you saw that when he passed Penhall in his second ride. He was faster out of the corners and just quick enough down the straights.

"He didn't make terrifically good starts that night. The Jawa used to spin a lot, they were a heavy block mass to get going, so there was a bit of a disadvantage there but we did our best to get it as good as we could. He was magnificent at White City when he won those two World Championship rounds in 1979 – it's horses for courses.

"There was a time, when Michael was at his best, that we had 13 machines on the go – including three long-track bikes. Even so, that was still a lot of bikes for that time and they were all 'runners' capable of being ridden to a win. It was a full-on job.

"We used to do all the same things that riders and their tuners do today and we were definitely on the ball. By using different compressions and altering the ignitions, we were as much to the forefront as anybody at that time.

"I used to write up our set-ups in an A4 book the day after each meeting. I'd log all the details in my own version of short-hand along the lines of: 'Rode at King's Lynn and used Mike Lee number one, two or three'; what the compression was; how many meetings the engine had done; his total points scored; and my own little bit underneath about how I thought the bike had performed on the night. I did it for every single meeting Michael rode in.

"I could stand to be corrected, but I don't think Michael had an engine failure in any titled meeting. Part of the reason for that was not that I was preparing the engines or doing them better than anybody else. It was all about knowing how

Father and son share a moment they had worked for since 1975.

"There were lots of speedway supporters on the plane with us. It took a while to sink in but when they announced it, I thought 'that's my Michael'. Before then I'd never really thought about him winning the World Championship."

far you could push certain parts. For instance, we'd never run with a connecting rod that had done more than 'x' number of meetings.

"The Jawa pistons were not of a very good quality, so we had to change those fairly often at one point. You'd only want to do about five or six meetings with the same piston but being as they were readily available off the shelf, it didn't particularly worry us. Con-rods would last fairly well but we wouldn't have run them in important events after, say, 10 meetings."

Although Andy Lee is rightly acclaimed as the engineering wizard who conjured vital tricks in the privacy of the Lees' workshop, Michael remains full of praise and respect, too, for the company who backed him with the machinery on which he won his two individual track racing World Championships in 1980 and '81.

"I've got a photograph of me posing with 13 bikes that Jawa supplied for me. They built up more on top of that and you needed it for the World Championship

Back home with Janet, son Jody and the World Championship trophy.

events – individual and team, plus England internationals and everything else. All those bikes were getting used. They were being carted off to Sweden, Denmark and Germany, etc, and without the backing I had from the Jawa factory all this would have been very difficult, if not impossible, so I must thank them for what they did for me.

"Hopefully winning the World Championship in 1980, followed by the long-track title the following year, helped repay the faith they showed in me.

"I was as chuffed to bits for them, as much as for myself, when I won in Gothenburg. They had been the dominant speedway bike since around 1966, until Weslake came in, and when Ivan, Ole and I were using their twin overhead cam engines as factory riders, I felt very proud to be associated with them.

Where do you go from here?

"When I first got the works contract in 1979, it meant so much to me – almost as good as winning the World Final, because Jawa didn't come along and give riders a contract unless they really thought a lot of you. Their sponsorship made me feel important."

Michael joined an elite band of world champions who have earned the honour and privilege of calling themselves the best. In attendance at Ullevi that momentous evening was a small sprinkling of all-time greats . . . Swedish trio Ove Fundin, Bjorn Knutson and Anders Michanek, plus Kiwi Ronnie Moore, who paraded around the track on vintage bikes before the racing got underway.

Glory came at a price, though. Michael reveals: "It was expensive in Sweden and after paying the travel and hotel bills for my three mechanics, family members and myself, I was actually out of pocket on the weekend by at least two grand!

His actual FIM prize money for winning the title was a pitiful £1,200. "But that didn't matter because I came home with the trophy," says Michael.

Randall Butt of the *Cambridge Evening News* says: "Significantly, I remember being on the Ullevi track when Dave Lanning was interviewing Michael for ITV. He asked him what he was going to do next after winning the world title, and

Michael about to take command in Heat 5 of the World Team Cup Final at Wroclaw, with Vaclav Verner, Scott Autrey and Edward Jancarz unable to resist.

Michael answered something like: 'I'm going to have a think about that – a big think'. Unfortunately his head didn't rule enough of went on during the decline and fall which eventually followed."

The day after the World Final, the local CEN dispatched a reporter and photographer to the Lees' cottage in Melbourn. A smartly dressed Michael was surrounded in the sunlit back garden by his parents and teenage sisters Belinda and Susan. They were photographed together drinking a champagne toast to the champion. It was a picture of happiness, the ultimate reward for what they had all contributed to over a long period.

Just 24 hours after his golden night in Sweden, the physically "shattered" World Champion went up to King's Lynn and produced a performance befitting the newly-crowned speedway king. Not only did he romp to an inspirational 12-point maximum in Stars' league win against table-toppers Hackney, but Michael also broke Jessup's track record with a time of 64.0 – even though his best bike was still on the way back from Sweden. Talk about happy homecomings. "He was absolutely superb," wrote Kevin Brown, the match reporter for *Speedway Star.*

Two weeks later, Lee scored 11 points (joint top scorer with Chris Morton) in Wroclaw as England regained the World Team Cup at the expense of the USA (Penhall scored a maximum), hosts Poland and the Czechs. It was the icing on the

10 CAMBRIDGE EVENING NEWS, Saturday, September 6, 1980

Cambridge ace leads East Anglian 1-2-3

World beater Lee reigns supreme

Mike Lee, the crown prince of speedway since his world debut in Gothenburg three years ago, was acclaimed king here last night.

The 21-year-old Cambridge star brought the world title to Britain for only the second time in the last 19 years with the most courageous performance of his meteoric career.

Three times he fought his way through from the back in the magnificent Ullevi stadium, on a track most of his opponents believed ruled out any overtaking.

After dropping a point to the pre-meeting favourite, Kings Lynn colleague Dave Jessup, Lee won his other four rides to finish two points clear of the field and

RANDALL BUTT from Gothenburg on the big night for speedway

needed and he produced it with only seconds of the race remaining.

As Collins was setting himself up to try to pass Jessup on the last but one bend, Lee went surging under him in the bravest, most audacious piece of riding of the night:

It was the psycholog... ...ded to ... has ... he u... m

first race but I reckon if I could have passed Collins earlier I might have taken Dave Jessup as well.

"The track wasn't the sort ... a lot of ...

The Daily Telegraph 25
Saturday, Sept. 6, 1980

World Speedway

LEE PIPS JESSUP FOR TITLE

By A Special Correspondent in Gothenburg

THE world individual speedway final here at the Ullevi Stadium proved a total triumph for England. Not only did Michael Lee of Kings Lynn take the title but his club-mate Dave Jessup finished runner-up.

So Lee, at 21, becomes youngest Englishman ever to take the world crown.

Heat three put the top Englishmen together and J... ed all the way from the ... ut a vital slip by Peter Co... n the last bend, allowed L... ake two priceless points ... econd place.

Two wins in a row for Co... ept him in the hunt but w... Reading's John Davis left him at the gate in Heat 14 his title hopes were ended. Jessup could have troubled Lee but, when he was headed by the Swede Jan Andersson in Heat 15, a second place wasn't good enough.

When Lee was fast away in Heat 16, he established a two-point lead over all his rivals and the title was his for the taking. Although fellow-Englishman Davis led the champion elect from the gate in heat 18, the youngster from Kings Lynn couldn't settle for second place and he stormed through for a triumphant victory and the title.

Jessup, having finished with twelve points, needed a run-off with the Australian Billy Sanders ...

SPEEDWAY STAR, September 13, 1980

LEE-DER OF THE PACK

1.	MICHAEL LEE	(England/King's Lynn)	2	3	3	3	3	14
2.	Dave Jessup	(England/King's Lynn)	3	2	2	2	3	12
3.	Billy Sanders	(Australia/Ipswich)	3	1	3	2	3	12
4.	Jan Anderson	(Sweden/Reading)	3	0	2	3	3	11
5.	Bruce Penhall	(USA/Cradley)	3	2	1	1	2	9
6.	John Davis	(England/Reading)	2	1	1	3	2	9
7.	Peter Collins	(England/Belle Vue)	1	3	1	1	0	8
8.	Chris Morton	(England/Belle Vue)	2	1	1	3	1	8
9.	Kai Niemi	(Finland/Eastbourne)	0	1	3	2	2	8
10.	Finn Thomsen	(Denmark/Hackney)	2	[illegible]	[illegible]	[illegible]	1	7
11.	Hans Nielsen	(Denmark/Wolve...	[illegible]	[illegible]	[illegible]	[illegible]	2	7
12.	Ales Dryml	(Cz...	[illegible]	[illegible]	[illegible]	[illegible]	0	5
							1	5
							1	4
							0	1
							0	0

Lynn News & Advertiser
Every Tuesday and Friday Price
Tuesday, September 9, 1980

Stars put Lynn top of the world — Special souvenir: Page

How I won—by champion Lee

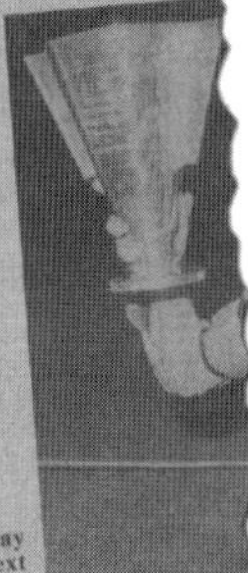

Sports Editor Chris Hornby sees Gothenburg triumph

MICHAEL LEE the newly-crowned King of Speedway ... from the sport in the next

SPEEDWAY SPECIAL... From DAVE LANNING in Gothenburg

HAIL KING LEE!

Mighty Michael wins the world crown with epic ride

MICHAEL LEE, of King's Lynn, became only the fourth Englishman since 1936 to win the World Speedway Championship at Ullevi Stadium, Gothenburg last night ...

place with Billy Sanders of Ipswich to give East Anglia its greatest night in motorcycle sporting history.

A breathless Lee, son of famous English scramble star Andy, said: "It ...

NEWS BRIEFING

Mike Lee is new world champion

Cambridge speedway star Mike Lee, aged 21, is new world champion.

He took the title in Gothenburg, Sweden, last night when he dropped just one point in his five rides.

It was his fourth attempt to win the world crown, and he is only the fourth English rider to win the honour in the history of the sport.

● Randall Butt's report ...m Gothenb... 10.

Mike Lee

HERTS & CAMBS REPORTER & ROYSTON CROW

FRIDAY, SEPTEMBER 12th, 1980 ★ ESTABLISHED 1855

WELCOME HOME 'KING' MIKE

Local lad, Mike Lee, came home at the weekend a World Champion and all set to make his million.

Mike, whose dream of becoming the world's number one Speedway rider came true in Gothenburg on Friday ... ing over the fields.

Friday's race in Sweden was the fourth time he has bid for the World Championship and winning it makes him the ...

STORY: JENNY ...

VM är över. Överst på prispallen tar Michael Lee emot lagerkransen och VM-bucklan. Därefter blev det stora kramen av pappa Andy, mekanikern som finjusterade Michaels cykel inför VM.

... för det var farsan Andy som låg bakom VM-triumfen!

ROSY LEE!

Mighty Mike roars to world title

from MIKE BEALE, Gothenburg

...ast night became ...gest - ever world ...pion—eight months ...jury threatened his ...

LEE'S THE KING

MICHAEL LEE, 22-year-old England and King's Lynn speedway star, won the world title in Sweden last night, beating anti-post favourite and team-mate Dave Jessup into second place.

● *Full report—Page 31*

Typical of the excellent national coverage speedway received in 1980, this is how the press reported Michael's victory in Gothenburg...

Trust Ivan to upstage the smartly dressed English World Team Cup winners at the RAC reception win his dickie bow! Eric Boocock, Dave Jessup, Peter Collins, Michael, Chris Morton and Ian Thomas complete the catwalk line-up.

cake for the team managed by Ian Thomas and Eric Boocock. With Michael having captured the individual title to follow Jessup and Collins' victory in the World Pairs, England had completed a unique World Championship grand slam. The £500 win bonus each rider received from the SCB was an irrelevance, though typical of the relative pittance on offer to our world champions at the time.

Thomas admitted in his 2006 book that he and Booey initially had "great reservations" about using Michael, saying he looked jaded and was doing too much, too soon after the back injuries he sustained at Birmingham in January. "But, I have to say, once we got down to business in the World Team Cup, he had changed and his dedication to the cause surprised me," Thomas said.

"I still have vivid memories of a race in the final in Poland when he missed the gate by yards and, in that class of competition, I feared a last place. But he stormed under everyone on the first two bends to keep us on track with a brilliant victory."

Everyone seems to have a favourite Michael Lee story and, like his former colleague Thomas, Boocock used his autobiography (also published in 2006) to recall Michael's drunken antics at the reception following the 1980 WTC final in Poland.

"We were invited to a big banquet in a huge mansion," says Booey. "All the bigwigs were there and our spirits were high. Michael, it has to be said, was very much the worse for wear, and disappeared for about half-an-hour. He reappeared just as the dignitaries on the top table had begun their speeches. The room was hushed as we all listened to what the man with the microphone had to say – until Michael burst in singing at the top of his voice. 'Dayoh, dayoh, dayoh' was the chorus as he bounced from pillar to pillar on his way back to our table.

"I was furious and told him to sit down and shut up, but he wanted to borrow £100. I gave him the money and said: 'Now f*** off and don't come back!' I don't know what he wanted it for but I wasn't in the mood to ask.

"I think he got away with it because he was a young lad, he was World Champion and he had just helped England win the World Team Cup, but it was very embarrassing for the whole England contingent.

"Michael¹s problems in later life have been well documented, of course, and I think he was already on the slippery slope then. It was the beginning of the end. When Michael became mixed up in drugs we all hoped it was just a fad and that he would quickly grow out of it. When those problems began to surface, it would have been naïve not to have realised he was getting involved in some way, although I think it's also fair to say that everyone makes mistakes. Remember, smoking wasn't the social stigma it is today, even though the government relaxed their laws on smoking cannabis.

"I should also point out that I never saw him take any drugs," added Boocock.

Michael recalled: "I wasn't a big drinker but the boys were celebrating because we'd won the World Team Cup and I was World Champion, so I decided to let my hair down. Not being used to alcohol at that age, I probably got pissed quicker than everybody else and must have started singing in my inebriated state. Don't ask me what I did with the 100 quid, but I guess it was used for more partying!

"I didn't mean to upset Booey, a super team boss who really looked after us. When we rode in Poland, he even brought cans of baked beans with him on the trip and cooked them in the pits on a little improvised 'stove' he'd made up before the World Team Cup Final to make sure we had something decent to eat!"

Ian Thomas continued: "Michael was a rider who could produce the goods when it mattered, as he proved so emphatically in Gothenburg. Perhaps his problem was that, on too many occasions, speedway didn't matter enough for him and, too often, he had off-track distractions which mattered more.

"He was his own worst enemy, the George Best of speedway. Both were wayward stars and, probably, both lacked the necessary degree of backing to help them cope with the trappings and pressure of fame and success."

One of the first changes Thomas and Boocock introduced after being appointed England co-managers at the start of '80 was to introduce a smart new dress code. The management duo and their team would arrive for international team meetings dressed in dark blazers and grey slacks, with the England badge embroidered on their breast pockets.

Thomas recalls that he had a job to convince Michael that this was the way it had to be, saying: "He seemed to like being seen as the rebel but Eric and myself put a lot of pressure on him to conform. We would have looked stupid with one rider different from the rest and, eventually, he reluctantly agreed to wear a blazer along with the other boys."

By the end of the 1980 season, Lynn had slipped two places in the BL table to sixth, while Jessup had, for once, just managed to overhaul Lee at the top of the team averages. But in the grand scheme of things what did it really matter to Michael, who had won the big one and picked up a second gold medal in the WTC in the space of a fortnight?

A year that had begun so badly for him ended almost perfectly – if you disregard the minor hand and back injuries he suffered in a fall during the BLRC at Belle Vue that forced him to miss the last few meetings of the season.

"I'd gone from lying in a hospital bed with a broken back in January, thinking my season was over before it had even begun, to World Champion. As I crossed the finish line in Sweden, it was certainly one of the happiest moments of my life," said Michael.

When asked immediately following the final at Gothenburg if Michael would go on to become a good World Champion, Leicester boss Martin Rogers expressed the view that "he may do – if he looks after himself", before adding that his former schoolboy prodigy had the God-given talent to win the title six times.

But Rogers was being typically circumspect and with good reason. He recalls: "When the World Final was in Sweden, Chris Hornby, then sports editor of the *Lynn News*, asked me for my 1-2-3 prediction and I gave him Lee-Jessup-Sanders in the correct order. When Michael clinched the title Bob Radford was in the Ullevi pits and asked me for my immediate reaction. It was: 'I hope he's a good World Champion'.

"Leicester had been due to open the 1980 Blackbird Road season with a Border Trophy match against King's Lynn on April 1, but it was washed out. It was rearranged as the last meeting of the season, and of course having the new World Champion gave it even more spice. But Michael cried off on the day, yet another disappointment for the fans and an embarrassment for the home (and away) promoters to deal with."

Michael himself immediately declared his intention to win more World Championships and not to treat the glory of Ullevi '80 as a one-off.

This should have heralded the start of a long run of sustained success for the 21-year-old whose schoolboy dreams had finally come true.

It should have been the springboard to greatness for a gifted youngster who seemingly had the speedway world at his feet.

Instead it was the beginning of the end for Michael Lee's racing career.

Drugs and the 'Wannabe Yank'

Under the influence of Americans

Chapter 17

WITHIN days of winning the 1980 World Championship, instead of taking a well-earned rest at the end of a highly eventful season before plotting how to build upon his greatest victory and continue along the path to speedway immortality, Michael Lee had other things whirring around in his young head.

The new World No.1 was busy instead in the USA, letting his hair down . . . and snorting cocaine.

Recalling his proper "full-on" experience of the expensive white powdery stuff also commonly referred to as 'Charlie', he reveals: "I was on my way to Aussie to race in their summer season but stopped off in California to take part in a Superbikers event near San Diego."

He was in the 'land of opportunity' to compete alongside other top riders in a series to test the all round skills of stars from different spheres of motorcycle sport. As well as Lee, American speedway No.1 Bruce Penhall also took part in the end-of-season fun event at the now defunct Carlsbad Raceway, a multi-motorcycle sports complex consisting of a quarter-mile drag strip, a seven-turn, one-mile road course, a moto-cross track and a speedway oval. Michael recalls US moto-cross legends Steve Wise and Kent Howerton also being involved, along with a couple of leading road-racers whose names now elude him.

"I didn't do that well, to be honest. I remember walking into the pits and seeing this flat track-style bike standing alone in the corner of the pits and saying to Penhall: "Hey look, some poor f***** has got to ride that dog today' – and it turned out to be me! All the other riders were using works factory machines that looked the business and performed much better than the bike they gave me to ride.

"As soon as I arrived in California there was a big party going on and the Charlie was on show. There were bucketfuls of it available and it's all going on, so that's when I tried it for the first time.

"At my third party in three nights, I met another young speedway rider there who is, and always has been, as straight as a die," says Michael, who refuses to disclose the identity of the person (though it should be stated that he is not referring here to his great rival and friend Penhall).

"I was on the Charlie and I talked this other lad that was with me into having a go too. He was apprehensive at first but I persuaded him, saying: 'Don't worry, you'll be all right, there's loads of young women about' and that kind of thing.

"Anyway, he tried some Charlie and thought it was great. We spent the night on it but the following day he must have freaked out about what had gone on

Michael with Billy Sanders (left) and Danish freelance rider Tommy Knudsen on the 1980-81 tour of Australia.

and, in a moment of panic, he phoned his father and confessed to him what we'd been up to.

"Straight away, the rider's father phoned my parents and told them what his son and I had been doing at the party. But by this time I'd already flown on to Aussie, so Mum and Dad had weeks and months to freak out about what I'd got involved in during my two weeks in America. My parents were aware that I smoked cannabis, though they didn't approve of it, but they didn't know at that stage about me doing coke

"In fact, the first time I'd tried coke was when I went out with friends after a meeting in Denmark. It perked me up and I didn't realise how much it had affected me. Then it came up again somewhere and I tried it again. I got the coke from someone who was involved in speedway but I will never name them, although I'm sure people will put two and two together."

When Michael touched down in Australia for his third tour of the country that he loves so much, there were other new angles to explore. Aussie-based tour organiser Nigel Boocock's brainchild was to bring two complete five-man teams from England and the USA to contest the first Tri-Nations Test series against Australia over seven matches, plus other unofficial meetings involving the same riders.

Captain Lee led a Lions team that also included Alan Grahame, Les and Phil Collins with Doug Wyer at reserve. The USA team was led by Bobby Schwartz and Dennis Sigalos, while Denny Pyeatt, John Cook and Shawn Moran provided back-up. Australia was spearheaded by Phil Crump and Billy Sanders, with most support coming from John Titman, Phil Herne and Gary Guglielmi.

Before the series began Michael appeared at the Sydney Showground against Ipswich's new World No.3 Billy Sanders. On December 6, 1980, in front of 16,000 on his home track, Sanders won a series of match-races against his East Anglian rival from the British League.

Australia easily defeated the Englishmen into second place in the opening match at Claremont but Lee and co. turned the tables and won at the two Victorian tracks, Mildura and Brooklyn (Melbourne), as well as the opening match of three in NSW at Newcastle. The Aussies hit back with two more wins, at Sydney Showground and Liverpool, before England won the final match and the series before a 9,000 attendance at Brisbane. Only in the Tests at Brooklyn and Newcastle did the Americans manage to avoid last place.

Lee lived up to his billing as the new World Champion by topping the overall scorers of all three teams with a combined haul of 80 points. Even so, not everyone was impressed by Michael's antics during the tour.

At the start of the 1980-81 Australian season in November, the speedway promoting rights at Sydney Showground were taken over by Frank Oliveri and his general manager Mike Raymond. They had made their reputations in the sport at Liverpool, a smaller track in the Sydney suburbs, where they later brought the World Pairs Final – the first FIM speedway World Championship Final to be held Down Under – to Liverpool in 1982.

Aussie journalist Steve Magro says of the ubiquitous Raymond: "He was, and arguably still is, our best speedway administrator-cum-promoter-cum-journalist. He was perhaps Dave Lanning, Len Silver and Reg Fearman all rolled into one.

"Mike ran the motorsport segment on the Channel Seven Sunday 'Sportaction' show and even anchored it for a while. A smarter, more savvy entrepreneur you'll not find anywhere."

But Nigel Boocock remembers the day his biggest crowd-puller, Michael Lee, upset Raymond with a prank that backfired. Booey explains: "The rest of the England team had already left but Michael stayed behind to appear on the Channel Seven Sunday sports show. He was to be interviewed by Mike Raymond but when Michael turned up wearing an 'I'm a Pommy Bastard' t-shirt, Raymond wouldn't have him on!"

Although no-one could question Lee's general standard of performance on the Aussie tracks and his leading points tally speaks for itself, it was evident to many involved in that tour that he also liked to unwind in his own way – and we're not talking about water skiing on the Hawkesbury River.

Over in Western Australia there was an unofficial match held at Bunbury. Michael withdrew and the announcer told the crowd that Lee had been overcome by heat exhaustion. However, that wasn't the case. Booey recalls that Michael was "stretched out on his back in the pits and out of it".

Doug Wyer, who earlier told how his admiration for Michael soared during their time together on the 1978-79 British Lions tour, confirmed Boocock's recollection of events at Bunbury. He says: "There is no doubt in my mind that on the 1980-81 Tri-Nations series tour he was influenced by some of the American boys. They would say to him: 'Come on, champ, let's go have a smoke' and he'd be off with them having fun.

"I knew all the American boys back then, I knew Shawn and Kelly Moran best because of their connection with my old club Sheffield and believe me, they were all good riders. But it was common knowledge that they most of them dabbled with drugs at some time – and I don't think it did them much good in the long run.

"When Michael was World Champion he even bought a big Yankee van to transport his bikes. It did about eight miles to the gallon. His two mechanics would drive it to all the meetings and Michael would follow them in his brand new Porsche. It was an ego thing and he was living the life," says Wyer.

But Dougie was also quick to point out that despite fraternising with the Americans, Michael remained popular with his English team-mates on tour. The former Sheffield and Halifax star says: "Michael was a great kid on tour. Whenever we had to ship our bikes and equipment interstate, he was there with the rest of us to help load and unload the trucks. He always did his share of the work even though he was the champ."

In fairness, Michael has never blamed anyone else for the mess he got himself to, least of all the Americans.

"I don't blame the Americans for anything I've done in my life. No-one was to blame for my drug problems except me," he says.

"People will always look to blame others for their actions and look for the easy option as an excuse, but I wouldn't blame the Americans at all.

"I wouldn't even say they introduced me to drugs," Lee countered. "Yeah, things happened but I wouldn't blame them for it. What I did could have happened anywhere – and it did.

"If they were to blame for me turning to drugs, then that would have been because I was a weak person who'd got sucked into it. But that certainly wasn't the case. I only ever did what I wanted to do.

"I used to hang out with the Americans so often that people used to call me a 'Wannabe Yank'. It wasn't that I wanted to be American at all – it's just that they liked to have fun and enjoyed their racing, although they could be serious as well when they had to be.

"Before I got to Australia I had two weeks' holiday in America and then moved on with their boys to Aussie, so I got quite friendly with the Yanks and spent a lot of time in their company.

"They were skateboarders and I bought myself a skateboard within a few days of arriving in California. We used to skateboard and surf together. We did all the car park runs – and got chased out of them too. It was pretty wild.

"But the Brits just weren't having any fun, everything was straight down the line. Perhaps it was that stiff upper lip reputation we were trying to uphold?"

Take a look at the size of those car 'mufflers' bolted to the exhausts of the bikes used by Michael and Billy Sanders during one of their battles at the Sydney Showground.

Michael responded to criticism from his former England colleague and World Pairs partner Malcolm Simmons. He says: "In his book, Simmo claims that the Americans were a bad influence on me."

Simmons wrote: "I think he was badly influenced by the Americans, particularly Kelly Moran, who I saw as his worst influence in his younger days. I know that Michael still says that the Americans didn't lead him astray but if wasn't them, then who else was it? Certainly no-one in the England camp. I think he's just being loyal to his American mates by saying that.

"I can understand why he was drawn to the 'fun-loving' Americans and why he describes us English blokes as 'boring' by comparison. While we wanted to be speedway riders the Ivan Mauger way, perhaps Michael preferred to do it the Penhall way?"

Michael responds: "Perhaps Simmo answers his own question of why I preferred the American boys when he admitting the English riders were boring in comparison."

Michael went on: "I became good friends with all the American boys and we had a great tour of Australia that year. I got on good with all the English riders, too, but none of them wanted to go skateboarding – and that was the thing. It ended up that I was a 'wannabe American' or a 'Yankee-doodle' but I didn't care what others thought of me.

"That's how I got the reputation because in the England teams I rode for, if the Yanks were around the place I think anyone would have thought I was on their

Hi ya, buddy! Michael and USA captain Bobby Schwartz before a Test match in England.

team rather than England's. I'd sit and eat at the Yanks' table at meal-times and they were quite happy for me to do so.

"But it should be pointed out that no-one raced them harder than me – I guarantee you that. They hated racing against me – Bruce will tell you that. Although we were mates and hung about together off track, the fact was that when we were racing against each other, I was probably more aggressive towards the Americans than any of the other English boys. That was because none of us wanted to be beaten – and the Americans felt the same way as I did about it. The Yanks always wanted to beat each other when they raced for their clubs or in individual meetings.

"They used to laugh about it whenever it was mentioned that I was a wannabe Yank. We all used to laugh about it – all except the England team manager, probably, and the England boys – the likes of Simmo and people like him who used to sneer at me because of it. 'You should be with us, we are a team,' they would said. "Yeah, but you're f****** boring,' I thought!

"I was having fun with the American boys – not crazy-fun, it was just that their whole lifestyle and outlook was different to the English. It wasn't like we were behaving idiots. Maybe on the odd occasion we might have done but that's just the way they were. I didn't want to sit around getting involved in politics and neither did the Americans. They wanted to go out and have fun – and so did I.

"I know circumstances change as you get older and now I do get involved in the politics of the sport, just like the Simmos, Bettsys and John Louis', the old stalwarts of the England team, did at times when I was a kid. But I didn't want to get involved and be part of that when I was in my early 20s. I wanted to be a bit footloose and fancy free.

"I didn't want to be forced to wear an England blazer with a badge on it and all that crap, although I do understand now that it's the professional thing to do so. So nowadays, although this may sound a bit contradictory, I do turn up looking smart and I'd tell the youngsters of today that it's the right way to be. If you're serious about your sport, you must do it – but no-one could ever tell me when I was their age!

"At the end of the day I let my results do the talking and providing I was doing that, I thought I could get away with the rest of it. When you have the off-the-wall life we had in racing, you need to be able to 'shoot off' a little bit at times. Although I know people will say that perhaps I shot off a little bit too much.

"We all knew what the craic was. If we had a smoke, it was always after the meeting. Apart from a couple of Yanks, none of us drank much alcohol in those days. We'd have a couple of puffs, go home, get up the next morning and work on our bikes again. So what? That doesn't make me a junkie."

It may be a tongue in cheek comment but there are still some who believe there is at least some substance to the notion put forward by journalist Randall Butt, who says: "There is a conspiracy theory that the American riders at that time, who knew they couldn't beat Michael on the track, encouraged his use of wacky backy and other things!"

If not Michael, then there is a long line of people out there who will still argue all day long that it was his friendship and natural affinity with the Americans that introduced him to the idea of drugs. It is also what his parents firmly believe, too.

Andy Lee says: "I believe it was circumstances that led him the wrong way and they were pressures that built up not from racing on the track, but from certain functions you were expected to fulfil as World Champion. I know he didn't like doing social functions.

"And the other factor, which we know all too well by now, is what I call the 'American influence'. I don't blame them for what happened to Michael but he was releasing pressure on himself by smoking with or without the Americans – and it got out of hand."

Val Lee is in no doubt: "I know who introduced him to cannabis," she says, unwilling to name names but probably more out of loyalty to Michael than to protect the identity of those concerned.

But she did dispel one myth when she quickly added: "No, it wasn't Kelly Moran. Kelly was a great character, a lovely guy and you couldn't help but like him. I know he did things but I think Kelly had a talk with Michael about what he was doing, although he didn't make much headway. Kelly also had a quiet word with me and expressed his concerns about Michael."

Moran, who finished one place behind Lee in the 1979 World Final, died in a

Los Angeles hospice in April 2010 after a long battle against lung and liver disease. Just days before he died weighing barely six stones at the age of just 49, he admitted to me that the years of heavy boozing and smoking since he was a teenager had finally taken its toll. He knew he had only days to live and, during the interview for *Backtrack* magazine, he briefly spoke warmly of his friendship with Michael Lee and the great tussles they had on the track for club and country. "He was a good boy, Mike," Kelly said.

Michael's mother recalls the first time she discovered a strange aroma pervading the Lee family home: "Andy was away at the time but I had a sneaking suspicion. I think it was soon after the 1980 World Final and I won't tell you the names of the top riders stood around in my kitchen at the lovely old cottage where we lived in Melbourn, but there were about six of them gathered together.

"I could smell something horrible and being a hay fever sufferer, it didn't agree with me. We had this huge ginger cat called Barney and I thought, 'why is the cat walking like that?' When I opened the door, the smell hit me. They had been trying to get the cat stoned – I could have killed them! But then I knew what was going on.

"I told them they were daft but they just laughed it off and Mike said: 'Go on mum, we're relaxing'. I think that was the start of Michael's downward spiral.

"He knew that I knew what was going on and that I was dead against it. I regularly had words with him about it. I used to say: 'Oh for goodness sake, stop smoking that filthy weed' and 'knock it on the head' but he'd just say 'I need to relax and wind down'. 'You don't need to relax with that stuff', I'd tell him.

"I knew what the Americans were doing and I was just upset that Michael fell into their lifestyle. The Americans were likeable lads and I got on well with all of them – they often called in to see us – but if they hadn't been there and introduced Michael to it . . ." says Val, her voice trailing away in barely concealed disappointment.

"I don't know, maybe he would have got into it at a later date anyway. Who knows? It hurt me but I could cope with it," she added.

Michael offered a wry smile when he heard what his Mum had said about him and his pals 'lighting up' in her kitchen some 30 years ago and how their actions had affected Barney the cat! But then he made a valid and serious point: "Everyone talks about how the Americans smoked dope but some English riders were also at it. And while I was in Australia, some of the Aussie lads liked to smoke the bush too!"

John Berry, probably the English promoter who understood Michael Lee better than any other and a man Lee has always respected, naturally has plenty to say on the question of drugs in speedway during that period and the part they played in Michael's downfall.

Berry, now a respected author and columnist for *Backtrack* magazine, who emigrated to Perth, Western Australia with his family in 1989, says: "When the

The USA Test side after their victory against England at Ipswich in 1982. Left to right: Shawn Moran, Bobby Schwartz, John Cook, Ron Preston, Dennis Sigalos, Scott Autrey, Bruce Penhall and Kelly Moran.

"I don't blame the Americans for anything I've done in my life. No-one was to blame for my drug problems except me."

Californians arrived in force in the late 70s/early 80s, they brought with them a drug culture. That is not to say drugs had never been heard of in the UK, or in speedway before that time. Indeed, there are several unproven stories of drug taking incidents in the sport prior to this. In my young day, amphetamines were called 'purple hearts'.

"But what the Californians brought along was a completely casual attitude to the using of 'recreational' drugs, specifically marijuana, amphetamines and cocaine. They had grown up with the idea that these drugs were quite socially acceptable.

"Anyway, many of the less strong-willed UK-based riders found themselves drawn into the drug web. Whilst, by and large, those Americans who partook appeared to keep their drug taking in proportion, Michael became hooked. We can talk about Michael, Gary Havelock and Mark Courtney in relation to drug taking, because the evidence is in the public domain, but there is no doubting that apart from these few cases the levels of drug use in speedway circles was pretty high during this period.

"I don't know if I am now the only adult left in the western world who has never experienced the taking of illicit substances. Sure, I enjoy a drink, and accept what many say in that alcohol is possibly even worse than the other recreational drugs, but alcohol is legally and socially acceptable.

"I freely admit it isn't a determination not to break the law that stops me from trying these other things. After all, even now I tend to break the law just about every time I drive my car (over the speed limit). No, my reason for not trying drugs is simpler than that. I just do not want to discover I might enjoy it.

"I once went to a talk given by a police drug squad officer. It was an excellent and informative evening, with the police officer being perhaps more scathing about alcohol, in terms of dependency and long-term damage to health, than the other 'lightweight drugs. But he also pointed out that once someone makes the step of taking illegal drugs, it is easy to slip from there into the 'heavy' stuff. More importantly, the amount of social damage caused by chronic users, and in particular the way in which they get the stuff and the things they do to get the money to pay for it, is just immense.

"If riders used them purely to 'unwind', in moderation, and not when they were going to ride speedway, then that was entirely up to them. However, it seems that most of these 'social drugs' linger in the body long enough to be detectable for some time afterwards – and one has to presume that if they are still detectable then they are also still having an effect.

"Now in all the time speedway has been operating, I cannot think of an incident when a rider has been done for taking performance-enhancing drugs. I recall one or two who have failed alcohol tests or had traces of marijuana but I am sure 'hangovers' are unlikely to be classed as performance-enhancing. Likewise, whilst I have personal knowledge of social drug-taking involving speedway riders, I have none involving performance-enhancing stuff.

"However, it would take a huge amount of gullibility to assume it hasn't happened. We are not talking steroids or the like here. After all, speedway riders are hardly famous for having Adonis-type muscles. But it would take a mug to think that stuff like amphetamines or speed wasn't being used.

"After all, although the taking of such reaction-enhancing substances has always been against the regulations, there was no random drug-testing until well on into the 80s. Discussions and gossip within the sport was rife, and circumstantial evidence was always there that some riders were riding under the influence. The finger was pointed many times at some Americans – you may be assured that in my time as England team manager there were several times when the England boys did not believe they were competing on a level playing field."

As is often the way, mothers have a simple yet very uncanny knack of putting their finger on a problem and I like this comment from Val Lee: "It was a shame when Terry Betts was no longer involved at King's Lynn because he kept an eye on Michael and I know Michael still thinks the world of him. Terry would have given him a clip round the ear and told him to pull himself together. There would have been no messing around."

Life in the Fast Lane

Arrest and rehab

Chapter 18

WHEN Michael returned from Australia early in 1981, his parents were not preoccupied with their son's defence of the world title. While almost everyone in the sport was expecting Lee to go on and add another string of major titles to his name in the season ahead, to cement his place in the annals of speedway history, and some even thought it possible he could go on to emulate Ivan Mauger's record-breaking haul of six world titles, Andy and Val Lee were worried sick about how they were going to get Michael off drugs.

They organised for him to attend a drug rehabilitation clinic in Cambridge but it didn't have the desired effect. On the contrary, Michael simply found a more ready supply of all the stimulants he could handle. And what's more, they were all issued to him legally and totally free of charge!

Explaining this bizarre early episode in his family's long and painful battle to get him to quit drugs, he revealed: "I did attend rehab for a while in the early 80s but it was an absolute waste of time. All they did was give me more drugs – any drug I wanted – and I even made money by selling them!

"The government appointed five drug specialists, psychiatrists if you like, and they could prescribe for you cocaine, heroin, anything. When you visited one of these rehab centres for the first time they weren't going to get you off drugs just like that, because the doctors didn't even know what was going on in your head. Some people are, of course, addicted to drugs but they don't understand what the addiction is. They've just got to have their coke or whatever.

"It's not a physical addiction, it's a mental thing. And if you can control your head, you can do what you want, when you want. With most people, their heads are shot away and they just want drugs for the sake of having them.

"Anyway, Mum and Dad knew from that phone call they received from the States at the start of our winter in 1980 that I was doing Charlie and they kept a close eye on me when I returned from Aussie in the New Year. But, unbeknown to them, as soon as I got back to England, the first thing I did was drive to London to score some Charlie.

"I think Dad soon twigged that I was up to something when he noticed me getting up later in the mornings and saw other tell-tale signs that showed I'd been on it for days and nights on end. Then he freaked out and confronted me about it."

Val Lee says: "Andy went berserk when he found out and he obviously had words with Michael. But it just didn't sink in with Michael. Andy felt very strongly about it and part of him also felt ashamed that his son had let him down, and that everyone would know about Michael being into drugs."

The King's Lynn Stars of 1981 – a troubled year for club and captain. Left to right: Mel Taylor, Pierre Brannefors, Robert Henry, Richard Hellsen, Nigel Sparshott, Dave Jessup and Craig Featherby. Al Littlechild joins Mike on the bike.

"I did worry about him having a lot of money at his disposal. I didn't want him to have an extravagant lifestyle and blow it all, which is unfortunately what he did."

Andy admits: "It was a very bad and sad episode in all of our lives. Like most fathers in these cases, I was probably the last to know. I certainly knew nothing of Michael's involvement in that scene at all, and for a long while I wondered what was going on.

"When I did get to know, I didn't understand it and probably didn't do the right things to counteract it. To us, as a family, it was devastating.

"I first knew something was wrong when he began getting up later in the mornings and became erratic in his behaviour, especially when he wasn't turning up for meetings on time and couldn't care less. These are all signs that I'm aware of now but I didn't recognise at the time.

"Sure, when I found out what had been going on I felt terrible frustration. While I was with Michael it was OK but you cannot be with your sons or daughters all the while, and I didn't want to be with him all the while. So maybe I was still doing the bikes and sending him off to do whatever he did. It's only natural – he didn't always want his dad there."

Returning to that failed attempt at so-called rehab in 1981, Michael continued: "Behind my back, my parents arranged for me to go and see Doctor Muller, one of five government-appointed specialists meant to help drug users to kick their addiction. Dad came with me to my first appointment but what neither he nor Dr Muller knew was that after talking between the three of us for a while, I'd disappear into the toilet to snort some Charlie before returning to join in their conversation. Although there were times when I was 'under the influence' in Dad's presence, I never physically took any drugs in front of him.

"Anyway, the doctor made a second appointment for me to attend his clinic five days later – but this time he asked me to come alone. I think he felt I'd been holding back a bit in front of Dad when he was questioning me.

"So I went back five days later, as arranged, and what did I get? No less than 14 grams of cocaine prescribed for me! The doctor's assumption was that the first thing he had to do was to stop me buying it on the street and mixing with other cocaine users, so for the next two months I was getting 14 grams of coke a week as prescribed by this doctor. I just went to the local chemist in Cambridge to collect it over the counter at no cost.

"It's white powder in a pot – cocaine hydrochloride, which is hydrophilic salt produced in laboratories here and not quite the same as the stuff sold on the black market. It's powerful but in a different way – it's too harsh and doesn't quite give you the high regular users would hope for. To be honest, I was still scoring decent Charlie elsewhere while also selling a bit of the stuff the doctor prescribed for me!

"I had another couple of appointments with him over the next two months. He asked how I was getting on and then he said he'd cut my cocaine allowance down to seven grams - but he would prescribe me amphetamine pills as well. The first ones he gave me were 'black bombers', which I'd previously scored on the black market anyway, and I didn't like them. They made you a bit edgy and uncomfortable. But when he offered them to me, I just said 'OK', because I knew I could flog them as well – and for a proper price!

"I actually phoned the doctor and told him: 'I don't like these black bomber things. If you're going to cut down on my Charlie, at least give me something else'. So then he gave me Dexedrine tablets, which were more acceptable. So now as well as my seven grams of cocaine, I was also being given 84 Dexedrine a week. Bloody hell! That's 12 a day – I'd have been rattling like a good 'un and totally off my head if I'd swallowed that lot every week! I thought, 'if only my Old Man knew what was going on . . . '

"The doctor even put me on a heroin substitute called Methadone, which is used to try and wean addicts off heroin, but after trying that once I told him I didn't want it again. It came in syrup form and made me feel out of it, and that wasn't why I was taking drugs. It also made you feel sick and once you puked it made you feel better and gave you a sudden rush. I thought, 'if this is what heroin does to you, no wonder you shouldn't touch it'. I told him to forget the Methadone, but to keep giving me the other stuff. 'Oh, that's a step forward,' he said. 'F****** step forward, mate! I wasn't making any steps forward.

"In the end, I decided I didn't want any more Charlie from him. If I wanted to score Charlie, I could always get better quality stuff myself from my contacts. When I told him, he thought I'd actually stopped doing it. So he left me on a long-running prescription of Dexedrine, which I was still getting from him a year later."

What Michael has described here seems unbelievable to those of us who have no understanding of drugs or the treatment administered to addicts. But in June 2010, under the headline '£44m Scandal of Jail Junkies', a *Daily Express* report reaffirmed the kind of thing Michael had experienced some 30 years earlier. The Express stated: "Figures from the Policy exchange think-tank claim that the government is spending £44m per year on providing drug addicts in prison with substitute treatments. The report argues that the increasing number of drug addicts in jails is a result of Labour policy, which focused on substitute treatments, rather than abstinence-based remedies for drug addiction."

"It came to the point where I stopped using Charlie and Dexedrine," continues Michael. "It wasn't like I was on and off it every other month. I actually stopped using Charlie for two years. And then one night I thought, 'oh f*** it' and got back into it again for the next four or five years. I stopped again for another year or two but then went back to it again before I met Nick."

Michael talks at length and in shocking detail about his fall from the dizzy heights of Gothenburg, as well as the woman who brought him back from the brink, later in the book. Meanwhile, let's remind ourselves of the World Champion's most high profile indiscretion during that wild and reckless summer of '81. While the country reeled from violent rioting that brought petrol bombings and police beatings to the streets of trouble spots such as Brixton, Southall, Toxteth and Moss Side, Michael Lee was rebelling in his own way.

Although rumours were rife among the speedway fraternity at the time that Lee and several stars of the American Test team were into drugs, in Michael's case very few people knew the full extent of his off-track problems. The stark evidence did not become clear to the wider world until the national press reported his arrest for possession of cannabis on Saturday, June 26.

It happened soon after he landed at East Midlands Airport in Leicestershire, having just flown back from the Denmark v England Test match at Vojens. Michael, who had top-scored for his country in their 60-48 defeat, was driving his Porsche 928 at high speed on the M1.

In addition to expressing their anger and concern about Michael's recreational habits, his parents were also worried about what he might get up to behind the wheel of one of the most coveted sports cars of its time and another sign of his decadent lifestyle.

Val says: "I did worry about him having a lot of money at his disposal. I didn't

The jubilant England team after their Test victory over the USA at Poole in April. Back tow: Wally Mawdsley (BSPA chairman), Malcolm Simmons, Dave Jessup, Len Silver (team manager), Chris Morton, John Lewsey (*Daily Mirror*) and Michael. Front: John Davis, Steve Bastable, Les Collins and Gordon Kennett.

want him to have an extravagant lifestyle and blow it all, which is unfortunately what he did.

"It worried me to death when I heard he'd bought a Porsche. I'd tell him to drive carefully but he'd give me that wry smile of his and I knew I was talking to myself. Once he was up the road and on the motorway, his foot would be down.

"To be honest, I knew what was going on. I thought, 'you're in the public eye and you're driving that blooming Porsche'. Because he was still a young lad, I was half-expecting it to happen at any time. I wasn't surprised when Michael was stopped by the police.

"Our local bobbies were aware of him and the car, too. They would make comments like: 'Mmm, he's driving a car like that and look at us' sort of thing. Two policemen actually mentioned to me that Michael was lucky to be able to afford a Porsche at his age.

"It still worries me now that he's got a motor bike!" Val added.

Martin Rogers was unable to recall Michael's specific pay deals during their five seasons together at King's Lynn but he was clearly earning more than most young men of his age.

"In the years 1976-79, his upfront payments were on par with riders of similar status," says Rogers. "One thing I did include in his deals quite early on, though, was the opportunity to earn a bonus payment if he placed well in any individual meeting – the thinking being the more he flourished, the more it spread the word that this was somebody to come and see on Saturday nights.

Calm before the storm . . . Michael lines up for England again, this time in the opening match of the Test series against Denmark at Hackney in June '81. Standing: Sean Willmott, Kevin Smith, Michael, Kenny Carter, Les Collins and Len Silver. Front: Chris Morton and Gordon Kennett, with skipper Dave Jessup on the machine.

"I sat in it and it was like an aircraft cockpit. So I've gone: 'Wow! How much is this?' I think they wanted 15 grand for it at the time, which was good value. I wanted this thing and I was going to have it no matter what, although it was probably a big mistake."

"I really don't remember the specifics of his deals, which I negotiated with him and all the riders during my time as general manager. Suffice to say he was able to afford a late-model Mercedes as a 19-year-old."

But Rogers added: "Certainly in that time Michael was never greedy.

"My recollection, though, is that he was decently paid - and that's why I said he should be fined a grand for the 4TT no-show at Sheffield in '79. To have punished him less would have been derisory given his earnings by that time."

Explaining how he came to own his first flashy sports car and the part its power played in his first arrest, Michael says: "Being the poseur I was back then, I acquired a Porsche 928 through my sponsorship by the Kim Cairns Car Agency in King's Lynn in about 1978-79. They had only the third 928 ever built, which was a left-hand drive model because Porsche hadn't yet made a right-hand version. I had to go up to Kim Cairns' showroom for an evening function to promote their new Ford agency and take along a speedway bike. But in the back of the showroom they had this 928, an HP claim-back by Lynn Regis Finance, the finance people for Kim Cairns, who also did a bit of sponsorship at the speedway.

"Being only the third one in the country, the 928 was creating a bit of interest under the spotlights, although realistically no-one was going to buy a left-hand model. I'd never seen one before. I sat in it and it was like an aircraft cockpit. So I've gone: 'Wow! How much is this?' I think they wanted 15 grand for it at the time, which was good value. I wanted this thing and I was going to have it no matter what, although it was probably a big mistake.

"I couldn't drive it away from Kim Cairns on the actual night of the launch because the car was due to be on display at the Norfolk Show two days later, which peed me off. I was very impetuous in those days - everything had to happen now. But they said it was booked for the Norfolk Show and it would be back at their dealership in three days' time. I think they thought my enthusiasm would cool off over that period and that I'd see common sense – but there was no chance of that happening.

"After three days, I was straight on the phone to them: 'Is the car back yet? I've got the money sorted out'. It was pushing me financially, I was only about 19-years-old, but I wanted the car so badly.

"My old man bollocked the hell out of me for buying it but I couldn't wait to pose at the wheel – and speedway meetings on the continent gave me the perfect opportunity to show off. I did a few trips abroad when I should really have flown out with the other riders but I found it so quick to get to these places in the Porsche."

Michael recalls one hair-raising trip in the GT-sports car with its five litre V8 powered engine in 1980, accompanied by his King's Lynn team-mate Richard Hellsen: "We had to get to the World Team Cup qualifier in Denmark and set off straight after Lynn's match at Ipswich on the Thursday night. He jumped in the passenger seat and asked: 'Do you want me to drive?'.

"I replied: 'No, Richard, you'll be all right'. He said: 'OK, I'll drive a bit the other side then'. No chance! No-one drove my Porsche except me!

"Anyway, we were due at Vojens for the Friday meeting. We went down to Dover straight after the meeting at Ipswich and we were at the track in Denmark before the people who flew there that day! They couldn't believe it. They thought I was barmy. I told them I knew I could get there in good time and before them. Once we docked at Zeebrugge, I reckoned it would take me about seven hours to drive to Vojens. But the others were going, 'no way, man, it's a 12-hour run. You won't do it in that time'. But I bloody well did!

"I think poor Richard was so shaken up by the journey, by the time we arrived at the track he didn't even want to ride for Sweden in that World Team Cup round, so I did England and the other two countries a bit of a favour by scaring the shit out of him!" (The fact that Hellsen failed to score for the Swedes, while England and the USA qualified ahead of the Danes, suggests that perhaps Michael wasn't joking!)

But what happened to him after he returned from another meeting at Vojens about a year later was no laughing matter. Michael recalls the drama that led up to his arrest in June 1981.

"When I arrived back from Denmark at East Midland Airport, I was in a Catch-22 whether to go straight to Halifax (where King's Lynn were riding that night) or go home first. I flew back in at about 10.30 in the morning and as I drove onto the M1 I thought, 'bugger it, I'll be home by half-past 12. We won't have to leave for Halifax 'till about half-three, so I'll have three hours indoors' – or so I thought.

"I've pulled out from the airport and was two junctions down the M1. I'm on the cruise control doing about 130 mph in the outside lane – there wasn't much traffic around on that Saturday morning.

"In the slow lane there's a white car – what I now know to be a 2.8 Granada carrying two cops – at the lowest part of the uphill rise on the M1, just where you go over the brow coming out of Nottinghamshire and before you're into Leicestershire. There they were but I just didn't bat an eyelid, probably didn't even notice they were cops. I just zoomed by. I got over the brow of the hill and I'm still cruising along at 130mph.

"But when I get down to Leicester Forest Services, a load of cop cars with their blue lights flashing are blocking all three lanes of the motorway. They're letting the traffic build up and filter onto the hard shoulder.

"So I've knocked the cruise control off and pulled in behind everyone else, still not realising anything was wrong. Then the police swooped and literally ran me up the embankment – they were all going for me.

"I'm stunned, thinking 'What's going on?'. I put the brakes on and parked up on the grass with cop cars surrounding me. There were policemen running in all directions. By the time I'd got my wits about me I was almost coming out of my car backwards. They were dragging me out.

"They thought I'd stolen the car. They're looking at a 22-year-old driving a rare 928 Porsche, which no-one has seen before because it's only the third one in the country. The cops have seen a young kid go flying past them doing 130 mph and you can imagine what they're thinking. They thought I was legging it, that I was on a mission!

"Anyway, they drag me out of my car, shove me in the back of a patrol car and tell me: 'Wait here', although it was a silly thing to say because I couldn't have gone anywhere even if I'd wanted to because I'm hemmed in.

"They start checking the motor over and ask me my name and when it all tallies up, they go: 'Is there anything in the car we shouldn't find?'

"It's then that it suddenly dawned on me. I'd left my little pipe and a tiny bit of hashish in the glove-box. And when I say tiny, I'm talking about 1.7 grams – less than the end of your finger nail. But it was there, in the glove-box, as evidence.

"It was pointless me saying that there was nothing for them to find, so I just said. 'Oh yeah, there's a pipe and bit of hashish'.

"As I'm admitting it, the older cop is getting out of my car with a big smile, my pipe and hashish in his hand and a look of 'I've got you!' written all over his face.

"They said: 'Wait there, we can't do anything.' They were waiting for the two cops I'd passed earlier to arrive on the scene, because they had to be the ones to charge me. It was them who'd radioed through to their colleagues to set up the road block ahead. Well, we must have waited a good three minutes for them to turn up, which shows you how fast I'd been going.

"The traffic control motorway cops also phoned the Drugs Squad, who then sent a member of their team to the scene to check out what had been found.

"Meanwhile, the two cops I'd passed at 130mph got out of their car huffing and puffing and swearing at me. 'What f****** speed do you think you were doing?' They'd obviously had it confirmed via their radio that the Porsche wasn't stolen, so now they're just pissed off because they couldn't catch me. 'I think I was doing nearly 100mph.' I replied, but they didn't believe me. 'Like f*** you were! We've been doing 135mph and we haven't even seen you'.

"I'd been on the gas, probably up around 145mph, because, as I say, there was nothing else on the road. But the two coppers in the first police car I passed let me go over the brow of the hill before they'd hardly moved, which meant I was well ahead of them by the time their colleagues set up the road block ahead.

"I was a little fortunate because the head of the drugs squad from Leicestershire Constabulary was a speedway supporter! He didn't let me off but he did fast-track it through. By now they realised who I was and that the vehicle was mine. So I was like: 'I'm racing at Halifax tonight, can we get this done quickly?'

"They took my car off to a police pound, drove me to Leicester police station and charged me – all in the space of about 15 minutes. The head of the drugs squad then drove me back to the compound where my car was waiting and said: 'See you later' – and that was it. I was on my way home again by about quarter-past one, although not doing 145mph!"

Michael didn't make it to The Shay, where Lynn managed to beat Halifax 42-36 without him. It was just one of a string of non-arrivals and disputes that blighted his season as World Champion.

"That was my first escapade involving drugs and the police and I got done £75 for it," he says, admitting: "It was really no more than a slap on the wrist."

But the police threw the book at Lee for a string of motoring offences, including speeding, dangerous driving, undue care and attention plus resisting arrest. "But I didn't intend to speed away from them – I just didn't know it was them behind me!" he laughs, recalling his first publicised brush with the law.

It was no laughing matter at the time, though, and his problems didn't end there.

He went on: "I already had four endorsements on my driving licence, so it all mounted up when my case came to court a few months later. I ended up with about eight endorsements and three was the limit. I was initially banned from driving for a year, which made life very difficult.

"That's when the story of my arrest and the fact that I smoked cannabis first came out in the press," Michael added.

There was another backlash in store. Studio Publications of Ipswich were due to publish a book on the World Champion and *The Michael Lee Story* was in fact pre-advertised at £3.50 in Studio's *1982 Speedway Yearbook* by Peter Oakes.

But when the shit hit the fan over Michael's involvement with drugs, Studio pulled the plug on the book and it never came out.

Michael's intended ghost-writer Laurence Rogers, a West Midlands-based school teacher and speedway jack-of-all-trades, recalls: "When the Sunday papers' scoop hit the headlines, production on the book was stopped just before it was due to be released.

"We were offered the chance to buy the unfinished book from Studio Publications for £1,000 but, in 1982, this was a substantial amount, so despite all the hard work that went into it, the book never hit the shelves."

Michael's motoring problems didn't end with the police car chase in Leicestershire either. He says: "About four or five months into my year's ban I did a stupid thing and was caught driving again. I needed to pick up something I needed for one of my bikes.

"I was at home one day and there was no-one available to drive me, so I jumped in the car. I drove from one side of Newmarket to the other, just to buy some nuts and bolts. I parked my car outside the parts shop and, as luck would have it, a traffic warden came along just at that moment. Because I wasn't meant to be driving the damn thing, the car wasn't taxed. Of course, with no tax disc in the window, the traffic warden called the police – and bang, I'm in trouble again.

"I ended up with a further six-month ban and also the threat of a prison sentence hanging over me if I was ever caught driving while disqualified again."

Michael says he has good cause to thank John Henley, an employee of Alan Littlechild's at the family business in Waltham Abbey, Essex, for driving him to meetings during his 18-month driving ban. "John drove a lorry for Alan and I got to know him well because after a fall-out with Dad in '81 I set up a workshop over at Alan's place. John was a similar age to me and he drove me about a lot until I got my licence back."

Michael may not have been driving himself anywhere for a while, but he was driving King's Lynn co-promoter Cyril Crane and the speedway authorities to distraction for much of a sadly lamentable '81.

Only Way is Down

Backlash and brickbats

Chapter 19

MICHAEL was once described as 'the most controversial World Champion' of all-time and not without justification.

News of his first drugs conviction following his arrest on the M1 raised the spectre of drugs in speedway for the first time. Although, in fact, just a week before Lee was caught with a small amount of cannabis, Speedway Riders' Association secretary George Barclay went on record to urge the SCB to introduce random drug-testing in the sport. Barclay expressed his genuine concern about drugs in speedway and said that he'd already held talks with Control Board manager Dick Bracher to alert him to the possible problems.

There was surely a knowing conviction in the words of *Speedway Star's* Peter Oakes (also promoter at Exeter at the time), an experienced national newspaper journalist who has enjoyed a close rapport with the top riders since he began covering the sport in the 60s, when he wrote: "I suppose it is only natural that the subject of drugs should creep into speedway – in the same way it has in other professional sports. Would it be any surprise if top international stars, facing the sort of schedule they do, turned to stimulants to keep them going when they must be ready to drop? Now is the time for the SCB to consider carefully the observations of George Barclay, never a man to cry wolf."

Despite the SRA's well publicised concerns, random drug-testing was not introduced until later in the 80s and no rider was punished by the SCB for testing positive until Middlesbrough's Gary Havelock in 1989. Michael Lee insists to this day that he never rode a lap while under the influence of any drugs – but that isn't to say that some riders weren't taking liberties for years, even after testing was belatedly introduced.

In fact, a totally reliable source confided to me that one international star of the 80s and early 90s – not Lee – tested positive for banned drugs on TWO separate occasions but avoided punishment by the SCB both times simply by producing a certificate from his friendly hospital doctor, who happily confirmed that the pills were prescribed to his pal for legitimate health reasons.

Never lost for words, King's Lynn's Cyril Crane was quick to react to the news of his top rider's conviction for possession of cannabis in 1981. It's interesting to reflect on the impact Michael's actions had on Crane and the club as a whole at the time . . . and then to compare what was said at the time with the benefit of 30 years' hindsight. Times and attitudes have certainly changed.

"It's crazy. I'm shocked and disappointed. This is obviously not good for the sport," said an outraged Crane, when asked in '81 for his reaction to Lee's arrest and subsequent court appearance in mid-summer.

"But King's Lynn cannot be blamed for this. This is an individual and everybody does their own thing and goes their own way. For a World Champion, Michael has not presented himself in the right manner.

"I don't know what repercussions there will be," Crane went on. "And I haven't the foggiest idea what action, if anything, the Control Board or BSPA will take.

"Michael earlier admitted to a Sunday newspaper that he had tried drugs. All this makes him downright ignorant.

"Michael probably doesn't realise what he has done but I feel he has done himself a great deal of harm.

PAGE 30 DAILY MIRROR, Thursday, September 11, 1980

MICHAEL LEE WORLD SPEEDWAY CHAMPION

Let's all share the glory..

EVEN the telegrams, cards and letters have not brought it all home to me yet.

I still can't believe it has happened.

The world championship trophy has finally come to rest on the sideboard of my mum and dad's house in Royston, Herts.

I have to keep looking at it and pinching myself to make sure my victory in the Gothenburg World Final was not a dream.

But now it is time to sit down and reflect on how my life will change as a 21-year-old world champion.

My main aim is to do as much as I can for the sport. I want to do for speedway what Barry Sheene has done for motor-cycling.

Publicity

It is all about getting more publicity and sponsorship for myself—and in turn helping to protect the sport. I want get into television advertising and to find big sponsor

BARRY SHEENE

for Peter Collins, Chris Morton and myself when we carry the English flag in the World Long-Track Final at Schessel, West Germany, on Sunday.

In Germany long-track racing is far bigger than speedway.

With speeds reaching 110 miles per hour on the straights it can be pretty hair-raising.

But I'm afraid all been concentra much on getting

Around three million *Daily Mirror* readers were treated to the controversial views of the 1980 World Champion.

"There is nothing worse than drugs or alcohol. Sponsors are hard to come by and obviously no sponsor wants to back a bad boy," said Crane.

"It wouldn't surprise me if Michael lost some of the people who have been supporting him. I know I wouldn't sponsor someone who has been convicted of possessing drugs."

Again, few outside Lee's immediate family circle and his closest friends realised just how heavily he was into drugs away from the track in '81, or that he was seeing a so-called rehab therapist.

Richard Clark joined *Speedway Star* when Michael was in his racing prime and he has edited the sport's only weekly magazine since 1996, a role he still fulfils with aplomb today. An intelligent, broad-minded 'man of the world', he is ideally placed to compare the contrasting attitudes of then and now.

"I think we firstly have to realise the moral compass has probably swung in quite a different direction since those days, or at least that's how it feels to me," says 'Clarkie'.

"Kids nowadays – there's a phrase to make you sound old! – seem to consume drugs openly, sometimes encouraged by their own parents' weekend experiments. Certain taboos, especially surrounding cannabis, have been deconstructed. Take a wander towards my local supermarket of an early evening and you'll almost inevitably pass someone leaving a trail of unmistakably sweet air behind them.

"But the response to Michael's 'dabbling', whether you think it an overreaction or not, was understandable and, probably, of its time. Alternative lifestyles were much more frowned upon then. These were Conservative times with a capital 'C', rightly or wrongly. 'Emotive' is the perfect word to use to describe the furore surrounding the subject of drugs.

"And speedway has always puffed up with pride at being a family sport. Michael was a superstar within that sport and many thought he was damaging its very fabric with his misdemeanours. I didn't personally, but I've always appreciated the other point of view, if not always been in agreement. Where I stand morally compared to, for example, Mary Whitehouse is the equivalent of one side of the universe to the other. But my morals, by and large, are my own business. It was Mary Whitehouse who chose to try and foist her beliefs upon others, including me.

"I do understand the argument that some children would have looked up to Michael and, therefore, he could be considered to have let them down.

"But look around these days, and you can see how things have changed. In a certain other major sport, for example, which long ago priced families out of its top tier in this country, it appears you can be involved in a very public beating, have an affair with a team-mate's former girlfriend, go shopping instead of take a drugs test, and still be considered for the job of captain of your country, and most certainly get a very vocal backing from your fans on the terraces. They're still heroes despite it all. Would that be the case if football sold itself as a family attraction?

"In Michael's case, I think it's important to stress the 'recreational use' part. If he chugged away at copious amounts of dope prior to a meeting, he'd probably still be on the last lap now. It's hardly conducive to sharpening your reflexes. So forget performance-enhancing.

"But is there any room for it in a professional sportsman or sportswoman's life? We're back with that moral compass again. Some argue these people have a duty to be squeaky-clean – but then we used to think that about politicians!"

Michael has always maintained that it wasn't drugs that accelerated his fall from grace as a rider. In his eyes, there were other mitigating factors.

It should be remembered that he won the World Championship at a particularly disadvantaged time in terms of the potential to cash in on his greatest triumph. Britain was in the grip of a deep recession, with soaring unemployment and interest rates. Many of speedway's loyal backers were running for cover, crowds were down and on the slide at many tracks. The sport was entering another period in the doldrums.

"We were finding it hard work to get any kind of sponsors. In fact, I had more support before I won the World Final than I did afterwards," confirms Michael, who told a gathering of SWAPA (Speedway Writers and Photographers Association) at the start of the '81 season that the World Champion should receive a £10,000 reward for victory.

"I even had a PR agency working for me. MRF Associates of Reading tried their best to find new sponsors but, commercially and financially, times were tough.

"Money was never a big issue for me, though. Winning the World Final wasn't about money. As long as you've got the will to win, the rewards should follow anyway. But when those rewards didn't come my way, it kind of knocked me a bit and left me feeling frustrated," he recalls as we continued to examine the different contributory factors that led to his dramatic downfall.

"I wanted speedway to become a far more professional and bigger sport but I saw us lose TV coverage and then snooker and darts, and every other sport you could name, suddenly seemed to be ranked above speedway in the eyes of the media and the general public. When I first started riding, speedway was, if not quite second to football as the biggest national sport, then very highly rated alongside a few others. I used to love to watch speedway as a kid on ITV's World of Sport on Saturday afternoons and it was big back then."

Michael developed a 'bad boy' image but then some have argued that he brought most of the negative headlines upon himself.

"Within reason, all publicity is good publicity," he counters. "I had a third-of-a-page column in the *Daily Mirror* once or even twice a week. Now that is major publicity for speedway, no matter what anyone thinks of me.

"But I wasn't getting help from any angle where the British authorities were concerned. I'm sure they resented a lot of the things I wrote about in *The Mirror* but it was the truth. I wanted to see speedway progress but it wasn't going anywhere. It was almost as if it was being suppressed for certain greedy people's benefit, so they could take advantage of it rather than the sport go out on a gallop and become bigger. I just wanted speedway to become a more professional sport and sometimes it was too amateurish.

"There was a little 'mafia' of promoters who controlled things and I felt they weren't pushing speedway forward enough to attract potential new supporters.

"The organisations that ran darts and snooker were going out and getting national sponsorship and big prize money worth 40 or 50 grand, while speedway was still giving its big meeting winners a pathetic £200. (Steve Davis received £20,000 for winning the Embassy World Snooker Championship in April 1981, though the total prize pot was £75k. A year later those figures were increased to £30k and £110k respectively.)

"Snooker and darts were getting national and international TV coverage like they'd never known before and yet by the mid-80s speedway blew it with ITV because someone in our sport wanted a back-hander, so the deal was blown out of the water. We'd gone backwards and I was getting more and more peed off."

He has a point. Apart from the financial rewards on offer, snooker legends of the 80s, Alex Higgins and Jimmy White, actually enhanced their popularity and status within their sport, becoming household names as much for their hard-drinking, womanising, hell-raising ways away from the green baize as than their

Before he was stripped of the title, Golden Helmet holder Michael with Andrew Edwards of sponsors *Motorcycle News*.

brilliance with a cue.

Of course, snooker and darts have always had a distinct appeal to the TV bods over speedway due to their sheer simplicity and the fact that a quick shower of rain was never going to affect the smooth running of the show, or wreck it altogether.

Randall Butt put speedway's perceived stature among the general public in the early 80s into perspective when he said: "As for Michael's affect on the local community after he became World Champion, that was minimal. He was born in Cambridge but lived in a village called Melbourn, south of the city, and was much better known in King's Lynn.

"I seem to remember he was introduced to the fans at Cambridge United FC after winning the world title. I was the United reporter for the *CEN* and knew that most supporters didn't have a clue about him or speedway. In the summer, cricket and rowing are what happens in Cambridge.

"At that time nearby Mildenhall were regularly attracting speedway crowds of two-to-three thousand (more than 7,000 saw the 1979 NL title showdown with Rye House) but the vast majority were from Suffolk and villages north of Cambridge. The *CEN* wouldn't even have sent a man to Michael's big meetings between 1977 and 1980 if I hadn't been a speedway fan who wanted to cover them," added Butt.

Some BSPA members were not amused by Lee's most critical comments that leapt from the pages of a national newspaper that then boasted a daily circulation of around three million.

Martin Rogers says: "I was interested to hear Michael talking about the promoting 'mafia' who wanted to keep things within their control, but I am not sure if he ever took the time to examine more deeply what the promoting caper involved, and why should he?

"But for any rider to take shots at the promoters of the day, accusing them of lacking vision, etc, was an easy way to score sympathy votes with members of the public who were conditioned to regard promoters as suspect.

"Graham Baker, who ghosted Michael's column for *The Mirror*, was a lovely man and a good mate of mine, and many of our contemporaries, but he milked these criticisms as only tabloid journalists can. It didn't do Michael any favours.

"He talks of being disappointed more rewards didn't come his way after he won the World Final but the fact is he was even then seriously flawed and pursued by bad publicity, which would have had most potential backers running a mile."

Michael went on: "The sport's governing bodies made my life harder after I became World Champion, as if I was being isolated from the scene. Dick Bracher was manager of the SCB at the time and if ever we bumped into each other, it was as much as he could do to even shake my hand. (Don't take it personally, Mike, 'Dastardly Dick' didn't go out of his way to warm to anyone!)

"I felt the authorities should have been encouraging me and the sport itself, rather than penalising me, so this also affected my attitude to racing. "

A few years ago, Ivan Mauger voiced the view that the British authorities have never made the most of the last four of their six individual speedway world champions. He says: "British speedway was patting itself on the back for too long when it was successful. They didn't capitalise upon Peter Collins or Michael Lee or Gary Havelock. They even had a chance as recently as Mark Loram.

"They could have put PC up on a pedestal when he was World Champion, because everyone loved him – we all did. Yes, he had his own manager in Dick Bott, but the BSPA needed a press officer then to ensure they promoted PC on a national basis, to gain the sport even more publicity.

"Michael Lee was a bit different to PC but they could have turned him into speedway's equivalent of a rock star. He was into drugs, drove a Porsche and did the sort of things that rock stars were famous for. He had strengths and assets they could have cashed in on. Michael had very good publicity value."

Was the relentlessly gruelling schedule a drain on mind and body, too?

"Yeah, but I'm not saying that's why things went wrong for me," says Michael. "It wasn't all the hard work that went into being at the top that caused me to go the way I did. But yes, come the end of the season, when you're feeling mentally and physically exhausted, and you're getting all the other crap from the authorities to deal with, I did start to wonder what it was all about. Many a time I recall thinking to myself: 'What the hell am I doing all this for?'

"I was riding too much, my appetite for it had gone. And yeah, maybe I did want to do my own thing a bit too. I started missing meetings and maybe that was because I was doing things I shouldn't have done."

His growing disillusionment with speedway manifested itself in a series of well publicised non-appearances at various meetings throughout his much troubled '81 season.

The campaign was barely a month old when he failed to turn up for the *Daily Express* Spring Classic at Wimbledon on April 16, when his King's Lynn team-mate Dave Jessup won in front of the ITV cameras. "Food poisoning" was the official excuse served up for public consumption but it looked a far from convincing one after Michael romped to stand-out scores of 13 and 17 respectively in away and home matches against Swindon on the following two nights. Again, typical Michael.

He turned on his form tap again to steer England to a Test series-clinching victory against his old mates from the USA to help get Len Silver's second tenure as manager off to a fine winning start in May. He was Lions' top scorer at Belle Vue and also in the decisive Test at Swindon, which underlined Michael's argument that although they were his mates, the Yanks always brought out the best in him on the track, if not away from it.

Come the start of flaming June, though, and the headlines turned black again. He failed to appear for Lynn's match at Ipswich but then things quickly got back on track again. After taking the *Motorcycle News*-sponsored Golden Helmet off winter holder Bo Petersen (Hackney) and successfully defending the monthly match-race crown against Les Collins (Leicester) without losing a race, Michael made it 10 consecutive helmet heat victories when he beat Gordon Kennett 2-0 in the first leg of the June challenge.

In fact, to complete a successful night at Saddlebow Road, he pipped team-mate Mel Taylor to snatch the Cavalcade of Speed marathon race and teamed up with Nigel Sparshott to win the Stardust Best Pairs.

But it was a familiar case of 'now you see him, now you don't'. Less than 24 hours after his efforts at Lynn, he failed to show at Eastbourne, where Eagles' star Kennett was awarded the leg and the Golden Helmet while Lee was stripped of his match-race title amid another wave of bad publicity for him and the sport. A fortnight after failing to turn up at Eastbourne came the police arrest described fully in the previous chapter.

His defence of the World Championship crown (unlike Peter Collins in 1977, the SCB claimed they couldn't seed Britain's World Champion to the international stages of the competition) began badly and barely got any better.

He scraped through the British Final at Coventry, usually such a happy hunting ground and a cut-throat meeting in which he'd not failed to score at least 14 points in the previous four years, by the skin of his teeth. After being controversially reinstated by referee Colin Tirrell following a crash with Ipswich's Kevin Jolly, Lee enjoyed another slice of good fortune when Jessup packed up while leading their race, and then another Lynn rider, Mel Taylor, let Michael

Slipping away . . . Michael losing his first race of the '81 World Final to Bruce Penhall.

through for the point that he needed to grab a top eight qualifying place – just one ahead of the last qualifier.

Michael couldn't blame his comparatively abysmal form on a busy continental calendar – Cyril Crane responded to his errant star's growing catalogue of missed meetings by banning him from taking on any personal or unofficial continental meetings for a month.

Crane told *Speedway Star's* Lynn correspondent Kevin Brown at the time: "I've not spoken or seen Michael for ages and it seems we are fighting a losing battle. He has broken his contract repeatedly this year.

"He should have attended all our meetings and with all the monies he has been receiving, it's King's Lynn Speedway who are the losers every time.

"The first time Michael missed a meeting for us we were up in arms," Crane revealed. "The second time we felt worse, but after five times you don't care. You get fed up with it and get the feeling that you can't bother anymore.

"What hurts most of all is that Michael hasn't even had the decency to ring me. I don't know what to do next, except to get on running King's Lynn to the best of my ability," said a despairing Crane.

"The public must have thought we were a load of idiots, but at least this shows that it is not the management who are to blame, but temperamental riders having peculiar ways.

"I don't want to see Michael leave King's Lynn," the Stars' chief confirmed. "But I don't want any riders around me, and there are others unsettled at Lynn, who don't want to ride. I will let them go whoever they are.

"But Michael has been with us since he was a kid. He is a terrific rider and not a bad lad to talk to. But what I would like to see is a different Mike Lee . . . mature, more stable and with the interests of King's Lynn at heart."

Lee's struggle along the rocky road to Wembley continued at White City in July, when he finished eighth out of 10 qualifiers from the Overseas Final. In the final, decisive heat, Jessup (who won the meeting) and Larry Ross kept out of the way, allowing Michael and Ivan Mauger to comfortably collect the points they both needed to scrape through to the Inter-Continental Final at Vojens in August.

The '81 Overseas Final is best remembered for the televised dispute involving Bruce Penhall and his new arch rival Kenny Carter, who slammed the American in front of the ITV cameras after the riders had tangled and crashed on the pits bend. It marked the start of their public feud that would dominate the sport for another 12 months.

Cradley Heath favourite Penhall was very much in the ascendancy as the season entered its final phase and he justified his odds of 7-2 to lift the world title by winning the Inter-Continental Final at Vojens on the last weekend of July, ahead of fast emerging Danes Erik Gundersen and Hans Nielsen.

Gareth Rogers, who has been involved in speedway as journalist, stadium announcer, TV commentator and promoter since the 60s, recalls an eventful trip he made to Denmark for that penultimate round of the World Championship. As he explains, a Porsche was not always a pre-requisite to land speed attempts: "I went with Michael and Kelly Moran to Vojens for the Inter-Continental Final," says Rogers, who was commentating for KM Video.

"Michael was driving the van between Esbjerg and Vojens and Kelly kept saying 'shwoop champ' as we were going along. That was the cue for Michael to do an impossible overtaking manoeuvre. You had to shut your eyes, it was unbelievable.

"When we got on the ferry I was sharing a cabin with Michael. The two of them disappeared but I said to Mike: 'Be careful what you're getting involved in'.

"Halfway through the night the purser came to our cabin and grabbed Michael for something Kelly had done – namely setting off all the fire extinguishers.

"Kelly had been given a lot of very good equipment by his Eastbourne promoter Bob Dugard but in the meeting itself he ended up scoring nothing. He was in such a dreadful condition.

"I'm like a walking chemist when I go anywhere and he kept borrowing paracetamols from me before the meeting at Vojens. He had to go to sleep in the van before the meeting too," Rogers added.

Once again, Lee just scrambled through, seven points leaving him two ahead of the last of the 11 qualifiers from Vojens for the World Final.

But his preparations for Wembley suffered another setback when he was left out of England's World Team Cup Final squad at Olching, Germany on August 18 – just three weeks before the individual final. At the time it was widely reported that was Michael was in no fit state of mind to race and that he'd "gone to Majorca" for a rest and to get away from it all.

He can now confirm, though, that he was ready and willing to ride for England that day and was "hurt" when Len Silver dropped him from the five-man squad. "I'm not saying we would have beaten the Danes if I'd ridden in the World Team Cup Final that year," says Michael, "but I was very disappointed not to be picked – and I told Len this only recently when we were chatting about old times."

Silver had problems of his own in the late summer and autumn of '81. Castigated by the English press for losing the WTC final by a seven-point margin to Denmark, he also had the responsibility of constructing the Wembley World Final track. He did a great job, too. The last World Final at the old Empire Stadium is fondly remembered as one of the most thrilling occasions in World Championship history. But it was a nightmare for Michael Lee.

While hot pre-meeting favourite Penhall lived up to all expectations to win his first title in dramatic style, his great rival Lee looked a pale shadow of the champion who had put the Californian in his place at Gothenburg 12 months earlier. Even during the pre-meeting parade the omens were not good when Michael was booed by a section of the Wembley crowd who clearly believed he had not been a good World Champion.

Ivan Mauger, arguably the greatest rider ever and certainly the most successful, was never a popular World Champion either and came to accept the stick he received from British fans as part of the job, a back-handed compliment he'd use as a spur to even greater things. Another multi-title winner, Ove Fundin, also loved nothing more than to ram the criticism he received right back down the throats of his detractors. Mauger and Fundin thrived on their unpopularity and it never did them any harm.

But Lee was never going to silence his critics on this memorable night in North London in front of 90,000 fans. He knew it was all over, his title gone, after running a last in his first ride (won by Penhall from Gundersen). And though he did well to hold off the typically tenacious Carter next time out, damaging Kenny's own title chances in the process, a second place followed by a last and then an ignominious fall (after his chain snapped) left Lee way down the field on five points.

As he trudged disconsolately across the hallowed turf back to the pits after sliding into the fence on the first bend in Heat 18, everyone agreed it was a sad way to relinquish the crown he had strived so hard to achieve the previous year. Afterwards, he told *Speedway Star's* Peter Oakes: "It didn't seem to mean a lot to me when I won the championship. But now I've lost it, I know how much it meant. I'll be back, I'm still good enough to win it again."

Lee switched bikes for his second ride and German superstar Egon Müller raised doubts afterwards about the former champ's loyalty to the Jawa factory when he told Oakes: "Michael is the most talented rider in the world – but his machines are not good enough."

Certainly, Michael was the only top line rider still putting his faith in the Czech

Battle of the Brits, as Michael leads Kenny Carter at Wembley.

machinery as the '81 season reached its climax. At the beginning of the year Ole Olsen sparked a mass exodus to Weslake when he ended 10 years as a works Jawa rider by setting up a Weslake agency in Denmark – and he rode the English power unit to second place in the Wembley final. Penhall became Weslake's first World Champion in five years, since Peter Collins in '76.

Lee had much to ponder in the closing weeks of his worst season in the sport to date. And his announcement immediately after Wembley that he wanted a transfer from King's Lynn did nothing to improve morale at the ailing Norfolk track, where even Cyril Crane was running out of ways to describe the latest disaster to hit the club he claimed had lost £80,000 over the three seasons 1979-81.

He said at the time: "Michael's timing has again been wrong, again hitting King's Lynn below the belt. This is another blow to Lynn and the financial implications could prove drastic.

"This is a further setback for our loyal fans who, despite everything, have stuck by Michael and have still been cheering him on.

"I don't feel angry or amazed," Crane went on. "I fully expected something to happen. Two years ago Michael made the same request but later signed a two-year contract!

"But I think Michael will be well advised to stay. He started here as a youngster and over the years there hasn't been that many success stories of riders who opted to move to another track.

"But I'm certain in the final analysis that if Michael can be a very professional,

Lonely walk back to the pits after his last race fall at Wembley.

clean-living rider he will become World Champion over and over again. In my opinion, if anyone is capable of beating Ivan Mauger's six world titles that bloke is Michael Lee.

"In all the years I've known him, Michael has never turned up with dirty equipment, he's always been immaculately equipped."

For his part, Michael told *Speedway Star's* Kevin Brown: "My decision to apply for a transfer was not a sudden one – I've been thinking about it for three years," he said.

"Two years ago I asked for a move but it got to the stage where Cyril Crane wouldn't let me go, making it hard for me, so I forgot about it.

"Now I have decided the time has come again. A move will do me good. There is no point in going on like we are at the moment. A change of club will make me keen again.

"Hull and Ipswich were down in the papers as my preferences but they're not. They are just two possibles from several possible new tracks. But mainly what I want is a midweek track, so I'll be able to ride on the continent at weekends.

"This has been the problem with King's Lynn being a Saturday night track and it has bugged me at times, plus the fact that earlier this season Cyril banned me from riding abroad for four weeks.

"Stopping my continental commitments lost me a lot of money and why the hell should I lose money? It isn't on. After all, it's my living.

"I wouldn't say it was desperate that I moved but I would like a transfer. If it comes to the conclusion that I can't get one, there's obviously nothing I can do.

"I won't be transferred this season, though, I'll see it out with King's Lynn.

I have no grudges against Lynn and I still want to win races and do the same for the club that I have in the past.

"But if you look at the record books, most riders move after six or seven years at one club. I'd like to stay and have a testimonial at Lynn but the main consideration is my long-term future. And I think I'll benefit more by getting away and making a fresh start.

"At the same time I feel bad and disappointed about the supporters who have left, although I can understand their reasons. Let's face it, King's Lynn isn't doing what it should be doing. It is getting me down, all the team down, and the supporters are disappearing.

"The truth of the matter is that the place isn't being run right. I don't like saying it and I don't like criticising anybody, but King's Lynn needs a big sort out.

"So it will do me and my results good – as well as my whole outlook on the sport – if I moved on. Because, at the moment, I'm pretty sick to the teeth of it.

"Maybe one or two tracks would be put off and weary of my reputation. But the problem is that most people don't know the reasons behind my absences this season, or whatever.

"People have no idea what was going on and generally how I have felt about the sport this year . . . pretty sick, I can tell you. I haven't been getting enthusiastic or keen about it.

"But at a new club I will want to do well and will be out to impress. Several promoters have told me they understand my side of the story and realise that I have been the target of a lot of mud-slinging.

"I have had a lot of 'stick' and bad luck, but I can't help that. What's happened has happened.

"But all this hasn't put a shadow over my racing. I'm still riding the same as I ever did. It's just that as a person, people don't seem to accept me as they did before.

"I admit that one of two things that have happened have been bad, the drugs thing and all that. OK, it's bad but these things are just not accepted and that's that. I don't touch drugs anymore anyway."

Lee continued: "But my future is definitely still in speedway. Certainly I've still got all my old ambitions. I'm not giving up what I have achieved over the years without putting up a fight!"

It never took much to rattle Crane's cage and, inevitably, he had the last word on the 'will he, won't he?' Lee saga at the end of '81: "He has repeatedly broken his contract this season," said Cyril. "I've taken legal advice and we could, I'm sure if we wanted to, start taking legal action against him for loss of revenue.

"What we have suffered this season has been a very harmful business," added Crane. "It seems probable that we might take the matter to the court because of the serious loss of earnings and damage inflicted upon King's Lynn Speedway.

"But I don't see how Michael, at the age of 22, has got the experience to express opinion about running a professional speedway track.

"So the boy – and that's what he is," Crane stressed, "is talking a load of rubbish. I defend every one of my staff. But the one thing I can't defend is the team in general.

"The least of all I can defend is Lee himself, because in my opinion he has brought King's Lynn to the unfortunate position it is in today.

"The fanatical King's Lynn fans will support Lee whatever he does, and will obviously defend him through this too. However, we have dozens and dozens of letters from supporters condemning the way he has treated both the fans and the management."

Crane then revealed how he'd earlier came to Lee's aid, claiming that he saved him from a possible ban for the rest of the term after a series of non-appearances, particularly his embarrassing failure to turn up for the Golden Helmet clash with Gordon Kennett at Eastbourne.

He claimed: "I saved Michael from severe punishment because some members of the BSPA then wanted him banned for the rest of the year. However, I told them that I would penalise Lee myself and everyone accepted that. (Do I hear more chuckling at the thought of the BSPA banning a rider, one of England's best, for failing to fulfil several club commitments?)

"But King's Lynn have suffered more than Lee ever has," added Crane.

You would have thought that, given the level of discord between promoter and star rider, there was no way back for Michael at Lynn. But Crane could be as explosive and unpredictable as one of Michael's 'black bombers' prescribed by Dr Muller. In the end, perhaps Crane and Lee decided that they needed each other in a 'marriage' of convenience.

Just as he did time and again when people thought he was down and out and were ready to write him off as a waster, Michael dug deep, tapped into that bottomless well of mercurial brilliance . . . and came up with a maximum to win King's Lynn's prestige Pride of the East for the first time in seven seasons! As parting shots go, it wasn't a bad way to remind the beleaguered Lynn management (and some disgruntled fans) that he wasn't all washed up quite just yet.

And despite all that had gone wrong for him in 1981 . . . those ridiculous drug counselling sessions that no-one but only the trusted few knew anything about, all the adverse publicity, his arrest for those shenanigans on the M1 and the backlash of the fans who were growing tired of his missed meetings and excuses, Michael still finished the season as Stars' No.1 with a 10.30 BL and cup CMA. You have to wonder now how much more he could have achieved had he always been fully focused on what he did best.

Cyril Crane didn't get to make his fortune as a builder in his home city of Norwich without making more than a few good calls at the right time. The organisers of the *Speedway Star* 'Speak-in' brought the pair face to face at the convention held over a long weekend at a Blackpool hotel in November, and it was in this north-west seaside resort where their differences were resolved – if only for the time being.

World Champ Again

Short route to long-track history

Chapter 20

LIKE a phoenix rising from the ashes, Michael Lee suddenly re-emerged from the depths of despair at Wembley and, just 15 days after meekly surrendering his speedway crown, he became a World Champion again.

This time he showed his class as a motorcycling all-rounder in the fastest form of oval tracksport to win the 1981 World Long-track Championship at Gornja Radgona, a city in the former Yugoslavia.

In simple terms, the main difference between the bikes used for speedway and long-track is that LT machines have two gears and a rear wheel suspension.

Tracks are typically three times longer than the traditional speedway circuits – hence the name of the sport – and the men on the machines don't exactly hang around. Riders exceed speeds of 100mph on wide, sweeping bends and long straights big enough to stage six-man races.

The sport, which drew its competitors from both speedway and grass-track circles, took off in the late 60s. Germany was, and still is, the hotbed of long-track racing, although tracks also sprung up in Norway (Oslo), Denmark (Aalborg and Korskro) and the Czech Republic (Marianske Lazne). There were several failed attempts to introduce the sport to Britain in the 70s, notably at Haldon (Devon), Chasewater (Staffs) and Motherwell in Scotland, but they proved to be no more than short-lived novelty experiments.

Ivan Mauger became the first-ever World Long-track Champion after the FIM granted the competition official status and introduced an individual World Championship in 1971. The six times world speedway No.1 has always been proud of his three LT title successes and appears somewhat irritated that riders who have excelled at this form of the sport don't tend to receive the credit he believes they deserve.

Ole Olsen and Anders Michanek were two other speedway World Champions who transformed their supremacy from one form of tracksport to the other during the 70s. In the following decade, Egon Müller and Erik Gundersen also completed the distinguished 'double'.

But in 1981, much to everyone's surprise, the elite trio of Ivan, Ole and Mich were joined by Michael Lee. And no-one was more stunned by his victory than the man himself.

The first Englishman to win the long-track crown, Michael says: "I'd had a poxy week after Penhall took my speedway world title from me at Wembley and, to be honest, I didn't go into the long-track final with much hope of winning it. I didn't even think I'd be in the running.

Michael showing great pace on the long-tracks of Marianske Lazne (right) and Scheessel.

"It was probably only the fourth meeting I'd ridden in over a distance of 1,000 metres and I was as surprised as anyone when I won it."

Lee finished third in his opening ride, behind three times champion Egon Müller and fellow Brit Phil Collins, but won his next two heats and semi-final.

Michael recalls an amazing afternoon at the venue, very close to the Austrian border, in the country that has been known as Slovenia since gaining independent status in 1991: "I'd only dropped two points from my first three rides and it was my mechanic Steve Burgess who first realised that I was actually through to the semi-final. 'Bloody hell, the semi-finals!' I thought. I'd become so cynical after what happened at Wembley that I couldn't believe I'd got that far.

"It was then a case of, 'right, let's go for it', and I just rode my tits off that day."

Lee had been the only rider to beat Christoph Betzl when they met in Heat 6 but the experienced German – bidding to become his country's fourth successive title winner – went into the final race with a one-point leader from the rookie Englishman.

He says: "All of a sudden, I've got the bull by the horns and I'm going for it. Everything that had happened in the previous few weeks was forgotten. It was a case of head down, arse up! I was a man on a mission."

The six finalists (from the inside, with points scores in brackets) lined up on the grid as follows: Michanek (16), Betzl (19), Müller (14), Gilgenreiner (15), Lee

His light, lanky frame was ideally suited to the big tracks

"All of a sudden, I've got the bull by the horns and I'm going for it. Everything that had happened in the previous few weeks was forgotten. It was a case of head down, arse up! I was a man on a mission."

(18) and Collins (14). Points were awarded on a 5-4-3-2-1-0 basis.

Wearing a yellow full-face crash helmet and with the No.14 number plate on the front of his bike, Michael (and Müller) gave the tapes a gentle nudge before they were all away. The title was effectively decided between the gate and the first bend, where Lee went shoulder to shoulder on the outside with Phil Collins while Gilgenreiner sneaked ahead of them in mid-track. But Betzl, the leading points qualifier and Michael's biggest threat, made a disastrous start and was trailing by miles as the other five screwed it all on into the first turn.

As they roared out of the massive first/second bend, it was Gilgenreiner who led down the back straight, hotly pursued by Lee in his slipstream. It's at this point that most riders in Michael's position, holding a comfortable second place with his main rival last, would have settled for what he had and taken the four points that would have comfortably clinched the world title.

But the instinctive racer in Lee wouldn't allow him to concede the race victory to the German. He hounded Gilgenreiner for a full lap and a bit before swooping round him in a brilliant, breathtaking manoeuvre that was one in the eye for the cynics who regard long-track racing as purely a test of speed with little skill required.

World Champion again. A surprised Michael claims top spot in the 1981 World Long-track Final ahead of Christoph Betzl (left) and Anders Michanek.

ITV commentator Dave Lanning drooled as Lee, his left leg trailing high above his machine like a loose twig gently blowing in the wind, hunted down Gilgenreiner and then passed him as if he was standing still early on the second lap. Lanning described Lee with his characteristic style as 'The Flying Hairpin' and suggested his stunning victory in the German-dominated sport was the continental equivalent of an English cyclist winning Tour de France.

Lee's thrilling last race win was surely the ultimate adrenalin rush that no drug he has shoved up his nose or down his throat could ever possibly surpass. The five points left him three clear of Betzl (who passed Collins) overall, while Mich grabbed the bronze medal after beating Gilgenreiner in a run-off.

It was also another triumph for the formidable father-son combo. The Jawa engine Andy prepared for his son was quicker than any of the Weslakes set up by the acclaimed German tuner Otto Lantenhammer, although Michael doesn't believe he had any significant advantage over his main rivals, most of whom were vastly more experienced on the long-track scene. Two of the other five on the start-line in the final race were past World Champions.

"Yeah, speed is crucial on the long-track but, to be honest, my bikes were not that special. Even before the final we were mixing bits from both bikes to try and come up with the right combination and couldn't make our minds up for a while.

"But I passed Mich, who was no slouch on long-track, twice during the meeting and also went by Gilgenreiner in the final.

"One of the most satisfying things about it is that the Germans were also shocked by what I'd done, and went home scratching their heads.

"I was well excited afterwards and couldn't wait to phone my old man to tell him I'd won. Because of what happened at Wembley two weeks before, he was as down as I was and so didn't come out to Yugoslavia. He just told me to go out there and do my best, and to enjoy it. His simple advice worked.

"I phoned him as soon as I got back to the hotel and when I told him I'd won, he was speechless. Whenever Dad was lost for words, I knew I'd done something big – whether it was good or bad!

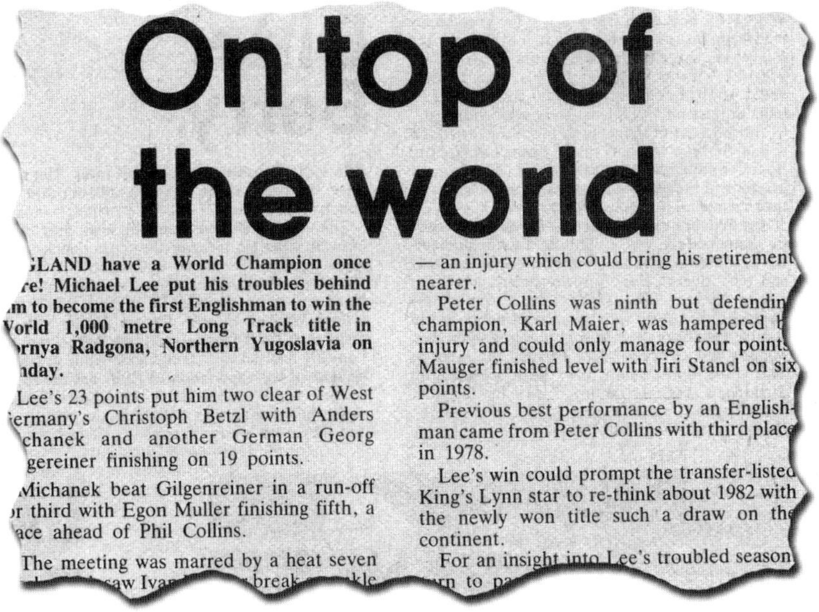

On top of the world

ɜLAND have a World Champion once ɾe! Michael Lee put his troubles behind ɹm to become the first Englishman to win the Vorld 1,000 metre Long Track title in ɾrnya Radgona, Northern Yugoslavia on ıday.

Lee's 23 points put him two clear of West ɟermany's Christoph Betzl with Anders ɔhanek and another German Georg gereiner finishing on 19 points.

Michanek beat Gilgenreiner in a run-off ɾr third with Egon Muller finishing fifth, a ace ahead of Phil Collins.

The meeting was marred by a heat seven ... saw Iva... break ...kle — an injury which could bring his retirement nearer.

Peter Collins was ninth but defendin champion, Karl Maier, was hampered b injury and could only manage four points Mauger finished level with Jiri Stancl on six points.

Previous best performance by an Englishman came from Peter Collins with third place in 1978.

Lee's win could prompt the transfer-listed King's Lynn star to re-think about 1982 with the newly won title such a draw on the continent.

For an insight into Lee's troubled season ...rn to pa...

Welcome headlines for a change.

Andy says: “It was an extraordinary achievement, because the long-track wasn't a British rider's sport and was dominated by the Germans around that time. I knew Michael's capabilities because I went to a lot of long-tracks with him.

“For me, it was just as fantastic as him winning the speedway World Championship. I say that because the long-track demanded a totally different riding technique – it looks the same as speedway, but it isn't because there are two gears on a long-track bike. The fact that he adapted to what was required and won it was pretty good.”

Like Andy, Michael regards winning at Gornja Radgona as probably as big an achievement as winning the speedway crown in Sweden a year earlier. “It was my third season in the World Long-track Championship but this was only my third meeting on a circuit of 1,000 metres or more. Scheessel and Pfarrkirchen, both in Germany, were also around that size but the other meetings I'd done in previous years were on smaller tracks, such as the German venues at Vilshofen and Plattling, which were around 700 metres.

“My first long-track meeting was at Plattling in 1979, although the two Jawa long-track bikes the factory gave me as part of my works sponsorship deal just sat in the workshop for about half a season until I received a letter through the post inviting me to my first meeting in Germany.

“At first I used a speedway engine, nothing like the super-tuned motors all the Germans were on. Then I realised that everything on the bike had to be lightened to make it go faster, so we were behind the others for quite a while in that respect. I wasn't competing with the Germans or doing any good – I don't think

The World Long-track trophy that Michael 'stole' from under the noses of the Germans.

"I received more bookings as a result of that success but I was in turmoil and on the slippery slope by then. I didn't exploit the fact that I became World Long-track Champion at all."

I even got beyond the semi-finals in my two previous World Finals.

"But I kept getting invites to go back to lots of different tracks. The German promoters saw that I was a proper racer who would always have a go and wasn't just going to turn up to collect my appearance money and then take things easy. I always went there to race hard and win."

In '81, Michael had qualified from the semi-final at Herxheim, another leading German track where Phil Collins topped the scorechart. The former Cradley Heath and England star, younger brother of Peter Collins, reveals that Michael played a significant part in him reaching the deciding race of the long-track final that year.

He explains: "I entered the World Championship for the first time in '81 but I didn't have a bike good enough to compete in my quarter-final round at Vilshofen – and that's where Michael came to my rescue.

"Tim Harrington, who was PC's long-track mechanic and also helping me, lived at St Neots in Cambridgeshire, which is just up the road from where

Michael lived. And when Mike heard that I was struggling for a bike, he kindly lent me one of his.

"Mike and I both got through that first round and I had my own bike set up in time to win the semi at Herxheim. I was actually leading the World Final after we'd all taken two rides each but then Ivan had his bad crash and that shook me up. I was due out in the next race but after seeing him taken off in the meat wagon, I was crapping myself. It was a horrendous crash – at first, we thought he might be dead!"

Thankfully, Ivan survived his frightening crash with German Josef Aigner on the home straight but a broken ankle in six places cast a shadow over the final in Yugoslavia.

"I was there with Michael, at the other end of the starting grid, in the last race of the World Final," continues Collins, "and although I made a fairly decent start, I should perhaps have lent on him a little more when we got to the first turn. Instead, I hesitated and got a face-full of dirt that virtually wiped me out. Still, I was satisfied to finish sixth overall in my first season on the long-track.

"Michael was the boy that day, though, and he deserved his victory. Now and again I watch the video of the final on YouTube and it always amazes me when I see his front wheel shimmering where he didn't have it balanced properly – you had to add little weights to the front wheel spokes to balance it.

"I had my brother Pete to show me how to set up my bikes but Michael was still a little inexperienced in this form of racing. In the film of the final you can actually see his wheel wobbling. That kind of imbalance on the front wheel causes blurred vision, so his eyeballs must have been bouncing around as he went down the straight at 100mph-plus!"

In addition to the unlucky Mauger and Peter Collins, others who failed to make the six-man final in Yugoslavia on Michael's big day included German aces Müller, plus Karl Maier and Alois Wiesbock, who had won the world title in the previous two seasons. Bruce Penhall only qualified as one of the reserves and didn't ride.

With typical humility, Michael recalls: "I thought I was going to Gornja Radgona merely to make the numbers up. To me, qualifying for the World Final was quite an achievement in itself, so to go there and win it was a bit of a shock.

"I received more bookings as a result of that success but I was in turmoil and on the slippery slope by then. I didn't exploit the fact that I became World Long-track Champion at all."

Instead, the lucrative long-track scene soon hailed a new hero from England. Simon Wigg won the world title at Korskro, Denmark in 1985 and dedicated himself to the sport to such an extent that he added four more World Championships to his name and established himself as the long-track king, earning tens of thousands of pounds on the continent almost every weekend of the summer. The sport lost a legend when he sadly died of a brain tumour in 2000.

"Wiggy became even bigger and more popular than the German riders in their own country," says Lee, who has nothing but respect for what his former England speedway team-mate achieved before his untimely death. "I know just how good he was, because I went to some of his long-track meetings with Steve Johnston in the 90s, when I was tuning Johnno's engines, and it was amazing to see all the crowds gathered around his large transporter, eager to talk to him and get a picture or an autograph. I always called Simon 'Herr Wigg' after that," says Michael, impressed by the charismatic Wigg's ultra-professional approach.

Again, we can only speculate how many more world long-track titles Michael would have won had he applied himself in the years following Gornja Radgona. Given his talent and with top class equipment at his disposal, he could feasibly have dominated this part-time sport for years and made himself a rich man in the process.

He may not have cashed in and earned the rich trappings of success enjoyed by Wigg or Kelvin Tatum, the three times champion who took over Simon's long-track mantle in the late 90s, but no-one can deny Michael his place in the history books.

"Whenever I play back the tape of that final race in '81, it still has me on the edge of my seat in excitement – I'm actually sitting there and willing myself to win! It wasn't until much later that I really appreciated the significance of what I'd done," adds Lee, who remains the only Englishman to have won both the world speedway and long-track titles.

Catch a Falling Star

When it's time to go

Chapter 21

GLORY in the World Long-track Final proved no more than a brief ray of sunshine amid the darkening clouds surrounding Michael's continuing downfall as a world class rider.

On track, the 1982 season began badly and just got worse. While still reeling from the tragic death of a good friend, Michael was dropped from the England team, then he suffered a wrist injury that sidelined him for two months and prevented him from defending his long-track crown.

He crashed out of the speedway World Championship at an early stage and ended the season back on the transfer list at his own request, after another unpleasant public slanging match with Cyril Crane.

His personal season-long struggle mirrored that of his club, with King's Lynn lurching from one crisis to another, on what seemed almost a weekly basis, before the beleaguered promoters decided to cut their losses and sell up at the end of another traumatic year.

Symptomatic of the general malaise permeating through Lynn at the time, Crane jumped the gun by relieving Lee of the captaincy even before a miserable 1981 had finished. After all the missed meetings and self-inflicted problems of the previous season, Michael could have no argument with the management's decision to appoint a new leader, even though he'd signed a new three-year contract that was meant to take him up to his testimonial season.

But their plans backfired on them embarrassingly when Dave Jessup flatly declined the offer of the captaincy.

"If Michael stays and I am appointed captain, I don't think I could do the job properly," said DJ, who was handed the England captaincy by Len Silver at the start of '81.

"There is no way I could captain King's Lynn while Michael is there because there is no way it will work. Michael is only human, after all, and I feel he will resent the change," Jessup added.

Crane then announced that he would leave his riders to decide who they wanted to skipper the side. Meanwhile, Jessup had made his mind up that he wanted away from Lynn after three seasons.

Stars' club record £18,000 signing was on a riding tour of South Africa in the winter of 1981-82 when he happily accepted an offer to join Wimbledon – his favourite track and much nearer his Kent home.

Michael was not exactly sad to see Jessup go. "There was rivalry between us and it was probably a bit more personal than that," he told *Backtrack* when interviewed in 2005.

"DJ used to turn up with the one bike on the car rack, while I'd arrive with two immaculate machines on a trailer or in the van. If something went wrong with his, he'd jump straight on my spare. So the next day I'd have two bikes to clean and prepare and yet I'd probably only ridden one of them myself.

"He was almost doing as well on my bike as he was his own – and it seemed to me that he was quite happy for that arrangement to continue for two or three months.

"It kind of wore a bit thin with me after a while and in the end I had to have words with people at King's Lynn about it.

"I never fell out with DJ, though – I haven't fallen out with many people – but it did get a bit personal at the time."

In another *Backtrack* interview, this time in 2007, Jessup responded: "There were times when I borrowed a bike from Michael if I had problems but, then again, he usually had two or three bikes with him every week, so he would never have needed to borrow mine!"

The rivalry between Lee and Jessup might have proved an expensive exercise for King's Lynn in the long-term but it definitely brought out the best in both England stars. "We had some really tough second-half finals," recalled DJ, who is almost six years older than Michael and completely different to him in many ways.

While Michael's idea of relaxing away from the track was a party and a joint, or maybe something more powerful, little Dave was never happier than when he was on the golf course perfecting the stroke play that has ultimately made him one of the most accomplished players on the pro-am golf circuit.

The strait-laced, serious-looking Jessup – a "loner," observed Crane - can now afford to laugh at being dubbed 'Cardigan Man' and admits he was never one to court popularity with the fans in the bar after a meeting or to let his hair down on overseas sorties with England.

He agrees, too, that while he consistently scored more points than Terry Betts did in his final season, he was never going to replace the club's all-time legend in the hearts of the Lynn faithful or, indeed, even the Stars' promoters. "Letting Terry go was the worst thing we ever did," was Crane's parting shot as Jessup left for Wimbledon and Colin Richardson came the opposite way in part-exchange at the start of '82. Jessup got it right, though, when he said: "No-one, not even the World Champion, could've replaced Bettsy."

Getting back to his rivalry with Lee, Jessup says: "We were meant to line up in one-to-seven order in the pits at King's Lynn but I don't know what happened to our No.2 because Michael always parked next to me, right at the far end!

"I wouldn't say we were big rivals, although it did rub it in a bit for me when, after the 1980 final, Michael was introduced to the crowd as the 'new World Champion'," added DJ, who never went closer to winning the title than on the night he finished runner-up to his Lynn team-mate at Ullevi.

Looking back now, Michael says: "I didn't disagree with Simmo when he wrote in his book that DJ was a tight bugger but some of the other things he said about him were uncalled for. You don't stab people in the back when you've known someone for as long as Simmo has known DJ.

"Another thing that annoyed me when I read Simmo's book was his comment that he saw me 'drop' something into Dave's bottle of orange juice in the pits during a meeting somewhere, implying that I was attempting to 'drug' my Lynn team-mate. Simmo must be a total idiot to even think that I might do such a thing!

"The trouble is, some people will have read that and actually believed it was true. I imagine them saying: 'Jesus! I didn't know that Michael Lee used to try and drug other riders!'

"I didn't like the way Simmo bad-mouthed certain other individuals either. He went on about 'selling races' and all that crap, which I thought was disgusting. What he chooses to admit to doing is entirely his business but to implicate Simon Wigg, who is sadly not here to defend himself, was totally out of order.

"I could tell you things about Simmo that would just stink, but I won't because I don't need to stick the knife into others to sell books. I will never name other riders who I know have taken drugs. I take responsibility for my own actions," says Lee, who will always respect Dave Jessup for the top line class rider that he was.

"I still see Dave and his wife Vicky when I go to Rye House, where DJ runs his spares service from his van in the pits. We probably get on better now than we've ever done," Michael added.

Jessup's departure from Lynn paved the way for Michael to form a new twin spearhead with Australian No.1 Billy Sanders, a good friend of his from past tours Down Under and their many on-track battles in East Anglian derbies involving Lynn and Ipswich, who became available after Hull closed at the end of '81. Michael talks about Sanders in much sadder tones later in the book but in the spring of '82 it appeared that Crane had found a way to revive sagging morale in the Stars' camp.

But when Jessup and another Lynn 'old boy' Simmons returned to lead Wimbledon to victory in the opening match of the season, the signs were ominous. And not just at Saddlebow Road, where Crane reported an operating loss of £30,000 in 1981. There was widespread gloom throughout the sport and *Speedway Star's* Philip Rising sounded another unheeded warning note when he wrote: "Tracks are losing money at an alarming rate. The BSPA is facing an economic climate the like of which it has never encountered before."

His depressing words might have applied equally at various other times in subsequent years and they are no doubt still a valid commentary on the sport today.

The issue of drugs wasn't about to go away either. Almost a year after SRA secretary George Barclay urged the SCB to clampdown on drug-taking among his members, random testing still hadn't been introduced and retired Swedish great Olle Nygren fuelled the rumour mill even further by alleging in a Sunday People article that he knew of one rider who had been spending £500 week to feed his drug habit.

Nygren: Ex-King's Lynn rider . . . long-time training school instructor at King's Lynn who paid the promoters a fee to hire the Saddlebow Road track . . . living in Norwich . . . it didn't take a genius to work out who 'Varg Olle' was referring to. Typically, the speedway authorities not only buried their heads in the sand, one or two – including Cradley Heath promoter Peter Adams (who, ironically, briefly acted as Lee's business manager in the late 70s) – came out from their ivory towers to condemn the wily Nygren's claims as "irresponsibility of the highest order."

Speedway invariably closes ranks when there's a whiff of scandal in the air and this was just another example of it.

The 1982 season is also sadly remembered for three tragedies in quick succession. Reading's American Denny Pyeatt died following a horrendous crash at Hackney in early July, shortly before Swindon's Martin Hewlett suffered a fatal brain haemorrhage. The first fatality of the season was much too close to home for Michael Lee, though.

On April 17 he top-scored for Lynn against rivals Ipswich in the League Cup but the meeting was abandoned following a sickening second-half crash that claimed the life of young Australian Brett Alderton.

The 18-year-old Milton Keynes rider, who was having trials at King's Lynn, crashed while trying to avoid fallen Ipswich rider Jeremy Doncaster as they raced down the back straight and into the third bend. He was catapulted head-first into the solid wooden board fence and it was later reported afterwards that he was probably clinically dead at the time of impact.

Along with Ipswich promoter John Berry and Witches' Danish star Preben Eriksen, Michael was one of the first to reach poor Brett as he lay unconscious on the track.

He recalls: "I ran over to where Brett lay and he was obviously in a state. I took his helmet and couldn't believe what I saw."

Just three days before the accident, the popular Alderton – in his second season of British racing – had been on cloud nine after scoring his first paid 15-point maximum since coming to England for Milton Keynes against Boston – ironically, the two National League tracks at which Cyril Crane held a promoting interest. Afterwards, a euphoric Brett rushed into the speedway office to phone his father, former Hull rider Dennis Alderton, at the family home in Sydney to tell him the good news.

How sad then that the next time Dennis got a call from England, it was to tell him that his son was in a critical condition and fighting for his life.

Alderton was immediately taken to King's Lynn's Queen Elizabeth II Hospital but medical staff there knew immediately that there was very little hope of him surviving the crash, so he was transferred to the Addenbrookes Hospital – the one in Cambridge where Michael himself had fought for his own life as a nine-year-old victim of peritonitis. With Papworth Hospital, world famous for its heart transplant operations, also in the city, doctors knew that by connecting Brett's body to a life support machine they would protect his vital organs and create the opportunity for him to become a donor.

That's exactly what happened – and Michael's mother Val was at the centre of the heartrending process as soon as Dennis Alderton landed at Heathrow Airport and headed straight for the Lees' home in Melbourn.

Visibly upset at the memory of the tragedy, Val said: "Dennis came alone from Australia because his wife Barbara had a heart problem and doctors wouldn't allow her to travel that distance by plane. We kept in touch with her by phone and I had to stand in for her when it came to the legal formalities at the hospital.

"Dennis stayed at our place throughout his time in England and Michael saw that side of it – all the heartbreak Brett's family went through."

It was thought that Brett had carried a donor card but as none could be found, his parents had to give their written approval for his organs to be used for transplant purposes. After three days word came from Papworth Hospital of a middle-aged family man from Surrey in urgent need of a new heart, so staff at Addenbrookes approached Dennis Alderton for his approval to go ahead with the necessary operation.

Val continues: "Brett was being kept alive by machines but we all knew there was no hope. Dennis and I talked and talked and he kept breaking down. Eventually, He said to me: 'Val, I'm going to stand back now and I want you to answer me this: If it was Michael laying there, what would you do? We've got to decide now what to do with Brett'.

"I replied that if Michael was in Brett's position, I would agree to donate his vital organs, so that part of him could live on in other people. I'm sure that's what Brett would have wanted – and Dennis agreed. I can remember standing outside Addenbrookes Hospital with him clinging to me and crying. It was so sad.

"We then went back inside the hospital to both sign the consent forms and be present when they switched off the machines.

"It took me a long time to get over the sadness I felt at the time and I know that it hit Michael very hard too. He and Brett were friends.

"Michael had seen his team-mates and rivals break their arms and legs before but seeing Brett's head injuries did have a marked effect on him. I know it did.

"But whether Brett's death had any underlying effect on what happened to Michael after that, I can't really say," Val added.

Michael says: "I was obviously very upset by Brett's death but I wouldn't say it had anything to do with what I did with my life afterwards. We all know when we take up speedway that it's a dangerous sport.

"The worst part of it, for me, was the night Billy Sanders and I drove to the

Friends Michael and Billy Sanders with Alan Littlechild at King's Lynn in 1982.

airport to collect Brett's dad, Dennis. It was a very unpleasant journey from there back to Addenbrookes Hospital because at that stage Dennis was still hoping and believing his son would, in time, make a full recovery. We just couldn't tell him how desperate Brett's situation really was.

"Billy was also riding in the meeting when Brett was killed. He was as cut up as anyone because Brett lived near him in Sydney and they knew each other very well."

Sanders and his Australian Test team-mate Phil Herne and his family also joined the Lees in rallying round Dennis Alderton and they were among the mourners at Brett's funeral.

What happened next to Michael in speedway terms is that he was back in the headlines again for the wrong reasons. He was picked by England's new co-management of Eric Boocock and John Berry for the first Test of the series against the USA at Wimbledon just 13 days after Alderton's fatal crash. He was there. But he didn't ride.

Michael had just flown back from the Jawa factory near Prague and although this time he took the precaution of actually appearing at the track rather than simply phoning to inform those concerned that he wouldn't be able to ride that night, his explanation that he was unwell due to food poisoning was unacceptable to Boocock.

Booey recalls: "Although we beat the Yanks 63-45 at Wimbledon, there was a major issue to deal with. Michael had turned up and was complaining he had a stomach bug – but I didn't believe it at all and I still don't believe it. He turned up looking terrible and said he'd been feeling poorly, so I told him not to ride if he didn't want to – and he didn't.

"I class riding for England as a big honour and anyone who doesn't want to ride for their country should just say so. Michael was just beginning to get a reputation as a wild child and wanted to pick and choose where he rode. If he was on form he was like lightning. But if he turned up with his head up his backside, he couldn't care less.

"I wasn't happy with Michael and I told the BSPA I wanted him dropped from the rest of the series, but the management committee insisted he kept his place. He was a big name and had been World Champion not long before, so I didn't get the backing.

"But, looking back, I was right because he rode like a big tart. He scored two at Swindon, seven at Ipswich, where he finished last twice, and one at Poole in the decider, which we lost heavily.

"We've mentioned Michael's personal problems before and I think by this time he was on the slippery slope. Michael was a smashing lad, and still is, but you can't mix business with pleasure at that level. Maybe, just maybe, a jolt like being left out of a Test series could have done some good but at that time I doubt it."

Trying to recall his showdown in the Plough Lane pits with Boocock, Michael says: "If I'd just flown back from Czecho, then food poisoning would have been my genuine reason for not wanting to ride, or I would simply have been too knackered from the trip. Having gone all the way to Wimbledon, I wouldn't have pulled out for any other reason."

Filmgoers in the summer of '82 were flocking to the big box office hit Poltergeist but who knows what demon spirits possessed Michael on that day, in June, when he bowed out of the individual World Championship in the British Final at Coventry with a paltry seven points – despite winning his first ride. A "sad sight" is how *Speedway Star's* match reporter described Lee as he trailed home last in Heat 18 behind the Grahame brothers (who filled the top two places on a big night of shocks) and Chris Morton.

Although Lee had been called up by Berry and Boocock for the start of the World Team Cup campaign (they could hardly leave him out for the Overseas Final qualifier at King's Lynn), he was dropped to reserve for the next, Inter-Continental Final round at Vojens, where he ran a poor last in his only ride and England were eliminated as Denmark and the USA went through to the final at White City in August.

Left out of all four summer Test matches against world champions Denmark, Michael's misery continued on July 24, the night Reading visited King's Lynn. He scored a maximum in the match but crashed in the second-half event and sustained a fractured scaphoid bone in his left wrist.

Despite a couple of abortive comeback attempts, the injury ruled him out of action for the next two months. And one of the meetings he was disappointed not to ride in was the Brett Alderton Memorial Trophy event at Milton Keynes.

The injured Lee could only watch the action from the pits as some of the sport's biggest names, headed by World Champion Bruce Penhall and Billy Sanders, gave their services free of charge to raise money for the fund set up for Brett's parents, who faced significant travel costs to and from Australia on top of the funeral bill.

A crowd of around 3,000, one of the largest ever seen at the Groveway track, came to pay their last respects to the tragic teenager who had paid the ultimate price for his love of the sport. The fund benefited by £6,257 but fund trustees – including Andy Lee and Knights' star rider Bob Humphreys – were outraged when it is emerged weeks later that MK co-promoter Cyril Crane, on behalf of the promotion, attempted to deduct around 20 per cent in expenses to cover the cost of stadium rental, track preparation, shale and programmes.

Crane banned Humphreys from attending Milton Keynes Speedway for making accusations against him, while an angry Lee also became embroiled in this unedifying spectacle. In a damning piece in *Speedway Star* pointing out that his friend had died on Crane's track at King's Lynn, Michael was quoted as saying: "I think it's disgusting. We all lost money getting down there, so why shouldn't the promoters? It's not a question of whether the figure is 20 per cent or not, it should be nil."

After the furore died down, I believe the Alderton family refused to accept money from the fund and decided instead to donate it all to a hospital in Milton Keynes.

Michael's wrist injury also ruled him out of the World Long-track semi-final in Germany, having qualified from his quarter-final at Marianske Lazne in May as joint top scorer with Dane Hans Nielsen. Had he been fit he would undoubtedly have sailed through to the final but he gave up his crown to Germany's Karl Maier without even a fight.

With his heart clearly no longer in it, Lee again informed Crane that he wanted a transfer from Lynn and during his continued absence Billy Sanders took over the captaincy. The Aussie had endured an unhappy '81 season at Hull but the switch to Lynn didn't provide the tonic he hoped it would. Mel Taylor also put in for a move in mid-season and as the team slumped towards the bottom of the BL table, the future at the Norfolk venue looked increasingly bleak.

The usually bullish Crane made no secret of the fact that his own enthusiasm for the sport had also waned and months before the '82 season ended there was repeated talk of Norfolk Speedways selling their speedway promoting rights at Saddlebow Road. Crane planned to continue running his regular car auctions at the stadium and benefit from catering revenue but needed to find someone to buy the speedway promoting rights from him and Vi Littlechild and then charge them a rental fee for the stadium. It was a big ask in a region troubled by rising unemployment and with a sport that has its finger perpetually hovering over the self-destruct button, but he managed to find a familiar figure who had the conviction to put his money on the line.

Martin Rogers, general manager at Lynn for seven years before he left Crane and co. to go his own way at Leicester in 1980, was delighted to add a second senior league track to his bow.

But there would be no place for Michael Lee under the new regime as Rogers reached for a new broom that he hoped would sweep away all the ills that he believed had plagued the club since his departure three years earlier.

Looking back on his winter '82 takeover, he says: "What Michael got up to after 1980 was not directly my business but I knew enough people at King's Lynn and saw for myself what an impact it was having there. By the end of the '81 season, when Leicester won there in the BL (Michael was missing for the last two or three weeks of the season, I believe), there was a noticeable dampening of spirits and lessening of crowd numbers.

"It seemed there was more of the same in 1982 when Cyril Crane was regularly making comments about how difficult it all was and, latterly, how he was thinking of shutting up shop or selling.

"I'd had a long-running and sentimental attachment to Lynn for years, Leicester was going really well, and the opportunity to buy the promoting rights at Saddlebow Road was irresistible. On reflection, it turned out not to be the best decision I ever made but I had a clear idea of how the place could be revived, some of the old values restored, and fancied the challenge.

"I didn't appreciate and severely underestimated the huge amount of damage that had been done in the three years we were away. I'm not saying it was all Michael's fault but almost certainly he and his actions accounted for a good part of it. Mind you, the promotion's handling of what no doubt was a very difficult situation probably left a lot to be desired.

"For that reason, and what I perceived as an urgent need to get back to the clean-cut, professional image I'd worked so hard to cultivate in earlier years, I didn't want Michael included in any deal I did with Norfolk Speedways.

"We agreed to purchase (the benefit of the contracts of) most of the riders but he was specifically excluded. Riders I talked to as potential signings (Peter Collins, Gordon Kennett, John Louis, etc) all knew and understood I wanted a complete image makeover."

Almost as if to prove Rogers right, Michael provoked yet another 'Lee goes missing' headline in the final days of a depressing '82 season when he failed to turn up for Lynn's Border Trophy match at Leicester, of all places. With an air of resignation, Crane said: "I just can't bother anymore. Over the past two weeks Michael has failed to turn up three times but most of al I feel sorry for the fans – and Michael himself.

"Team manager Alan Littlechild saw Michael on the day of the Leicester match and said he was perfectly all right. He was bright, healthy and alert. He didn't look ill and wasn't in a bad state.

"Apparently he just said: 'Damn it, I'm not going'. The explanation was that he had simply lost interest, which is ridiculous.

"But the funny thing is, I like Michael and I don't want to push him down anymore. But I think he has got to have a good look at himself in the winter months. I aim to see him and his father Andy to discuss his future.

"I hate to see talent go to waste and I believe Michael still has a rosy future. But it is all up to him now," Crane added, with the zeal of a man who knew he still had a prime asset left on his books that he was looking to sell to the highest bidder.

Today, Crane can look back on those difficult days at the helm of a sinking ship with the benefit of hindsight but his opinion of Michael hasn't changed. "He was too easily influenced by others – namely the Americans," says Cyril from his home near Norwich. "They could handle drugs because they were used to them but Michael couldn't. It's the same with youngsters today – they get in with the wrong people and it ruins lives.

"In the final analysis he is right to blame himself for what happened to him but if the people he mixed with at the time hadn't been around to party with and get into a life of drugs . . . well, what can you say?

"Alan Littlechild, who has always got on great with Michael, and still does, used to go round to his house on a Saturday morning to check that he was OK. He'd usually be working on his bikes and looking fine but come about 6.45pm, I'd be on tenterhooks and thinking: 'Oh my God, is he going to turn up?'

"One time the Control Board and BSPA got on to me, saying that Michael was owed money by us – I had letters from the promoters' association manager, Ann Gillespie, and all sorts. But in our contract with Michael it clearly stated that if he failed to turn up for a meeting without a doctor's certificate, he'd be fined £250 each time by the club.

"One year he failed to turn up 16 times, home or away, so that was £4,000 we saved!

"Michael did a lot of harm to King's Lynn while I was promoting there but whatever he did to me I've always liked him as a person. I'd only put him down for his actions. He is a very likeable, friendly bloke. There are no problems between us now. I saw him at Mildenhall Speedway last year and we're always glad to see each other, and we still remain good friends.

"Terry Betts was the best rider King's Lynn ever had, or ever will have, but Michael was the most talented and easily the best on ability."

Although Lee just held on to the No.1 position at King's Lynn when his 35 official league and cup matches were added up, his 9.65 CMA (around half-a-point better than Sanders') was the first time he'd dipped below a final double figure average since his first full top flight season for the Stars in 1976.

Only Poole finished below King's Lynn in the final 1982 BL table, and that's just where he was heading . . .

Fired up at Poole

Silencing the critics

Chapter 22

MICHAEL'S transfer from King's Lynn to Poole at the start of 1983 was just what he needed to reignite his enthusiasm and hunger after eight seasons with the same club.

Cyril Crane and Martin Rogers have highlighted his shortcomings and the grief they claim he caused King's Lynn. But the fact is he established himself as the Stars' No.1 rider and a world class superstar from the age of 18 and, save for the '81 campaign when Dave Jessup just pipped him to top spot, he remained their biggest points scorer and drawcard until he left at the end of '82.

So King's Lynn didn't get a bad return on someone who hadn't cost them a penny when he pledged his future to the Stars at 16.

Let's be honest. The fact that King's Lynn were not good enough to win anything bigger than the 1977 Knockout Cup during that period was no fault of Michael's. Actually, wasn't it a typically brilliant last lap manoeuvre from Lee that secured Lynn's cup final victory against Reading.

Aside from Terry Betts in the first three seasons and then Jessup, it was the rest of the team – often short of a genuine third heat leader and lacking match-winners at reserve – who didn't come up to scratch often enough? It was easy for the lesser lights in the Lynn side to blame Michael for damaging team morale with his actions but there was also a sense that Lee became an easy scapegoat for management, team-mates and supporters alike.

The under-performing riders should have taken a long, hard look at themselves in the mirror and questioned why they didn't do better, instead of grumbling behind the back of their much more accomplished team-mate who often carried the them in away matches.

Even though it was a pity that his departure from Saddlebow Road at the end of a dismal '82 – two seasons short of a due testimonial – was surrounded in acrimony, it was still the right move for all concerned. In hindsight, it should have happened a year earlier.

But who would take a big gamble on a rider whose tarnished reputation for unreliability and use of recreational drugs had been public knowledge for some time? Whoever bought his contract knew they would be taking a calculated risk.

As Rogers didn't want Lee included in his takeover deal with Crane, Michael's BSPA contract remained an asset of the former King's Lynn promoting company, Norfolk Speedways Ltd. There was initially talk of Crane selling Michael's registration on to the Palmer brothers, a couple of wealthy farmers closely associated with Lee's local National League team Mildenhall, but the Speedway

Control Board understandably frowned upon freelance ownership and moved swiftly to veto the plan. Around the same time, the BSPA blocked Mildenhall's bid to enter the British League.

After weeks of continued speculation, Poole dropped their reported interest in Coventry's New Zealand star Mitch Shirra (he joined Reading) and splashed out to get Lee instead.

The Pirates had a similar record to Lynn in that they rarely threatened to challenge for the main honours – their British League championship success of 1969 looking a dim and distant memory. They had not won any major silverware since then and had just finished rock bottom of the BL, one place below Lynn.

Fresh start on the south coast at Poole.

But Poole boss Reg Fearman, one of the sport's most experienced promoters since the early 60s when he was a major driving force behind the formation of the Provincial League, has always had a bold belief in his ability to make the right moves. It had been almost four years since he bought the promoting rights at Poole from the Knott family and he saw 24-year-old Michael Lee as the catalyst for transforming the Dorset club's fortunes after too many years of under-achievement at Wimborne Road.

The Pirates' fans needed a new hero to support following the acrimonious sacking of their former hero Malcolm Simmons at the end of 1980. American star Scott Autrey announced he was quitting British speedway and returning to the States after two mediocre seasons as the second heat leader to John Davis and in Lee, Fearman hoped he had just the man to get Poole moving in the right direction again.

Davis spearheaded a mainly young side, with the emerging Kevin Smith, Andy Campbell and Neil Middleditch all expected to improve. Wild Czech Vaclav Verner was guaranteed to keep all his team-mates on their toes, while Australian Stan Bear (doubling-up with NL Weymouth) and young Dane Brian Jakobsen were also expected to progress.

Neil Middleditch, who has always retained the greatest respect for what Michael stood for as a rider, recalls: "I'd known Michael for a number of years and the news he was coming to Poole created a real buzz in the town.

"As a rider, the opportunity to race alongside someone as talented as Mike was a chance many of us would have jumped at."

When approached to recall Michael's brief time at Poole, Reg Fearman made no attempt to hide his lingering contempt for Lee and the damage he believes he ultimately did to the promoting company that went bust the following year. No doubt most of his bitter comments are badly coloured by his company's collapse towards the end of 1984, so perhaps we shouldn't be surprised by his general antipathy towards Lee, although it would be ludicrous for anyone to blame Poole Speedway's demise as a top flight club in the mid-80s on the actions of one rider. There were a number of other mitigating factors that Fearman appears reluctant to acknowledge as genuine factors in his downfall at Poole.

Reg readily agreed to talk from the serenity of his lovely Provencal home in the South of France – a world away from the turmoil he experienced at the track where he spent his last days as as an eminent British promoter. Firstly, he recalled the prelude to Lee's arrival on the English south coast – and the warning signal he chose to ignore.

"I talked to Andy, Michael's father, who told me he was not sure that Michael had turned over a new leaf," Fearman reveals.

Andy and Michael were barely on speaking terms at the time due to Michael's continuing drug habit.

Fearman continues: "My wife Joan and I met Michael and his then partner Janet in a West London hotel on a Sunday afternoon and discussed him coming to Poole. He was very polite and very plausible, convincing me that 'drugs were a thing of the past'.

"But the leopard didn't change his spots, as we were all to discover over the following years."

Fearman still keeps copious personal files at his home – he also owns a townhouse at sought-after Henley-on-Thames in Berkshire – chronicling a lifetime in speedway, which he says may one day form the basis for his published memoirs. In the meantime, he raided his files and confirmed the financial terms of Michael's transfer to Poole.

"The deal for Michael's transfer was £39,000, which we agreed to pay over three years - £13,000 for each season he completed," he says.

Fearman confirmed that Poole's personal deal with Michael for 1983 was structured as follows: In the main match or meeting he would be paid £4 per start and £25 per point; and £4 per start and £8 per point in the second-halves. In addition, he was to receive three payments of £1,000 each on the first day of April, July and October.

The former BSPA chairman admits he had no difficulty agreeing terms with his expensive new capture. "Michael was easy to deal with. It was the fact that he was going to move to Poole lock, stock and barrel, and that the 'grass would be greener there' in the Poole area. I believe I did invite him down to Poole during the

Front wheel off the ground and in flying form, Michael leading Larry Ross and his old mate Louis Carr at Belle Vue.

winter and showed him the beauty of the area. Andy had a contact with Heron Homes and I'm sure it was one of those that Michael moved into at Verwood."

The sea air did a rejuvenated Michael a lot of good in terms of his scoring power for the Pirates. New England manager Wally Mawdsley also recalled him to the national side, although he struggled to impress in the 3-2 series victory over the USA and was left out of the first two Tests against Denmark.

But, yet again, it was typical Michael. Just when his critics were ready to write the epitaph to his international career, he came up with an inspirational match-winning 16 points to lead the Lions to a series-clinching defeat of the Danes in the third Test at Hackney in early July.

In the World Championship, Michael clearly meant business again after two years of bitter disappointment. He followed victory in the British semi-final with second place (behind Chris Morton) in the British Final at Coventry and was runner-up again in the Inter-Continental Final at White City, splitting Danish stars Hans Nielsen and Erik Gundersen on the rostrum.

While in the build up to the World Final in Norden, Germany, Michael sent out a clear message of intent to his big English rival Kenny Carter that he wasn't going to have things all his own way after two years as the self-proclaimed England No.1. While Lee was losing his way in 1981 and '82, Halifax tyke Carter had been the one to emerge as Bruce Penhall's main threat. Penhall won their bruising showdown in the '82 World Final in Los Angeles but when the American announced his retirement from racing immediately after retaining the title, everyone believed it was only a matter of time before Carter fulfilled his

Battle of the Brits as Michael leads Kenny Carter in their Golden Helmet clash at Poole.

obsession to become the sport's top rider.

Lee had other ideas, though. Nominated by the BSPA to challenge Carter for the Golden Helmet, he beat the Yorkshireman 2-0 in the first leg at Poole on August 3 and then crushed him 2-0 again on August 20 in the return leg at The Shay – a result that stunned Carter.

Doug Wyer, who rode in the same Halifax team as Carter that night and watched Kenny's shock defeats from the pits, recalls: "Michael made Kenny look very ordinary that night and won both races by a full straight. Kenny did some incredible things at The Shay and was very hard to beat there.

"It was quite unbelievable to see how far in front Michael was and how easy he made it look – as if Kenny wasn't in the same race," Wyer added.

Like most riders of that era, Lee never did care much for Carter, who failed to win the World Championship before he shot dead his wife and then himself in a tragic double shooting at their Yorkshire farmhouse in May 1986. "I neither liked nor respected Kenny," admits Michael.

"We had major rivalry and I used to hate riding against him because he was like me – neither of us wanted to be beaten. It was a battle every time.

"The difference was, Kenny would try and win the battle any way he could rather than accept losing it. He'd rather take me out and cause us both to crash than let me win.

"Thinking about some of the things he'd done in the past, it was quite scary at times. He was full-on and you had to be quite smart against him. I wasn't scared of Kenny but let's put it this way, when I raced against him I made sure

England's top scorer in the World Team Cup Final dives inside Ole Olsen at Vojens.

"It was quite unbelievable to see how far in front Michael was and how easy he made it look – as if Kenny wasn't in the same race."

I was cautious and calculating and had my act together, because I knew how dangerous he was.

"He was a hard rider and did whatever it took to win. Yeah, he could ride a bike – you don't go as fast as he did without being able to do so, but sometimes I didn't like the way he went about it. No-one can win everything and occasionally, or quite a few times, you have to accept that you will be beaten by a better rider on the day. But Kenny could never accept losing to anyone," added Michael, who top-scored for England in the World Team Cup Final at Vojens, where the Danes ran out fairly comfortable winners.

Carter scored 10 points in the 1983 individual World Final – one less than the man who deposed him as England's No.1 that year. A last in Michael's third ride proved costly, although two more wins in his last couple of rides at least saw him back on the rostrum in third place – a point behind his mate Billy Sanders but a clear four behind the runaway champion Egon Müller. The German, revelling in a distinct home track advantage, was simply unstoppable on his GM that day, although Michael's 'gold top' Weslake was hardly lacking speed.

"Michael used the Weslake with the gold top rocker box cover for the '83 final," says Andy Lee, "and other riders tended to fear him whenever they saw

On parade before the 1983 World Final at Norden.

SWAPA's Rider of the Year had a late night with a couple of boozy hacks!

him using it. To be honest, though, we used to fool them sometimes by switching the gold cover and putting it on a more standard engine that wasn't up to World Final standard!"

But Andy's wry smile quickly disappeared and his face wore the serious look of a concerned parent again when he revealed: "Before the '83 World Final I was on absolute tenterhooks and really worried, because Michael was still in the throes of his ups and downs.

"I remember he rode at Halifax about a fortnight before Norden and all through that time, right up until the World Final, it was a tip-toe period for me. I was trying to keep things on an even keel. He was trying to get off drugs but he was not in a stable state of mind generally and it was very worrying."

Even so, if the World Final had been staged anywhere other than in Germany that year, the chances are Lee would have won it, or gone even closer to regaining the crown, although Sanders would still have been a strong contender too. Reg Fearman was at Norden to see Lee become the first Poole rider since Malcolm Simmons in 1976 to finish in the world's top three but he argues that Michael's outstanding form on the world stage and his season-long brilliance for the Pirates was of no benefit to Poole Speedway's finances.

On the contrary, Fearman claims: "No, I don't think it made a hoot of difference. The Poole public had already shown their colours regarding

Among greats at the SWAPA dinner in '83. Left to right: Ole Olsen, Barry Briggs, Michael, Freddie Williams, new World Champion Egon Müller and Peter Collins.

"At the Poole end-of-season dance, several riders arrived after the start and within a short time were 'merry'. I knew it was not alcohol and kidded the boys in to 'treating' me. I was taken outside by several to the car park and to a van where something resembling a cigarette was offered. I learned it was cannabis. That has been my only experience of that vile habit."

the signing of Michael Lee but I was trying to win them over."

As with Crane in Lee's last couple of seasons at King's Lynn, it appears that Lee became an obvious scapegoat for a promoter finding it increasingly tough to make speedway pay.

Let's examine the facts: Only Neil Middleditch and Andy Campbell rode in more matches than Lee for Poole in 1983 (just one meeting more in both cases). Michael appeared in 42 official league and cup matches – the most he ever featured in during any one season and his highest appearance tally since way back in 1977. So the spate of missed meetings that so badly tarnished his image at King's Lynn were a thing of the past.

And just in case anyone at Lynn may have forgotten his capabilities, he returned to Saddlebow Road at the end of Martin Rogers' first season as promoter and won the Pride of the East.

Poole's new No.1 finished the '83 campaign with an impressive 10.43 CMA in the BL – the fourth best rider in the league (behind Dennis Sigalos, Hans Nielsen and Erik Gundersen) and the highest placed Englishman.

It was the first time a Poole rider had finished a season with a double-figure average since Simmo topped the BL charts in 1978.

So you would have half expected Fearman to have been patting himself on the back for his capture of a world class rider no-one had dared to touch.

Fearman describes his working relationship with Lee in '83 as merely "compatible", although he admits he had no disciplinary problems with the rider. "I don't recall any problem other than towards the end of the season, when he would arrive very late for the start of home meetings," Fearman added.

"I was probably more conscious of the perils that were rising in that I knew drugs were abounding," he continued. "Jack Fearnley and I took an English team to Denmark for a weekend. I travelled in Michael's van-cum-transporter with three other riders. At one time a pipe was produced from the glove box and Michael said it was 'the best hashish'. It was then a case of pass the pipe for a 'drag'.

"Prior to that there had been 'banter' and it was said that 'Reg is OK'. I went along with it to find out just what was going on.

"Also, at the Poole end-of-season dance, several riders arrived after the start and within a short time were 'merry'. I knew it was not alcohol and kidded the boys in to 'treating' me.

"I was taken outside by several to the car park and to a van where something resembling a cigarette was offered. I learned it was cannabis. That has been my only experience of that vile habit.

"The whole of British speedway was aware that there was a drug problem within the sport – random drug-testing was taking place and the odd rider managed to escape, as he or they claimed they didn't know where to give the urine sample and went home!

"Several of the American riders had also been arrested at Heathrow for bringing into the country drugs that were legal in California but not in the UK, and they therefore got off lightly," Fearman said.

Michael admits that he was still using drugs during his time with Poole. "As well as cannabis, I was also on amphetamines by then," he says, before confirming his former promoter's claim that drugs had become rife in British speedway by 1983.

"Without doubt they were. I'd say that around 30 per cent of British League riders were smoking dope by then – at least one per team," he estimates.

"I'm not saying riders were turning up for meetings stoned. No, they would take a joint to smoke on the way home from the meeting."

Some in speedway still believe the problem was more serious than that.

In October, *Speedway Star's* Richard Clark and I had the pleasure of Michael's company well into the small hours that followed the annual SWAPA awards dinner at the St. John's Hotel in Solihull, near Birmingham. The Poole star had rushed straight from Poole's match at Sheffield especially to collect the richly deserved Rider of the Year award.

Michael has always been good company and Clarkie and I saw no reason to pass up the opportunity to chew the fat with him over a few more beers and share a few drags of what Michael had brought along with him for his own relaxation at the end of a long night in the West Midlands. I've never smoked a cigarette in my life, let alone tried cannabis, but my curiosity was aroused.

Richard smiles at the memory of what he describes as "my night of marijuana madness with a former World Champion!"

He says: "Well, it didn't seem quite like that but, surprisingly, I do remember it well. It was long past the official function and, with the bar shut, we retreated to the hotel foyer where we kept the night porter from his beauty sleep. I don't think a single joint was ever going to compete with all the bottles of beer consumed.

"As an avid rock concert-goer at the time, I can't imagine the appearance of a single jazz cigarette would cause even a ripple to be honest.

"And, of course, I'm sure nobody inhaled!"

I'm certain that by the time we all finally made it to bed at around 4.00am, Michael would have been the most sober and coherent among our little group.

But within a few weeks of the start of the following season, he was back in big trouble and his speedway career had gone up in smoke.

Turning Point

Beginning of the end

Chapter 23

SATURDAY, March 31, 1984 is a day Michael Lee will never forget. Like the season itself, the night began so well for him when he returned to King's Lynn with Poole and beat Dave Jessup – back to lead the Stars again after two years at Wimbledon – in the opening race of the League Cup match.

On paper, Heat 5 looked like another banker three points for the visiting No.1 as he lined up at the gate alongside his team-mate Neil Middleditch and the home pairing of Steve Regeling and Richard Hellsen.

But when referee John Eglese released the tapes, Michael rocked backwards and forwards in the manner he had developed over the previous seasons in an attempt to be moving forward as the tapes rose but referee John Eglese waited until he was moving backwards before raising the tapes. Lee was left at the start as the other three raced into the first bend.

Feeling aggrieved when a re-start was not called, he rode slowly towards the 30-metre mark before turning around and coasting back to the start-line, where he parked his bike near the inside of the track just as the red lights came on and the race was stopped.

Michael's white exclusion light indicated that he was the cause of the stoppage and was ruled out of the rerun, but he didn't let it end there.

He grabbed the phone on the centre green adjacent to the starting gate to try and make a verbal protest to the referee but says: "Eglese just hung up on me".

The anger erupting like a volcano within, an incensed Lee then decided to pay the Midlands-based referee a visit in the officials' wooden box perched high underneath the main stand and accessed only by ladders. He went marching up them to remonstrate with Eglese.

Michael admits: "I was very abusive to him and, shall we say, quite aggressive. I told him what I thought. I had my hands on his throat and said: 'I'll f****** have you, mate'. But I didn't strike him. Track staff were there dragging me away from him.

"I felt so angry as I left the box that I leapt from the top of the ladders to the ground."

Michael was immediately fined £100 by Eglese, suspended from the rest of the meeting and reported to the Speedway Control Board for his actions. The outcome of their disciplinary tribunal and its devastating effect on his career is covered fully in the next chapter. But let's first record the views of several key witnesses to those stormy events at King's Lynn.

Lee's Poole race partner Neil Middleditch says: "Yes, I remember 'That Race', although not all the details. What I do remember is coming out of the first turn, looking across and seeing Michael going back up the track towards the start line – on the inside and causing no danger to anybody else in the race.

"He hadn't even entered the first turn. I think he felt there should have been a re-start – and the rest is history.

"They (the authorities) wanted Michael. The ref was so out of order, he completely overreacted. This was the final straw that broke the camel's back."

Ipswich boss John Berry watched the drama unfold from the pits and says: "As a person, Michael was impossible not to like, even though he was a bit scatterbrained. There was always a ready smile, and I never had a cross word with him except on the day when, for him, the racing died.

"I was at that meeting at King's Lynn when he rode the wrong way along the track whilst a race was in progress. The sole reason for my going to that meeting was to try to speak to Michael like a Dutch uncle but he had given me a mouthful before the meeting started when I tried to speak to him. He had obviously turned up in a foul mood and in any case was not prepared to listen to anyone by then.

"Although the idea of him riding into oncoming riders is nightmarish, that is really not what happened. Feeling aggrieved because he had missed the start, he pulled up in the first turn whilst the other riders continued.

"He parked his bike on gate position one on the track – where a flag marshal would stand to wave his flag at the end of a race. It was an act of defiance and calculated to cause a stir but it was not dangerous."

"He then rode back to the start line, going the wrong way but not on the racing line.

"He parked his bike on gate position one on the track – where a flag marshal would stand to wave his flag at the end of a race. It was an act of defiance and calculated to cause a stir but it was not dangerous.

"Michael's subsequent actions in visiting John Eglese in the referee's box and accosting him were, in my opinion, far more worthy of serious penalty, but it was his riding the wrong way along the track that people all focus on."

Martin Rogers was the King's Lynn promoter on the night in question and he, too, confirmed that Lee in no way endangered the lives of the other riders.

He says: "As regards the infamous 'wrong way round' part, I have to say it was sensationally reported upon but the reality is after being left at the gate, Michael rode towards the first bend, did a U-turn and rode back towards the tapes right on the inside line.

"The riders coming round to complete their first lap and start their second were not inconvenienced or endangered by him despite all suggestions to the contrary. Steve Regeling who was in the race, told me he didn't even see him."

The SCB had introduced tougher new starting regulations at the beginning of 1984. To try and eradicate cheating at the gate and clamp down on riders who rolled at the start, the new rule stated that riders would be excluded merely for touching the tapes. Previously, a rider had to break the tapes to be thrown out of a race.

Michael prided himself on being one of the sport's fastest starters, with lightning-quick reflexes and possessing almost a sixth sense about referees and when they were about to hit the tape release button. It became a battle of wills between him and them.

In an interview with Peter Oakes for *5-One magazine* in 1995, he said: "I was such a good starter and not a cheat. The job was to get to the first corner in front and, fair enough, if you anticipate the start you're not cheating.

"You're beating the referee and that was a part of the excitement of it. There's a difference between a big rolling start and anticipating the start. I was good at anticipating. I was used to sitting there and going – bosh! It was as if I was connected up to the referee.

"When I was confident and things were going well, it was like I was actually pressing the button. The green light came on and you just knew when it was going to go and it was time to drop the clutch. Sometimes I would hit my head on the tapes.

"Michael was a lightning-fast starter and often people couldn't accept that. I think Michael's tape exclusions wound him up a bit and in the end I honestly think both he and the referees became paranoid about the whole situation."

"It used to pee referees off. Sometimes they would stop the race and I would do exactly the same again. You use your own psychology and take control of the referee and certain referees knew that. If you did it three times on the trot, you would get excluded and that started to bug me.

"I'm out to win a race for myself or the team and I haven't broken the tapes but I've been excluded from that race. I didn't like it."

Andy Lee says: "I believe referees at that time were as paranoid as Michael was. There was one particular ref who was so concentrated on watching Michael at the gate that the other three riders might as well not have been there.

"Michael was a lightning-fast starter and often people couldn't accept that. I think Michael's tape exclusions wound him up a bit and in the end I honestly think both he and the referees became paranoid about the whole situation."

The most high profile example of Lee's losing battle to come to terms with the new starting regulations came 37 days after the King's Lynn incident, when

Neil Middleditch was Michael's partner in 'that race'.

Michael again found himself at loggerheads with a referee, this time during the televised England v USA Test at Ipswich officiated by Frank Ebdon.

Ebdon was one of the new breed of referees who applied the regs to the letter of the law and wasn't fazed by riders' reputations. As a fan at Wimbledon he'd grown tired of seeing riders repeatedly delay the starts, so when he passed his referee's exam and joined the SCB's appointed list he resolved to penalise the antics of riders like Lee to ensure fairer starts for all.

At Ipswich, with millions at home watching the controversy unfold on World of Sport, Ebdon twice penalised the Poole star (Bobby Schwartz and Richard Knight were also excluded for tape-touching) and a bitterly frustrated Lee became so sick of this perceived injustice that he finally walked out of the meeting. England manager Carl Glover, who pointed out that all the riders were reminded and warned before the meeting of the new stringent starting rules, and home promoter John Berry both tried to talk Michael out of leaving Foxhall Heath early. Indeed, Berry did manage to persuade him back from the changing rooms after he'd been excluded.

But what caused him to finally walk out was that he got a flyer, the race was restarted with all four, and then he got caught going backwards again and the race was not stopped, as at King's Lynn a month or so earlier. He got as far as the first turn, rode across the centre green and into the pits and home when the race had finished.

After all the aggro at King's Lynn a month or so earlier, Michael regarded this as another nail in his coffin and left the stadium as England plunged to their worst-ever home defeat (36-72) by the rampant Americans.

"I'm so jarred off with speedway nowadays, and the way referees are ruining the sport, that I may well retire," Lee told ITV's interviewer before heading home. Given the impending tribunal it was possibly not very sensible to sound off like that on national television. It was bound to work against him.

Lee's frustration with the sport was palpable. He looked jaded and several late arrivals for big meetings, including the Test matches at Cradley Heath and Ipswich that spring, were another sign that his lifestyle was continuing to take its toll on his mind and body. Without his father around to relieve some of the pressure on the tuning and preparation side, Michael was spending very long hours in the workshop. In fact, his workload had increased because, by now, he was also tuning engines for other riders.

Even so, he could still turn it on better than anyone when he was in the mood. After pulling out of the first Test against the USA at Swindon on the eve of the match because he said he didn't have a bike that was competitive enough, he bounced back brilliantly to top-score in the next two matches at Sheffield and Cradley Heath. At the end of the series, which England lost 1-4, Michael had the highest average (11.37) of the 18 riders used by Carl Glover, whose hopes of containing the Americans were dashed by the absence from four of the Tests by the injured Kenny Carter.

"I back what Michael had to say about the referee spoiling the meeting. The people had come along to see the likes of Michael Lee and Bobby Schwartz race, not have them excluded for what, after all, is a mere technicality. If I'd paid to come I would not have been at all pleased with what happened."

I'm inclined to agree with Michael that speedway lost some of its excitement when the SCB began to exclude riders for tape-touching. There has always been so much emphasis placed on starts, it's still where the majority of races are won and lost, and the shenanigans in the moments preceding the release of the tapes added to the drama. Those who welcomed the new rules introduced in '84, and which still apply today, would argue that they have survived the test of time and that starts became much fairer.

But supporters pay good money to see four riders contest each race and a more lenient approach to tape-touchers – say, a warning followed by a 10-yard handicap for a repeat offence – would leave the customers feeling less like they have been robbed of full value for money entertainment. When Emil Sayfutdinov was rightly excluded for slightly nudging the tapes in the tense semi-final of the 2009 Danish Grand Prix, it killed the drama that had been building to a crescendo as the Parken meeting progressed. Some would say that's a small price worth paying to ensure fairer starts across the board, but I'm still not convinced.

Billy Sanders didn't condone Michael's walk-out at Ipswich but he did sympathise with his friend when he said afterwards: "I back what Michael had to say about the referee spoiling the meeting. The people had come along to see the likes of Michael Lee and Bobby Schwartz race, not have them excluded for what, after all, is a mere technicality. If I had paid to come I would not have been at all pleased with what happened."

One who has always been convinced of the merits of the stricter starting regs is Sanders' former promoter John Berry. He says: "Michael believed that the starts of races were a three-way contest between himself, the other riders and the referee.

"The Big Daddy of the technique of giving yourself an edge at the starts was Ivan Mauger and many riders subsequently studied and copied Ivan's methods of unsettling the other riders. I suppose the likes of Michael and Erik Gundersen would claim their methods were their own, but Ivan was the undisputed master when it came to the psychology of starting technique.

"Now there are two ways you can look at this practise of disrupting the starts. Lee/Gundersen/Mauger (and others') supporters might well argue that using gamesmanship was part and parcel of racing, whilst us 'purists', for I count myself in this group, feel the responsibility of a referee is to come up with a fair start which gives everyone a chance to race on equal terms.

"Generally, the younger, stronger-minded referees were of the latter view, and began stopping and re-starting races if one or more riders gained an unreasonable advantage over the others. Such starts were 'unsatisfactory' as laid down in the regulations.

"There is a fine line between having faster reactions than the other riders and gaining an unfair advantage, but I would say referees understood the difference. In this respect you can say Michael, among others, was targeted."

Michael Lee and many others firmly believe he was also victimised by the Speedway Control Board.

Trial and Error

Miscarriage of justice

Chapter 24

AFTER the furore involving John Eglese at King's Lynn and his walk-out at Ipswich, Michael's 1984 season continued to fall apart. The Poole management suspended him for six days after he failed to turn up for an inter-league challenge at Weymouth and when he missed the second leg of his Golden Helmet match-race challenge with Shawn Moran at Sheffield, having lost the first leg 2-0 at Poole the previous night, he was stripped of the title.

The rejuvenation and hunger he showed in his first season with Poole had given way to a growing disillusionment with the sport and the men who ran it. Aside from whatever drugs he was continuing to indulge in at the time, the Pirates' skipper was also permanently exhausted.

Neil Middleditch explains: "Michael had his workshops at Verwood and later moved them over to my place - in fact, we still call the workshop 'Michael's Room'. He tuned for me for some time, along with many other riders – probably too many if truth be known, as he put so much pressure on himself to deliver a good engine.

"When I won the NLRC in 1985 it was on one of Michael's engines. His workmanship was first class and attention to detail second to none.

"I spent a lot of time with Michael during his time at Poole and was his mechanic at the Norden World Final and a number of other meetings. His preparation was meticulous, the attention to detail on the tiniest things on a bike amazing. Everything had to be just right, no half-measures.

"I think perhaps the tuning did take its toll on him because riders needed their engines and sometimes parts would arrive late, which put Michael under even greater pressure to deliver the engines on time. Sometimes he'd be working all night to try and not let them down but no person can maintain that sort of workload over a sustained period of time."

Despite his ongoing problems on and off the track, Lee served notice of his intent to have another serious crack at the World Championship by romping to a maximum in the British semi-final on his home track. He had qualified for the British Final at Coventry but he would be denied the chance to ride in that meeting and the three England v Denmark Tests for which he'd been selected in June.

For Michael's world fell apart after the Speedway Control Board held its disciplinary tribunal in London and ruled that his actions at King's Lynn on March 31 would be punished with a savage five-year ban from racing.

The actual wording of the SCB's draconian suspension read: 'Michael Lee is

The wooden officials' box where Michael paid John Eglese a visit at King's Lynn in 1984.

suspended from taking part in any motorcycle or automobile competition, nationally and internationally, for five years from June 1, 1984.'

It was said at the time that Michael did himself no favours by failing to attend the hearing, held at the headquarters of the RAC/ACU and offices of the SCB in 31, Belgrave Square, Pall Mall, and by not notifying the Board of his non-appearance. His explanation was a valid one, though – Janet had given birth to their second child, Jordan, in Poole the previous day (May 30).

A stunned Michael learned the severity of the Board's verdict the following afternoon, in a phone call from the *Daily Star's* Peter Oakes who broke the devastating news to him at home while he was sat alongside his partner and newly-born son.

Immediate reaction to the ban was one of widespread outrage and disbelief, even among Lee's biggest critics, and it still seems incredible today. Five years for supposedly endangering the lives of three of his fellow riders? It seemed like a sick joke, except Michael wasn't laughing.

Speedway Star editor Philip Rising summed up the general bewilderment of many when he wrote: "A five-year ban is completely over the top. Once again, as with the attempt to suspend Ivan Mauger's licence 18 months ago, the administrators of power seem to have no real awareness of what their verdict actually means.

"It is all too easy to sit behind a desk and hand out sentences without realising the real consequences for a man who earns his living racing motorcycles.

"Even those who stubbornly support Michael are occasionally embarrassed by his misdemeanours. But any form of punishment must fit the crime.

"A five-year ban will spell the end of his career. They might just as well have handed out a sine die suspension. The result would be the same. No rider would sit out five years and then attempt a comeback. And what about Poole? Their supporters? Speedway in general?

"The Control Board didn't use a big stick to punish Lee, they shot him with a gun."

Reflecting on Michael's ban today, Martin Rogers says: "The ban of five years was so over the top he couldn't fail to successfully appeal it.

"There is no doubt Michael behaved badly on the night (at King's Lynn) but it is debatable whether his actions were so terrible in the greater scheme of things. If that alone, or even the sum total of his misdemeanours over the years, amounted to 'conduct prejudicial to the sport' (and there would have been a fair weight of evidence to support that), then it was within the sport's controllers' power to hit him with some disciplinary penalty. But obviously not five years or even anything approaching one year," Rogers added.

Neil Middleditch says: "In truth, Michael was a bit of a rebel but a ban for something so trivial was mind-boggling. I just couldn't believe it."

Michael's first reaction to news of the ban was to quit but he had the wholehearted support of his family, his club and supporters - not just from Poole, but all over Britain. A petition protesting against the original five-year suspension carried more than 6,000 signatures. The SOS (Save Our Star) message to the Board read: 'We deplore the action taken by your body regarding the excessive ban imposed on Michael Lee and feel that, if the SCB has any conscience whatsoever, they should lift the ban immediately.'

So an appeal was launched and a new SCB tribunal hearing date set for Wednesday, June 20. Poole Speedway paid all the costs of the appeal, which were £3,500.

Reg Fearman quickly organised legal representation for his top rider. "It was I who contacted Ronnie Teeman, a sports lawyer in Leeds, and gave him the brief," he recalls. "He came to my attention after successfully defending Ian Thomas on a drink-driving charge sometime previously."

If Michael had a valid excuse not to attend the first hearing when sentence was passed, his absence from the appeal tribunal was enshrouded in a dark sense of foreboding.

Fearman reveals: "I'd arranged to pick Michael up at his home in Verwood at 7.00am on the day of the hearing. I duly arrived in good time to find him and Neil Middleditch in the garage workshop – they had been working throughout the night.

"Michael said he would get changed quickly and went into the house. I waited a while before asking Janet to see where he was and to hurry him up. She came downstairs and said he was fast asleep on the bed.

"I went up to the bedroom and shook, prodded and pinched Michael, but to no avail. I'm positive that he was in a drug-induced sleep.

"I insisted that Neil Middleditch accompany me to the hearing in London to substantiate that Michael had been taken ill. I telephoned from the house to a doctor friend of mine, who was also the Poole track doctor, and asked him to visit Michael soonest, which he did within two hours. He confirmed to me later that it was impossible to awaken him.

"We had an early morning appointment with Ronnie Teeman for Michael to answer some final questions from him before going into the Court Of Appeal."

Although understandably "pissed off" at Michael's failure to attend, Fearman admits: "I'm sure the presence of Michael would have made no difference to the result."

Middleditch recalls: "I remember the day of the court appeal. I'd not been working with Mike that night but had gone over to his place to meet him before going off to the hearing. He'd been working all night, as he often did due to his heavy workload tuning engines, plus also his own racing.

"When he went upstairs I think he was genuinely exhausted. Also, having spoken to him, he felt the verdict against him was a foregone conclusion and that his presence at the hearing would have little or no bearing on the outcome, which turned out to be the case."

Recalling the early morning scene on that fateful day, Michael confirmed Reg and Neil's accounts, saying: "I'd been working late tuning a stack of engines for three or four days non-stop. I think it was six o'clock in the morning by the time I got the last engine done and Reg was coming round at eight to go up to London.

"I remember going inside the house, up to the bedroom and thinking 'I'll lay down here for 10 minutes, sort myself out and then get ready'. But I laid down and didn't get back up.

"I remember Reg arranging for the Poole track doctor to come to the house to examine me. Although I was basically in a semi-coma, subconsciously I was aware of what was going on around me. I could hear Reg and the doctor talking and, because he was so angry, Reg was physically hitting me trying to wake me up. "Wake up you f****** bastard!" I heard him say. He was really giving it some.

"I knew what was going on but I wasn't going to wake up. I didn't want to know, so I just let them get on with it. In the end the doctor arrived and Reg pushed me back onto the bed.

"Then the doctor got hold of my hands and started sticking pins in them but it still didn't register with me. I thought, 'you carry on, mate, I ain't moving'."

Michael admits: "I just didn't want to face the appeal hearing. I hadn't done what I'd been accused of (endangering other people's lives), so I didn't believe I should have to go there in the first place. It was all bollocks.

"It was maybe wrong of me not to accompany Reg to the hearing but my heart had been ripped out because of what had gone on at the initial hearing. I really didn't care anymore."

The hearing lasted for around eight hours before the four-man tribunal panel decided that the ban on Lee would be reduced from five years to 12 months. They cleared him of the most serious charge of endangering the lives of other riders but found him guilty of three lesser charges. However, he was fined an additional £50 and ordered to pay £500 towards court costs.

Five years would have been criminal. One year was still extremely harsh. In Michael's eyes it was a disastrous verdict – but his Poole promoter still considers it an appropriate punishment.

"I was not at all confident that Michael would be found not guilty after receiving an earlier five-year ban," continued Fearman. "I do believe that Ronnie Teeman 'won' the case in so far that the sentence was reduced to one year. What else could one hope for after such serious charges, including assault?"

Fearman remains convinced that Lee's barrister did all he possibly could on his client's behalf. "Absolutely and without any doubt," says Reg. "Ronnie Teeman gave examples of not only the law but also similar cases in the High Court. I believe a major point that he made was that the referee put on the red stop lights when Michael turned around from the first corner and therefore the other three riders were no longer in any danger."

"I don't have any complaints about how my legal representative handled my case," says Michael. "Reg also stuck by me in court. Angry though he may well have been with me, he stood by me and I'd never knock him. He was good to me and never let me down.

"I fully understand that Reg would be unhappy with me over what happened because, as my promoter, he copped the brunt of it. He didn't get his money's worth from me," Michael agrees.

But, in apparent contrast to the majority, Fearman does not believe Lee was treated unjustly by the authorities. "Not at all," he says. "In Michael Lee's own words, he put his 'hands around the throat of the referee' in the official's box after climbing the steps from the race track. It could well have led to a prison sentence in a civilian court."

Fearman's view is shared by his former BSPA colleague John Berry, who says: "What Michael did on the track that day was childish, provocative and unnecessary but, in my opinion at least, it was not dangerous.

"Far more important to me was that he went into the referee's box and accosted him. In Michael's own words, he had his hands around the man's throat. That was absolutely unacceptable and deserving of hefty suspension, although maybe not a five-year ban."

In hitting Lee with a sledgehammer, the SCB ignored their own precedent set eight years earlier, when they charged Hackney promoter Len Silver for assaulting referee Martin Palmer in his box at Swindon following the controversial exclusion of Hawks' Zenon Plech. Silver, who was also England team manager at the time, received only a one-month suspension for behaving in much the same way as Lee did to John Eglese.

In the early 90s, when John Eglese was SCB manager, Rye House star Martin Goodwin was fined £900 and banned for six months for throwing his crash

Mike and his Bike - the one he built especially for the 1984 British Final but couldn't ride.

helmet through the glass window of the referee's box at Hackney.

OK, so Silver and Goodwin didn't have the 'previous' a serial offender like Lee had but, then again, the SCB tribunal wasn't meant to pass judgement on his previous misdemeanours.

Berry went on: "What I suspect Michael got the threat of five years for was continuing to stick two fingers up to the speedway authorities by shouting his mouth off in public and refusing to attend the tribunal. This, on top of a long period of tantrums and unreliability. In the end I reckon the one year suspension was about right.

"Had he, at any stage, shown the remotest contrition – and meant it – instead of continuing to maintain a fight he was never going to win, I am certain that the powers that be would have fallen over themselves to help him get back on track. Whichever way I try to look at it, I can only see him as his own worst enemy.

"In any case, had it not been this incident, I'm sure there would have been another that would have seen him suspended. By then he really was out of control."

Many, especially Michael, believe to this day that his destiny at the hands of the tribunal beaks had already been pre-determined before the appeal hearing.

Middleditch says: "Certain people within the sport were out to get Mike and that is exactly what they did."

Fearman added: "I believe that when the five-year ban was imposed, the tribunal members thought it was a good way to get rid of a bad and disturbing influence on British speedway. There was no doubt that Michael was also inviting bad national and international publicity."

Berry also saw it coming, saying: "I believe the SCB finally reached the stage where they decided he was such a liability that it was time for him to take a 'rest', so in that respect I think Michael was correct in thinking he was being victimised."

And Martin Rogers agreed that a hefty punishment for speedway's 'bad boy' was also inevitable: "I went to the appeal hearing and said my piece. The underlying feeling here, though, was that officialdom definitely was 'out to get him' one way or another. And this incident gave them what they thought was sufficient to hang him.

"A lot of promoters, a lot of SCB people, many fans, sponsors and others were absolutely over fed up with Michael Lee and his continuing succession of incidents, arguments and clashes with authority on and off the track, inside and away from speedway.

"Of course, the ban was central to Michael's career. It knocked the stuffing out of him and in my opinion (at the time and since) smacked of officialdom getting its payback and saying to Michael, in effect: 'You have knocked us, criticised us and by some of your deeds, actions and words done the sport many disservices over the years – now it's payback time, we'll show you who is the boss, take that and stick it up ya!'

"There were people on the then SCB and RAC, and you might suspect some in the BSPA, who were so sick of his ability to generate unfavourable publicity. The central players (SCB) always were desperately concerned about image, including their own. That said, I fancy the manner in which the case against Michael was mounted and conducted – albeit by some of their big guns who had legal credentials – was extremely flawed.

"The screaming headlines which accompanied the 'riding the wrong way' part of it all were very misleading and helped form opinions which could be said to have almost certainly played a part in pre-judging the case.

"Also, as far as I recall, none of the three other riders in that race were called to the hearing. I'm quite sure none of them would have said anything to support the contention that Michael acted in a manner to endanger anybody.

"The questioning at the tribunal was quite brief and it is worth pointing out others in the box at the time of the Eglese confrontation, Edwin Overland (announcer) and H.H. Howard (timekeeper), were not, as far as I know, invited to give evidence in any shape or form."

And what of John Eglese, the former Coventry track raker who gave up refereeing to become the manager of the Speedway Control Board following the retirement of Dick Bracher in 1990, four years before his tragic death?

Berry says: "Michael singles out John Eglese as his *bête noir*. John was a very forthright person. Some might even say he was officious and dogmatic.

He certainly did not shirk confrontation. He was part of a new breed of referee who wanted to actively improve the sport and particularly to make the starts to races fairer. For that aim, he had my respect. However, great referees like Graham Brodie also have a touch of humility, or humour, or both. If John had that side to him, it was not obvious.

"I don't believe John Eglese singled Michael out for special treatment. Rather, I believe he simply wanted to make the starts fairer to all riders. Michael had by then become possibly the biggest culprit in the league when it came to shenanigans before the start of races. He didn't need to do it. He was good enough without all the messing about.

"With Michael's single-minded determination to beat the new more rigid starting system, and John Eglese's own single-minded resolve not to let anyone put one over on him, a confrontation was inevitable.

"By the time the matter had come to a head in March 1984, Michael was already seriously into drugs, had become unpredictable and unreliable, and was showing classic symptoms of paranoia. He had decided the whole world of speedway was out to get him. All the world of speedway wanted was for him to accept the new regime and conform to it. Given his state of mind by then, it wasn't going to happen.

"By this stage, I was pretty jaded with the sport myself. If Michael is critical of the way things were going in speedway at the time, I would have to agree with him. Unfortunately his antics, both on and off the track, were by now a part of the problem."

Rogers added: "Michael was convinced John Eglese was 'out to get him'. I'm not sure, and we will never know, but I thought Eglese was a referee and a personality who considered his job to get the riders away to a fair start however much any of them didn't want that to happen."

The anger Michael felt towards Eglese, not for the incident that led to his ban but for the damning evidence he gave to the court of appeal, is as tangible today as it was some 26 years ago.

I've rarely heard Michael say many bad words about anyone else in his life but the mere mention of Eglese still make his hackles rise. Eglese died on February 15, 1994 following a car crash near his Warwickshire home but, even so, Michael can never forgive him.

"John Eglese was going to get me back at all costs because of what I did to him in the ref's box," he says.

"He ruined my career by lying to the court. He drew a diagram on a piece of paper to support his claim that I'd ridden the wrong way on the track and had forced the three other riders to scatter around me.

"Yet we had 2,000 signatures from people who were at the meeting, plus Martin Rogers and the other three riders in the race all testifying that I hadn't endangered anyone.

"I knew the court had already made their minds up – they believed Eglese. I'd been pre-judged, it was all cut and dried. And I was so dumbfounded. Everything had gone and it was the main turning point for me.

"When Eglese later became manager of the Control Board, it all fell into place," he went on. "It was all nicely controlled and suddenly, I didn't want to be part of this little game anymore.

"I hope people aren't offended by what I've said about him, because the man's gone, but that's the way I honestly feel. I thought he was trying to destroy me and my career, like he was trying to break me.

"I've spoken to a few announcers who shared the officials' box with John Eglese and they've told me they felt certain there were some riders he looked out for and would try and make life difficult for."

Despite Reg Fearman's protestations and Lee's own view that he had the best possible representation at the appeal hearing, I still believe the one-year ban was excessive. Yes, of course Lee had a long list of missed meetings and walk-outs against his name but he was not a dangerous nor aggressive rider and had never been involved in any violent incident. He had been fined on numerous occasions and paid the price. To accuse him of endangering the lives of others was a calculated insult.

"Legally speaking, it (the one-year ban) probably couldn't happen today, not for the circumstances that surrounded my case anyway. I understand that some sports impose life bans on competitors who take drugs, which is why I never rode while under the influence. But for the Board to take my livelihood away from me...

"My appeal was heard in London on the same day as the British Final and to show how hopeful I was that I'd be cleared to ride in that meeting, I actually had my bikes prepared and ready to go to Coventry for the meeting that night," says Michael, convinced he would have re-emerged from his early morning stupor to grab a top eight qualifying place from the meeting won in controversial fashion by Kenny Carter.

"But from the moment the SCB told me I had to serve a full year out of speedway, my whole attitude changed. I knew that it was really the end of my career, everything had been taken away.

"I could have accepted it if they had real reasons for banning me but they tried to make me look a prat by saying the punishment was for riding the wrong way round a track, as if I'd endanger the lives of my fellow riders. It was ludicrous and totally out of order.

"Why was I banned for five years for something so f****** trivial anyway? I never rode the wrong way round the track. They were out to get me.

"If I was innocent of the main charge, how could they drop my ban to one year? If a person's innocent, there should be no penalty whatsoever.

"That was the point when I decided I was going to do something else in life.

I started tuning engines and also got fairly heavily mixed up in the drugs scene."

While Lee did whatever he did for the next year of his ban, Poole Speedway struggled on for the rest of '84 without him. Although all payments from the club to Lee ceased with immediate effect, and Cyril Crane received no further instalments of the transfer agreed in 1983 beyond the initial £13,000 payment, Fearman says he never considered that Poole were entitled to any compensation from either the SCB or BSPA for the loss of its star man.

"If any was due perhaps it should have come from Michael Lee himself," says Fearman, still clearly dismayed by events that precipitated his own unhappy departure from British speedway when the promoting company, Poole Speedway Ltd, collapsed early the following year. "I don't think he even acknowledged what we had done for his benefit or the horrors we had gone through due to his lack of self control. The only compensation Poole Speedway had was the use of a guest rider and that was more a dispensation.

"The high profile that Michael carried did inestimable damage not only to Poole, but to speedway racing as a whole. I do believe that his behaviour was a major contribution to the ultimate collapse of the promoting company, but I wasn't to know that then.

"There were many riders taking drugs. I'd learned some were on the payroll of Poole Speedway but they and others at other tracks kept a reasonable low profile."

Lee has been through some desperate times in his life, more of which we'll come to in the remaining chapters, but he still believes that none of his other bad experiences can compare to the gut-wrenching feeling he had in the pit of his stomach on the day his speedway career effectively died.

"It was my lowest point," he says unhesitatingly. Prison wasn't a problem for me, I did my time, but the day the Control Board dished out my five-year ban . . . and then at the appeal hearing when they found me innocent of the charges but still kept my ban in place for a year . . . they were the real lowest points of my life.

"I can't change what happened and I can't alter people's opinions of me either. But I can live with myself. I genuinely feel that I was let down by speedway, while people in speedway at the time will say that I let the sport down. It's a matter of opinion.

"The powers that be who were running the sport at the time will know what I'm talking about. No-one else will, because they didn't suffer as I did by what was decided in that courtroom. What happened to me in that courtroom that day . . . that's what really destroyed me," he says.

Prodigal Son

Final fatal attraction

Chapter 25

HAVING the ban reduced from five years to one seemed at the time a token victory. Everything suggested that Michael wouldn't ride again. He had just about run out of tracks who would be prepared to take a chance on him.

But like Reg Fearman before him, Martin Rogers gambled.

"Much changed on the speedway landscape in 1984-85, most notably the BL losing tracks to NL, and emerging for 1985 as effectively the 'super league' some promoters had been pushing for over several years," Rogers explains.

"Early in the '85 season King's Lynn were in big trouble. The previous year had been good, results-wise, but unprofitable. Then along came the so-called super league. Costs escalated, riders who had been heat leaders in the bigger league wanted more money, but most produced less by way of results, and genuine top men were thin on the ground.

"We had a good, competitive team in '84 but realised it would be much more of a struggle in '85, and soon discovered it was even more than that. Olli Tyrvainen was refused a work permit, so we used Mick Poole early on but he was just a first-year kid and thrown in to an ultra tough situation. We needed a recognised heat leader, fast, and where was one of them to be found?

"Answer: Michael Lee, approaching the end of his 12-month ban, living down near Poole, doing engines, but not contemplating racing."

It was a decision that both Rogers and Lee would have cause to regret. In his book, *In My View*, the former King's Lynn boss explained why the 'fatal attraction' between club and its prodigal son ended in tears.

"It was an all-too familiar catalogue of missed meetings, promises and pledges to reform, continuing uncertainty and fractured morale, more of the same merry-go-round which had so frustrated and deflated promoters, colleagues and fans in the latter part of his first stint with the club.

"He had the ability to drive everyone to distraction, pulling back hundreds of missing supporters as soon as his return was announced, then alienating them and plunging the whole operation into turmoil all over again. It started encouragingly but after a couple of unproductive meetings the problems began.

"There are few more melancholy experiences for a speedway promoter than standing at the gate, waiting in vain for your main attraction to arrive . . . the sinking feeling as another nightmare unfolds, the annoyance and disappointment and frustration as the news is spread among several thousand fans whose day is about to be ruined.

"Michael failed to turn up for the home match against Belle Vue on Spring Bank

Holiday Monday – a fixture which attracted the biggest crowd for a domestic fixture at the track for five years – took a break, came back, went missing again, returned once more, then disappeared yet again.

"Claiming he had no machine to ride, he had to be dragooned into turning up for a League Cup match at Sheffield and collected three points on junior Ray Morton's bike in a horrific 63-15 slaughter, not surprisingly a record for the club.

"Thrown yet another olive branch after he moved back to East Anglia, things went along reasonably for a while before he opted out in the closing weeks of the season. He was 'suspended indefinitely' and few people expected to see him again. The chronicle of uncertainty could not do anything but once more hugely affect morale, in the pits and on the terraces.

Michael's state of mind was further destabilised when, in April '85, he received the tragic news that Billy Sanders, one of his best mates in speedway, had taken his own life. The Ipswich skipper couldn't cope after his wife Judy left him to be with his Australian Test team-mate Gary Guglielmi. Aged 29, he was found dead in his fume-filled car in woodland at Nacton, Suffolk.

"It was John Cook, Billy's Ipswich team-mate, who phoned me," recalls Michael. "I knew something was wrong straight away and after a long, silent pause, Cookie just said: 'Billy's killed himself'.

"I was stunned and all I kept thinking was 'why?'. I hadn't seen Billy for about year because I'd been out of speedway due to my ban but we were proper mates – like brothers.

"I stayed with him and his family at Rooty Hill when I visited Sydney on my first trip to Oz. And when Billy joined me at King's Lynn in '82 he, Judy and little Deano came to stay with us at Newmarket until about six weeks into the season, before they'd sorted out a place to stay.

"I think a lot of speedway riders are spur-of-the-moment people, which is what makes them successful at what they do. I don't know if Billy's death turned me into a 'wild boy' but we were really close," Michael added.

"The end of the 1985 season was the finish of Michael Lee as far as I was concerned, and in case there was anybody out there who felt that I was wrong or that they could deal better with the problems he presented, I would have passed the baton there and then," said Martin Rogers.

If it had not been for Bury St Edmunds property developer Peter Thurlow, that would have remained the case.

Rogers continues: "The ultimate dilemma with a Michael Lee-type situation is how to be able to plough through the emotion and come up with an objective response. When a rider is potentially such an important member of a team and component of a track's business, a whole season – at least – can stand or fall on the decisions taken.

"Contrary to all expectation, Michael did ride again in 1986, with Peter the catalyst in getting together a package which we all desperately hoped would provide the organisation and back-up support to make things work.

"His Abbeygate Group of Companies came up with an offer which was designed to establish once and for all if Michael had a contribution to make.

"There had been one or two enquiries as to whether he would ride again, if he might be tempted by a National League club, and as usual he featured a few times in the winter rumour mill.

"What did become clear was that if he rode, it would only be in British League, and from King's Lynn's point of view, it could only work if he turned over a completely new leaf and accepted the responsibilities involved.

"Peter, who backed Terry Betts and Dave Jessup for more than a decade, was nagged by the thought that given appropriate support, surely Michael could still do a job. He was an enthusiast, a shrewd and successful businessman, an organisation man, minded to try to find out what made the guy tick – and, more to the point, what it would take to ensure his undiluted commitment and reliability.

"The pair met to have those questions asked and answered. Machinery? No problem. Facilities? Sure. Transport? Easy. Back-up support? All he had to do was ask.

"After spelling out to Michael that in return, he expected nothing less than 100 per cent and that this was a once-off, last time offer, Peter put up a convincing case which, to a club and promotion in need of a minor miracle, was one of those classic offers that you couldn't refuse.

"Not without reservations, it was all agreed but with the understanding that one let-down really would be the last.

"For several weeks, it looked good. He came, he saw, and if he didn't exactly conquer (a 7.74 average and one maximum) he was at least an ever-present and from time to time showed he could still win races.

"But by June he was gone, without prior warning failing to turn up for a meeting at Sheffield – scene of the previous year's horrors – inevitably disowned by Peter Thurlow, suspended by the club initially for a month, then indefinitely."

Speedway Star revealed that behind the public farce there had been growing concerns. 'Even before his Sheffield let-down when he claimed that he had 'worked for 18 hours to get my engine done but didn't make it', there had been signs that not everything was completely right.

'Lee's role in the abandonment of Lynn away matches at Wolverhampton and Belle Vue provoked ill-disguised grumbles; after reporting bright and early for opening matches he had in recent weeks reverted to his old habit of dashing into the stadium with only minutes to spare.

'And twice in vital matches, against Coventry last month, then against Cradley a fortnight ago, he had failed to beat the two-minute time allowance and was excluded from last heat deciders at King's Lynn.'

It was almost, but not quite, the last King's Lynn fans were to see of Michael Lee. When a couple of years on Bill Barker and Malcolm Simmons bought the

A frustratingly familiar scene of waiting and head-scratching, as Martin Rogers has words with his enigmatic star.

"The ultimate dilemma with a Michael Lee-type situation is how to be able to plough through the emotion and come up with an objective response. When a rider is potentially such an important member of a team and component of a track's business, a whole season – at least – can stand or fall on the decisions taken."

promoting licence from Rogers in January 1988, they (as Rogers had done five years earlier) baulked at the idea of paying a chunk of money for Michael's registration which Rogers still held.

"They argued, reasonably enough, that Michael had surely closed the door on his career and would never ride again," Rogers said. "They were persuaded, or convinced themselves, that you should never say never."

And although three seasons elapsed before the next little chapter, sure enough, in 1991, when Lynn were back on struggle street, Barker handed the errant ex-champion another go.

Barker had planned to use Lee a year earlier but had to wait 12 months because the intransigent SCB had banned him again – this time for an unpaid £50 fine dating back FIVE YEARS, to his non-appearance at Sheffield on June 12, 1986. They ruled that he would remain suspended for a similar length of time to that which the fine remained on the books unpaid.

It meant Lee couldn't race again until March 1993 and he had to confine his speedway activity in 1990 to engine tuning and watching Stars' home and away matches from the pits, where he would readily dispense advice. After pressure from supporters demanding Lee's return, the Board finally relented and gave him clearance to resume racing from January 1, 1991.

And who was it that made Lee wait another year before he was eventually cleared to race again? Speedway Control Board manager . . . John Eglese.

But by then, Eglese had much more serious issues to concern him that winter. A couple of riders had tested positive for banned substances at the end of '90, while England star Gary Havelock – the sport's new 'bad boy' - was hauled before the SCB again to answer charges of indecent exposure, for which he was cleared. Havvy had a three-year suspended sentence hanging over his head having already served a one-year ban for failing a drugs test at the 1988 BLRC.

When the news of Lee's belated reprieve broke, early in November '90, Michael revealed in his regular column for *Speedway Mail International* magazine that family and friends organised a celebration party for him at his local pub, The Bell, in Kennett, where a strippagram added to the evening's fun and frolics!

Towards the end of January '91, Lee attended a supporters' meeting and it was reported that he had signed a three-year contract – and accepted the added burden of the captaincy. He invested heavily in three new machines (GM engines in Jawa frames) and was delighted to be leading a team brimming with young talent such as Henka Gustafsson and Mark Loram.

Newmarket-based Pam and Ray Rudge announced they were reviving the Michael Lee Fan Club they'd run five years earlier while new sponsors came forward in the form of Silkolene Oils, NGK Spark Plugs, MBI Video, PJS Ignition Systems, Lynford Motor Co, and Trackstar Equipment. It was all systems go.

England team manager Eric Boocock even spoke optimistically about him and Colin Pratt reopening the international door to Michael. "He could still win a World Final because he's a good gater," Booey told *SMI*.

But the promotion, with Dave Jessup as team manager, did suffer a setback when they realised there was not going to be a reduced average for Lee on his return to the sport, despite having a verbal agreement for a reduction at the BSPA conference, and that meant some late team changes. Lee stayed at 7.74, his average from 1986, instead of having a reduced CMA of 6.50. The promoters probably felt they had collectively given him enough 'second chances' in the past not to warrant any more favours. As a result, Lynn's proposed starting line-up was half-a-point over the 40 maximum limit, which meant Richard Knight being jettisoned to Berwick.

Before the start of the Sunbrite First Division season, Lee nipped over to Australia to improve his fitness with appearances at the Wayville Showground in Adelaide and the once-a-year Melbourne Showground event promoted by former rider John McNeill, where he was beaten into third place in the 'Mr Melbourne' final by Aussie stars Todd Wiltshire and Troy Butler.

Michael with Chris Morton and his mechanic Ged Blake at the 1986 World Final.

Lee's eagerly awaited UK comeback on March 16 attracted the biggest opening night crowd for several years but, after beating Reading's World No.3 Wiltshire on his long-awaited comeback, a handful of meetings suggested that the old spark was not quite there. Michael managed 15 appearances (5.52 CMA) but clearly was not the force of old, not even close to his 1986 incarnation.

Terry Betts later told *Speedway Star*: "I honestly felt he (Lee) rode too hard and was desperate to do well. Mike has been out for a long time and I felt he tried to come back overnight. He was plunged in at the deep end and, of course, the spotlight is always on him."

Michael's last-ever appearance in the green and gold came at Cradley Heath on Saturday, June 1, 1991.

Recalling why he again felt victimised by the speedway authorities in 1991, Michael says: "I'd been asked to take a random drug test a couple of times and proved negative but the one time I got peed off was when I came back and they tried to test me on the day I was only a track reserve – No.18 – for the Commonwealth Final at King's Lynn. I only agreed to turn up there as a favour for promoter Bill Barker, who phoned me on the morning of the meeting begging me to help out. I'd been World Champion and really didn't want to be riding in this qualifying round as a stand-by reserve. It felt a bit insulting."

A reluctant Lee, then 31, thought he was going along simply to make up the numbers but found himself taking one meaningless ride as a replacement for the injured Craig Boyce in Heat 18. On a wet track, he just kept out of the way and didn't trouble the scorers. It was a sad way to complete his last four laps but, as ever, there was a dramatic postscript to that final competitive track appearance on June 2, 1991.

Michael at the start of his final 1991 season.

"Amazingly, my name got pulled out of the hat for the test and I'm being asked to sign a consent form even though I was only a stand-by reserve. When they told me I had to provide a urine sample, I thought 'you bastards' - and I legged it! I went to the dressing room, got changed and walked out. I put my bag in the car and pissed off.

"Of course, by the time I got 10 miles out of King's Lynn my mobile's going like there's no tomorrow and I'm being told to come back for my own good, but I just went: 'Get f*****! You just stitched me right up'.

"By now I'm thinking, 'why am I doing this again? Do I really need it?' It wasn't good."

He was immediately suspended for failing to take the drugs test. Five weeks later he pleaded guilty at an SCB tribunal and, after a forceful mitigation plea by top lawyer Jeffrey Care, he was let off with a two-year suspended sentence.

King's Lynn '91 wasn't quite the final curtain call on Lee's turbulent speedway career. A few weeks later he made his last abortive comeback attempt back at Poole – with near disastrous consequences.

"I was practicing with John Davis after the meeting one night when a con-rod in the engine broke at the end of the straight and the bike just spat me, headlong, into the fence.

"I knew straight away that I was finished. I broke four vertebrae in the lower section of my back and spent four months in hospital.

"It took me a long time to get over that injury, my worst ever in speedway. I've never ridden a bike competitively since then, for fear of doing permanent damage and ending up in a wheelchair."

Michael now regrets even attempting his failed comeback bids in 1985, 1986 and 1991, saying: "My heart wasn't in it, I didn't have the same level of dedication anymore. With my lifestyle being what it was by then, and having had a year off, I wasn't focused on speedway.

"I was in a Catch-22 with the engine business. I knew I needed to concentrate more on my own riding career but, at the same time, I didn't want to let down my customers either. I thought: 'The speedway authorities might ban me again next week, in which case I'll need those customers to pay my bills'.

In fact, after his last appearance for Lynn under Martin Rogers in '86, Michael turned his attention back to the workshop. He tuned engines for Belle Vue's England star Chris Morton and was a key part of Mort's pits back-up team at the World Final in Katowice.

A year later he prepared the engines Ipswich's American star John Cook used at the two-day 1987 World Final in Amsterdam. Michael was also involved as the World Final tuner for Shawn Moran and Richard Knight (Bradford, 1990), as well as Ronnie Correy (Gothenburg, 1991).

During his five-year lay-off from speedway between '86 and '91, Michael competed successfully in the British Moto-Cross Championships.

But he also had more off-track headaches to contend with when he was made bankrupt in 1987, although he viewed this setback as a blessing in disguise.

"I hadn't paid tax for four or five years and the tax office came in with a demand," he explains. "They wanted 62 grand but, around two months after reaching an agreement with the Inland Revenue to pay them off in instalments, the VAT man came in and demanded his £1,900 in full.

"When I told them I couldn't pay, they decided to bankrupt me. We had the bailiffs round but they didn't take very much, while the bankruptcy did me a big favour. It meant my case with the revenue was discharged."

From his home on Australia's Gold Coast, where he resumed his career in journalism and collaborated working on Ivan Mauger's 2010 autobiography, Martin Rogers says: "I felt sorry for Michael after he resumed his career in 1985-86 but because of a combination of reasons simply couldn't properly get it all together.

"By then, though, any sorrow I felt was very much conditioned by the collateral damage he left behind him at a very tough time when Lin and I were desperately trying to keep King's Lynn in business.

"In summary at this distance, I'm sad his career and his life spiralled into such disarray and that unfortunately overrides the memories of the exciting, often thrilling ride which took him to the top. Being associated with it was absolutely brilliant for a few years and then, later, absolutely awful.

"I wouldn't say our stint with Michael in '85 and '86 prematurely turned us away from promoting speedway, but it was a big factor in convincing us that we didn't want to be in anything remotely like the same position again with a rider who carried so much baggage."

Reflecting now on his last comeback attempt some 19 years ago, Michael says: "I gave it a go but I probably should never have come back. I should have retired when they gave me the ban and gone off and done my engine tuning business full-time. My business suffered after I made my comeback and once my racing career folded completely, I went full-on into drugs."

Busted

Drug-dealing and the cocaine lifestyle

Chapter 26

WE have read about Michael's use of drugs at various stages of his speedway racing career but many will probably be shocked by the sheer scale of his involvement after he hung up his leathers . . . and became a self-confessed drug-dealer.

"After my ban which stopped me from riding I needed some kind of excitement in my life," he says. "Because I wasn't racing at the time, I started to circulate and got deeper into a world of drugs. I'd go to buy my own stuff and then think: 'Bugger me, I can buy a £20 bag this big but if I buy a £200 bag I'll have so much more'.

"I started buying it in pubs and then I got to know suppliers of drugs. In the pub there would be a few little wraps for sale, whereas I remember going down to meet known suppliers in flats in London and seeing cannabis resin stacked like bricks against the wall. These were major suppliers. I'd go: 'So how much is that?' and they'd say: 'That's two hundred pounds worth'. When I broke that down in my mind into, say, 10 kilos, I realised I could make money out of it.

"I then started to buy quite large amounts because I got to know where I could get rid of the stuff. I actually started to become a supplier myself and it just escalated from there.

"After leaving speedway I was happy to sit around people and I wanted to know who the drug suppliers were. The people I was mixing with obviously weren't going to take me to their suppliers just like that because it's undercover, but I soon got to know who and where they were to be found.

"For instance, I'd go to one supplier for my own drugs and then say to him, 'I'll have the whole lot off you, mate'. Then when I asked for more than he was able to sell me, he'd offer to take me to his supplier so that I could buy my stuff direct. I'd give him something as a 'thank you' for introducing me to his main supplier.

"Drug-dealing in this way is talked about much more often and openly these days but it's been going on in Britain for decades.

"I wasn't the sort of dealer who went to pubs pushing it. I only sold to people who were looking for it and wanted to buy from me. Someone would come up and say 'there's an old boy here who wants this or that', I'd go and meet them. That's how it operates. I've never forced anyone to do anything they haven't wanted to do.

"But before you knew it, I was moving quite a lot of drugs. I was making thousands of pounds a week - and that was back in the 80s. The best week I ever had was a profit of £14,000, hence the reason why I wasn't that keen on going back to speedway.

"In the early days I could easily make between £1,500 and two grand a week. When it really escalated in the late 80s and early 90s, I was getting pretty full-on and then the coke came along too, so we're talking big money."

As Michael admits, he needed to keep selling cannabis, marijuana, or whatever you wish to call it, to feed his own expensive cocaine habit.

"You're dead right there. The fact is, when I went to buy a bag of cocaine a lot of it was going up my nose. I was living it and it wore me into the ground' in the end.

"There's no doubt in my mind, if I hadn't stopped snorting cocaine like I was doing, I guarantee you I'd be dead by now. Or if I wasn't dead, I'd have a massive hole on the front of my face.

"I was just living for today. When I was 25-years-old I didn't think I'd reach 30. It was never in the equation. And when I made it to 30, I honestly believed that my 40th birthday was definitely never going to happen. At the time I didn't even care whether I made it to 30 or 40. When you're not on the drugs, all you're thinking about is when you'll be on them again.

"I was back on the Charlie in my 40s and I'm thinking 'where do I go from here?'. I started to think, 'I can't really do this anymore' and yet when I was 40-years-old I didn't expect to make it to 50. But, touch wood, I'm here and I'm still healthy. I'm a survivor!"

Michael talks candidly about his use of cocaine and other substances that consumed him before and after his racing days were over. He was once offered £20,000 by a Sunday tabloid newspaper to reveal all about his former coke habit but he turned it down and now the one-time World Champion tells here just what those dark days were really like.

"Every day now I seem to pick up the paper and read about one so-called celebrity or another admitting to the world 'I have a cocaine habit', as if it's something new," he smiles knowingly. "I think it was the *News of the World* who approached me about selling my story. It was sometime around the mid-80s and they offered me 20 grand to tell all about my cocaine lifestyle. I didn't even consider it, though, because I didn't want to do anything that could jeopardise the lifestyle I had going by then in any way.

"I was such a coke-head at one time. I'd left speedway and coke was my life. I was using bucketfuls of the stuff. And it wasn't like nowadays where the coke is all cut and the user is getting only 20 or 30 per cent coke. I was actually getting 90 per cent pure cocaine before all the commercial, villainous, money-making crap came into it.

"I was that deeply into it that I had my own test kit to measure the quality of my cocaine. It's like my racing and now my tuning, when I get into something I'm full on. When I do something, I never do it half-heartedly, so I was totally into my drugs. I was dealing cocaine and I had the money to ensure there was a bottomless pit of it coming my way. It was my life.

"I gave up coke three times but for one reason or another I ended up going back to it. I haven't got time for the stuff now but while I say I'm anti it, I also believe that everyone should try it once. I have this funny logic about it because I don't believe you can make assumptions about things without trying them. Then again, I wouldn't try heroin or anything that was going to get the better of me physically."

Presumably, one would apply the same twisted logic to the notion of jumping off a 25-storey tower block or sticking your head inside the jaws of a great white shark. Until you've actually tried it, you'll never really know if you'll do yourself much harm!

Anyway, Michael continues: "Cocaine is a mental drug in the sense that it grabs hold of you psychologically. There's a feel-good factor and when you have it you don't want to let it go. Whereas heroin physically affects your body and your body hurts if you don't have it.

"I was regularly among junkies who stuck needles in their arms but I'd never do that and I would never take heroin – or whack things up myself, as they put it. That would make me sick. I would snort more than those people ever could but I could never put a needle in myself."

Snorting coke gave Michael the buzz he'd missed since he stopped racing. A line of Charlie replaced the adrenalin rush he experienced when he used his skill to outwit the very best opponents on track all those years earlier, when he was still enjoying his speedway.

He explains: "It sounds stupid but I actually liked the life I had when I was doing coke. I was roaring about the country – London, Manchester, all over the place – and I always tried to be with semi-sane people, not junkies. There wasn't a seedy side to it, as people might imagine, it was very much a business thing.

"Because I had good quality cocaine in my possession I was supplying respectable executives who wanted maybe only three or four grams a week. If they had a meeting coming up in which they wanted to impress someone and needed to feel super-confident, they'd do a line of coke just before they went into the room. I used to laugh at that side of it, because I never used it to improve myself or try and impress other people. But the trouble was, recreational use soon became all day long."

Speaking with the lucidity and insight of a Senior Lecturer at the School of Pharmacy, Michael explains the effects of cocaine and what this powerful stimulant did for him: "It's a social drug. It stimulates your mind and makes you talk a lot. You can sit and talk about things that would usually seem quite boring but have a really in-depth conversation for hours on end. But it ends up in all talk and no action.

"I'd sit down with my mates – some of them had stacks of money as well – and we'd have these grand ideas and make projections about investing in office property developments and launder our money through different business ventures. We'd sit and talk about all these things but they never happened – and that's what coke does to people. It gives you bright ideas that never come to anything. Maybe for some people they do come to fruition but I doubt it because most people end up at rock bottom if they don't sort themselves out."

Naturally, Michael's health did suffer as a result of his drug abuse.

"When you've been abusing yourself for as long as I was, you're not going to be in the peak of fitness, although I wasn't really in ill health either. Probably the one reason why I managed to maintain some kind of sanity is that if I ever went three days without a proper meal, then when I did eat I ate good food. I wouldn't go somewhere and just have a burger. With all the cash I had, I'd eat out at restaurants almost every night. The lowest my weight dropped to was eight stone," added Michael, now looking a much healthier 11st.

He accepts, though, that he was on a relentless downward spiral. "Too much coke does wear you down physically. It burns your immune system because your body is not meant to be going at that pace all the time.

"Before you knew it, I was moving quite a lot of drugs. I was making thousands of pounds a week – and that was back in the 80s. The best week I ever had was a profit of £14,000, hence the reason why I wasn't that keen on going back to speedway."

"I'd go for 48 hours on coke and then stop and collapse, and you wouldn't see me for the next 36 hours. Then I'd be out again and have another 46, or even 56 hours on it. My record was 14 days, non-stop, on coke and amphetamines. Then I'd sleep for two-and-a-half days solid. Sometimes I'd go to bed but because I was on such a high I was unable to sleep, so I'd get up and just carry on."

His total abuse of his body became complete when, in his early 30s, Michael started mixing drink and drugs.

"Although I wasn't a big drinker and was virtually teetotal until I was about 32, I will say that when you are out all night snorting cocaine and drinking alcohol, it's the coke that is keeping you sober. You can drink like a fish.

"But in the end that lifestyle will kill you. When I was on Charlie, sometimes I'd drink a whole bottle of vodka or tequila and have a proper conversation with people. The booze half relaxes you but it's the coke that's keeping you in the ballpark. I don't touch spirits now, just a beer now and then.

"I was more into amphetamines in the early days but your body can't take that and coke after a while. So I'm glad I stopped. What started out in the late 70s as cannabis for relaxation, in the end became too much. It was dawn 'till dusk."

Michael was heavily into drugs while still living with Janet, although their long-term relationship was on the rocks and would end for good soon after his release from prison.

He says: "We'd moved from Poole back up to Newmarket and she knew all about what I did. I continued doing it when we moved to Red Lodge and again when we lived in the little village of Chippenham. And we were still together when we moved to our luxury bungalow and I was busted big-time in the 90s.

"She was living a bloody good lifestyle out of it. She wasn't complaining and seemed quite happy to go along with everything while the money was still coming in. Without sounding bitter about it, while I still had money she seemed quite happy to put up with it. People can say what they want, and Janet can say what she wants, but while there were good times she was about."

In the early 90s Michael, Janet and their four children lived in a luxury bungalow in Holywell Row at Holywell, near Mildenhall Speedway. It was set in 22 acres of farmland with 18 adjoining stables.

"Total luxury," recalls Michael. "The rent was £1,200 a month, which was a lot some 20 years ago, and the place would easily cost at least half-a-million to buy now.

"This says it all. I didn't even have a job. I was paying for our lifestyle by dealing a lot of drugs. When I look back on it now, I shake my head and think 'f****** hell!' It was mad.

"It wasn't until after I had the longest prison sentence that it changed for Janet. I came out with nothing and she'd had to move from the rented bungalow at Holywell and was living on benefits in a semi-detached at Red Lodge.

"The one thing I am sorry about when I look back at that period of my life is that our children were brought up in such an environment. People, my mates, would come to the house and the snorting and smoking would go on quite openly. I'm not proud of it.

"In a way it educated our kids but it probably wasn't the best way to educate them. Maybe I should have kept the drugs side of things more out of the way but with the lifestyle I was leading, being so engrossed in it, that was never going to happen.

"I regret that now but in a way, it educated them about life and what goes on and they have come through it quite well. It's put in front of most kids today and unless you wrap them in cotton wool and never let them out, I guarantee you that every child is going to come across drugs at some point."

Jordan Lee, Michael and Janet's second eldest son, provides a fascinating insight into his life at that time in a later chapter.

Michael vividly recalls the moment, in the summer of 1997, when his lavish, cocaine-fuelled lifestyle came crashing down around him. Though thankfully his demise was not quite in the bullet-riddled style of Tony Montana in Scarface, his recklessness was bound to catch up with him sooner or later.

"I never thought about the possibility of being caught and arrested," he says.

Michael pictured back at Mildenhall, where his speedway career began, in 1995.

"I was that deeply into it that I had my own test kit to measure the quality of my cocaine. It's like my racing and now my tuning, when I get into something I'm full on. When I do something, I never do it half-heartedly, so I was totally into my drugs. I was dealing cocaine and I had the money to ensure there was a bottomless pit of it coming my way. It was my life."

"You try and plan everything carefully and cover your tracks but eventually it does happen and you can't get away from it. Sooner or later the wrong person hears something they shouldn't, or someone you're connected with gets caught and they haven't got the balls to take the consequences.

"It was quite a shock when it happened. I was sitting at home feeling nicely relaxed and doing my thing. I'd actually just skinned a big spliff up – and that was the thing, from dawn until dusk I was either selling drugs, taking drugs myself or being involved in them in some way. It was non-stop, like running a supermarket.

"But this one day, it was mid-afternoon and I'd just rolled a joint up. I leaned back on the sofa to fire it up and all of a sudden two or three unmarked police cars came howling down the big, long drive way leading to the bungalow. They screeched to a halt and when I looked out of the window I thought: ''F*** - drugs squad'. I turned to Janet and quickly thought 'what can I hide?' but then realised that there was no bloody point in even attempting to hide anything or trying to run for it. All I did was slip the half-a-gram of coke, which was in a little wrap for my personal use, inside the top of the rubbish bin.

"The front door rattled and in actual fact I still had a joint in my hand when I answered the door to the cops! I've gone: 'I know what you want' before walking back into the kitchen. Of course, there was one copper on either side of me and they told me to sit down and wait while their colleagues carried out a full search of the property.

"They obviously radioed in because the next thing you knew there were four or five more cop vehicles on the scene. They were everywhere - dogs, vans, the lot. There were no sirens, though. The second lot came in nice and peaceful and it was all sorted.

"The first thing they spotted was the electrical cables leading to the loft, where I'd been growing cannabis plants, along with a set of ladders. They went up and I heard one copper say: 'F****** hellfire, look in here!'

"They found 264 plants up there. The whole L-shaped loft was just green with skunk-weed plants.

"I was sitting there saying 'yeah, yeah, you've got me now' and then they were asking if there was anything else. I told them I was just growing a few plants, so the cops got a bit sarky about it. 'A few plants?' one of them said. 'There's enough here to supply the whole of East Anglia!'

"But I still had the spliff in my hand while talking to the cops. I'm not thinking properly now. Not only was I wasted on that, man, but I was wasted on the fact that the cops were all around me. As I fired up the spliff and was taking the first toke, I went 'oh shit!'. The copper next to me said: 'What's that you're smoking there?' I said: 'Yeah, I thought it was a cigarette but it's a joint'. So I stubbed it out and they took it away as more evidence.

"Then the dogs were brought in and they found the 15 kilos of hash stashed away in the garage. I think there were 46 bars all stacked up. Then they found the half-a-gram of coke I'd tried to hide in the waste bin. If they had found lots more coke on me, I would probably have got another six or seven years on my sentence.

"Finally, they found 90 grand in cash that was in my bedside drawer. It was wedged full with 50 and 20 pound notes. Very frustrating."

Michael was arrested and taken initially to Mildenhall police station before being transferred to Bury St Edmunds, where he was detained in a cell overnight. "They then took me off to Norwich prison, where I was remanded in custody until my first bail application was heard in court.

"I'd hoped to get bail at the first attempt, and my solicitor thought I would be granted it, but I was taken from Newmarket magistrate's court straight back to prison."

But, on this occasion, not to the familiar walls and relative safety of HMP Norwich.

Michael recalls the horrifying moment he suddenly discovered he was being transferred down to London, to be locked up with some of the most notorious and violent criminals in the country.

"When the prison van left the court in Newmarket, it started to head towards Norwich but then, all of a sudden, it stopped and the driver did a U-turn and began to go in the opposite direction.

"I was in the van with two other prisoners, who had both been convicted of very minor offences, and we were told that there had been a 'lock down' at Norwich and we weren't allowed to return there that night.

"It was mid-afternoon and I'd just rolled a joint up. I leaned back on the sofa to fire it up and all of a sudden two or three unmarked police cars came howling down the big, long drive way leading to the bungalow. They screeched to a halt and when I looked out of the window I thought: "F* - drugs squad'."**

"The screw who was driving said that he'd been told to take us to Pentonville Prison in North London, which freaked us all out. But as we were driving along the A1, he received another message to say that Pentonville was full, so we were re-directed to Wormwood Scrubs in West London, which was just as bad.

"But it was getting late and, with all the traffic in London, there was another sudden change of plan. It was decided that we wouldn't be able to reach the Scrubs in time for their 10.00pm curfew, so we were finally taken to Brixton prison, in South London, instead.

"We'd been cooped up in a tiny cubicle each for about six hours. All you could do was sit on a little plastic seat and stare at six feet high partition walls with your knees jammed against the door. Being tall, it wasn't a pleasant journey and the two other blokes in the back of the van were fuming at me because they blamed me for the fact that they'd landed up in a hell-hole like Brixton.

"I didn't go a lot on that place," says a typical understated Michael. "They put me in with a black cocaine-dealer. I found the place intimidating.

"The Old Bill were basically 'playing' me. They thought that if they sent me down to Brixton, or one of the other bad London prisons, I'd give them information on the people I was involved with."

Without wishing to sound like he is trying to reclaim some higher moral ground, Michael says: "Every time I've been busted, I've taken the consequences on the chin and no-one has ever been grassed up by me. I don't want it on my conscience that maybe 10 years down the road, I have an enemy who is going to want to retaliate. You do your time.

"After two weeks in Brixton, I was taken back up to Newmarket for further police questioning. They again questioned me about my associates but I wouldn't give them anything. I was angry by now and I told them: 'You bastards – are you going to send me back to Brixton if I don't grass?' I was almost wiling them to do it, because just the day before I'd managed to get myself a job in Brixton. The first thing you do when you're sent to prison is to get yourself a job so that you can get out of the cell and occupy your time, and actually try and use your head a little bit.

"But they must have realised that their tactics had backfired on them because when they didn't get what they were hoping for out of me, they sent me back to Norwich instead."

Although police vigorously opposed Michael's application for bail, he was very fortunate that his father came to his aid once again.

Andy is understandably saddened when reminded of his son's dramatic downfall and the circumstances behind it, but he agreed to talk about this sorry chain of events for this book: "I paid his bail and nearly got into trouble myself by trying to help out."

"For some reason they tried to claim that Dad was in some way involved with me and the drugs, which was totally ridiculous," added Michael.

Andy continued: "He was in deep trouble when I bailed him out because the court wanted an awful lot of money. I had to put up £150,000 and it was just fortunate that I was in the process of selling my business at that time, so I was able to prove to the court that I had enough surety for bail. It's no good saying you have a house worth £150,000 – you actually have to prove you've got that amount."

Val Lee said: "I told Michael he would be caught - he was mad. He deserved to have the book thrown at him. He apologised again and I told him he'd been an idiot.

"I went to his court trials – it was just another thing to face. You wondered what tomorrow was going to bring but it was always a case of 'let's face it when it happens'. Andy found it more difficult than me to attend the different court hearings."

"Despite all we'd been through," says Andy, "I still supported Michael as much as I could in the background. I went to see him in prison, which, to be honest, was quite a job to do. It was absolutely terrible."

Michael doesn't feel the need to apologise or make excuses for many things he has done in his life but there was genuine remorse in Michael's voice when he added: "My parents didn't deserve this. They couldn't understand what I was doing or the extent to which I'd been doing it."

But Val added: "I realised Michael had hit rock bottom when I had a visit from some not very nice people. I was on my own. They came inside the house and said they were 'looking for the bloke with the Porsche'.

"I said: 'Sorry, there is no Porsche and I don't have a clue where he is'.

"They were getting a bit threatening and said: 'We've got to find him, he owes us money'. I said: 'Don't look at me, I'm not paying you' I told them before giving them one minute to get off my property before I set the dog on them. I had a 'guard dog' sign put up on the outside of the cottage.

"But what they weren't to know was that all I had were my two King Charles Spaniels!"

"Anyway, the two men went and sat outside in their car for a while before driving off. Thankfully, I never saw them again.

"I realised then that Michael's money had run out and that he'd hit rock bottom. I told him what had happened and he shrugged his shoulders and said 'I'm sorry - I'll sort it'.

"I was worried about the physical and mental damage he would do to himself if he kept it up but, fortunately, he got off the coke. I quite expected him to have to go on a rehab course but he just gave it up like that."

Yet again, though, Michael let his parents down badly. He reveals: "Within seven to eight weeks of being released on bail, I was at it again. I managed to score cannabis after getting it 'on tick' from a supplier I knew, which meant I owed him.

"When I came out of prison at the end of 1998 it was to nothing – the bungalow had obviously been reclaimed by the landlord - but I managed to sell three or four lots of drugs and quickly build up a bit of money again. I was pumping it out as quickly as I could to get some money in for myself and to pay back the bloke who'd given the cannabis to me in the first place.

"I'd buy two or three hundred quid's worth, which I could make about £100 from each time, and it just escalated again. I had about several hundred pounds worth of hash on me when the police raided my place again. That was it – I was back off to the nick.

"They took me straight to prison and because I'd breached my bail conditions, I had to stay there for the 18 months I served of my original three-year sentence."

Michael had previously served two small sentences at HMP Norwich, a month each time at the end of the 80s and again in 1993 for minor drug offences. "I was caught with about an ounce of cannabis, it was an inconvenience really."

But this time he got what he describes as "The Big One."

Prisoner FA3549

The inside story

Chapter 27

FOLLOWING his arrest, Michael immediately accepted the stark reality of his situation and, just like every challenge he faced on the track, met this one head-on too.

"I knew I'd be going to prison," he admits. "At first you kind of think 'how can I get away with this?' but, logically, there was no way out. Not in my wildest dreams did I think that I'd avoid a prison sentence.

"I'd previously appeared in Bury Crown Court and Newmarket Magistrate's Court but when I heard that my trial had been switched to Ipswich Crown Court, I feared the worst.

"When you're inside, you do your homework on the likely consequences based on the charges against you. I was constantly checking out the various judges and finding out what their attitudes were to drug offenders. The two I was most likely to face were real hardliners on drugs, so I expected to be severely punished."

He pleaded guilty at Ipswich Crown Court on September 19, 1997 and was convicted of 10 charges involving producing, possessing and being concerned in the supplying of, or with intent to supply, Class B drugs cannabis, cannabis resin and amphetamine, plus possession of the Class A drug cocaine. On January 22, 1998 Michael was brought back to the same Ipswich courtroom for sentencing.

He says: "The solicitor who'd been representing me on legal aid put me in touch with a good barrister and in the end I got away with a three-year sentence - but the judge could have given me as much as five years. If I'd splashed out, say, 10 grand I might have got a lighter sentence – I've learnt that it's often a case of who knows who, people doing favours and a bit of 'nudge nudge, wink, wink' – but, realistically, I knew what was coming my way."

With a reduced sentence for good behaviour, Michael knew that he was at least looking at an 18-month stretch and, all being well, a release date of December 1998. He would spend most of that term banged up in Norwich prison, which he was already familiar with.

All prisoners are given their own personal number on arrival. Michael Andrew Lee had been World, England, King's Lynn and Poole Number One.

In HMP Norwich he became known as Prisoner FA3549.

Of course, he would have received a lighter jail term had he been willing to 'grass' on the ringleaders higher up the chain in his drugs conspiracy but, as he has said, that was never even a consideration.

"It's a shock to your system when you first go in there and it's hard to start with," says Michael, whose first cell was located on A-Wing, where the remand prisoners were housed.

"Because I'd been racing speedway not that long before I arrived at Norwich, for better or worse, quite a lot of fellow prisoners and screws knew who I was. Some of them you wouldn't want to know but there were others who gave you something to talk about. You could actually shut off from the situation you were in for a few minutes and talk to them about speedway and, being in Norwich, most of them either supported King's Lynn or had been to the speedway at some point.

"I didn't feel any shame at being recognised, because these people were in there for crimes they'd committed too. I can't say I enjoyed the recognition either – I've never liked that side of speedway. We'd chat about speedway and I'd usually go: 'Yeah, that was back in the old days . . . now I'm in here for selling drugs'. And they'd go: 'Yeah, yeah, we heard'.

"The majority of people in prison know about drugs anyway – they are rife in prisons all over the country. And if you don't know about drugs when you first go in, you soon learn and you'll certainly know a lot more about them by the time you come out.

"At one stage I was brewing 35 litres of hooch at a time! I used to brew it in five-litre plastic cleaning canisters. If you did the lid up too tightly, because the yeast grows, they would explode! And once that happened, the whole wing would stink of alcohol."

"My first priority aim was to get myself a job that would enable me to leave my cell, which isn't an easy task. The first job I had was sweeping the landing. People might say: 'Bloody hell, that's a bit of a come down, isn't it?' but I didn't care. It's not a come down when you're in prison because anything that gets you out of your cell, when you're banged up for 23 hours a day, is good news. If you didn't have a job, you were only allowed out for an hour's 'association'."

Michael had been used to living on his wits and he quickly adjusted to prison life and learned how the 'system' worked and, occasionally, how to beat it.

"I swept the landing for about a week and then I managed to arrange for some hashish to be smuggled in to me by a friend at visiting time. If ever I felt stressed out, I found it the ideal way to relax.

"In prison, drugs are currency and by having a small amount of hashish I could improve my situation. You share things with people, do favours here and there, and it helps. I was celled-up with a bloke who worked in the kitchen and before long I got a job in there too.

"At first I did a few odd jobs and then I started working in the bakery, where I was taught for six weeks by the head baker. When he was transferred to another prison, I took over from him and kept the job of head baker throughout the 13-14 months I spent at Norwich, before finishing my sentence at Hollesley Bay."

Just like on the track, it was all about being in the right place at the right time and remaining alert and vigilant.

"I'd be up at 6.30am every morning and go straight to the kitchen and start cooking for about 640 people. I quite liked it because I've always done a bit of cooking anyway.

"Everything went from the kitchen to the wings and I was making bread and, what you could loosely call 'sponge deserts'. Only they never had much yeast in them, so they didn't rise and tasted more like bits of brick!

"But at the end of the day it didn't matter. The point was, I was getting lumps of yeast back to the boys on the wings, which meant I was more in favour, and it just went from there.

"It was great because those of us in the kitchen were out of our cells from 6.30am until about 5.00pm every day. Once the food had been cooked and distributed to the different wings, we'd walk back to our cells with the trolley, get changed out of our kitchen clothes and start eating ourselves, if we wanted to. But one of the benefits of being in the kitchen was that we could eat more or less as much as we liked all day, so we were eating decent food regularly."

There was another bonus that became part of Michael's cunning plan to improve prison conditions and day-to-day existence on the inside, and which also explains the shortage of yeast in the 'sponge deserts'.

He reveals: "The big bonus of being the baker was that I could get my hands on the yeast, which was kept under lock and key in the screws' fridge. I would never nick it from under their noses but somebody else did and it was my job to get it back to the wing one way or another.

"I'd cut the yeast up into thin strips and stuff it anywhere I could. One day, instead of cutting the block of yeast in half, the others nicked the whole block and I had a job to conceal it from the screws on my way back to the wing, which was about 300 metres from the kitchen. It was roughly the size of a packet of 200 cigarettes and I hid it under my jacket sleeve.

"I thought I was going to get nicked because one of the screws kept deliberately bumping into me – he must have known something was up – but I clamped onto the block of yeast and managed to get away with it. I got on well with that particular screw and I think he let me get away with it that time.

"The next problem I had was getting rid of the stuff in case the screws raided my cell looking for the missing yeast. So instead of going straight to dinner, I was hacking the yeast up into slivers so that I could distribute it to the others.

"And because everyone knew what I had, there were soon phone cards appearing on strings from everywhere, dangling in front of the bars on my cells.

A £2 phone card would pay for a bit of yeast, which was used to make alcohol. I'm not kidding, there were phone cards being dangled from about 20-odd different cells, four storeys high – about 80 windows!

"The phone cards were another part of prison currency. If I didn't want to use them myself, to make calls to people on the outside, I'd 'sell' them for a bit of puff.

"The other problem was that half the blokes who ended up with some yeast didn't know how to use the stuff properly. I was the prison expert at brewing hooch but that in itself created another problem I had to deal with.

Michael shortly before his arrest in 1997.

"At one stage I was brewing 35 litres of hooch at a time! I used to brew it in five-litre plastic cleaning canisters. If you did the lid up too tightly, because the yeast grows, they would explode! And once that happened, the whole wing would stink of alcohol.

"It would take two or three days to get the brew going well, using orange juice, a bit of water and sugar mixed with yeast. So, of course, everyone on the wing is bloody ordering extra sugar and extra orange juice and it's getting out of hand. The screws aren't stupid and every cell was being turned over.

"They turned mine over, too, but they couldn't find it. At one time I hid as many as five of the five-litre containers beneath the shroud cladding that covered the pipes in my cell. The screws kept looking at it but were satisfied in their own minds that my hooch couldn't possibly be hidden anywhere inside the shroud or the piping because if they couldn't open the safety screws around it with a normal Phillips screwdriver, then they were convinced that I certainly couldn't either.

"I had to stand outside on the landing while they ripped my cell to pieces trying to find my brew, but they couldn't figure it out.

"What they didn't know, though, is that I'd made up my own special tool. Using two metal screws I'd nicked from the kitchen, I then attached them to a cigarette lighter to form my own makeshift screwdriver! It used to take me 20 minutes to half-an-hour to unscrew the shroud – but that's where I kept my booze hidden.

"And because there was a bit of heat coming through the pipes, it even helped the brewing process all the more. That night, after lights out at 8pm, other prisoners were sending down all their bottles on string for me to fill up and send back to them. I got rid of four of the five-litre bottles I'd brewed and kept the last one for me and my three other cell-mates. And did we all get hammered that night!

"I pulled that trick about four or five times and never got caught. I had to knock it on the head because I knew that if they did catch me, they would whack another two or three months on top of my sentence as punishment.

"The screws turned their backs for 30 seconds and this bloke was beaten to a pulp and cut to ribbons with razor blades cut into tiny pieces and then embedded in the back of tooth brushes. It's not nice and just made you think, 'don't mess with these people'."

"As it was, the maximum number of phone cards you were allowed was seven. But when they spun my cell one day, they caught me with more than 200! They left me with 14 – seven more than I was meant to have – but it gave the screws knowledge that I was definitely up to things.

"There was a guy who was getting cannabis smuggled in but I'd give him a number of my phone cards and distribute it for him. I was totally engrossed in prison life, it was a new challenge for me."

As well as enjoying some of the 'perks', Michael saw plenty of the dark side, too.

"At one stage I had to share a cell with five other inmates," he continues, "but worse things happened. I once saw a prisoner – apparently a grass – who was totally mutilated. The screws turned their backs for 30 seconds and this bloke was beaten to a pulp and cut to ribbons with razor blades cut into tiny pieces and then embedded in the back of tooth brushes. It's not nice and just made you think, 'don't mess with these people'.

"Someone committed suicide in the cell next door to me. You think we would've heard something but we didn't hear a sound. He hung himself from the bars. I don't know why he did it – I'd spoken to him a couple of times but you don't get too close to anyone in prison."

Apart from the half-hour allowance to watch television each day, Michael spent some of his time writing letters to family and friends. "I'd write lots of personal letters, expressing regret for the grief I'd caused them, which was good, even if I didn't end up actually posting all of them. It was something to occupy time," he recalls.

"My parents, Janet and the kids all came to see me. I'm glad the kids came, although I wouldn't have wanted to put them through it any more than I did.

Some mates also dropped in. I received a lot of letters from people in speedway – fans, mostly – telling me to keep my chin up. They would say nice things like 'you're really a nice person and probably don't deserve this', when I knew that I did deserve it. And then they would go, 'you'll come out the other side better for it' but when I came out nothing changed for a while.

"Still, it was nice that people remembered me, although you don't want to think about people or things happening on the outside because that's when you start struggling to cope with whatever it is you're missing.

"The worst times were after visits. The feeling of going back to the cell was one of complete emptiness. It was horrible, you almost reached the point where you felt it would be better to have no visitors at all. You'd try and put on a brave face and appear happy when, inside, you weren't happy. It wasn't easy."

Towards the end of his sentence, Michael requested a move from A-Wing to the more docile C-Wing at Norwich, which he recognised as the right path towards his eventual transfer to the open prison at Hollesley Bay in Suffolk, where prisoners who commit much less serious crimes are sent. It was there that he was reminded of his speedway past when he spotted Kevin Teager, the former Ipswich, Crayford and Hackney rider, who was working there as a prison officer.

"C-Wing is a drug-free wing, unlike A-Wing which is as rough as guts and is the place where all the unruly remand prisoners are held. Even though they drug-tested me on three occasions and I came up negative each time, the screws knew I smoked dope because they could smell it in my cell.

"They told me that my best chance of applying for a transfer to an open prison was to get myself on C-Wing and prove to them that I wasn't using drugs and was therefore less likely to re-offend. And that's what I did. I stopped taking drugs for about three weeks while I was still on A-Wing and then stayed clean for the month I spent on C-Wing. I went from there to M-Wing – supposedly the 'open' part of Norwich – for the next couple of weeks and then I got my move to Hollesley Bay, where I served the last two-and-a-half months of my sentence.

"At Hollesley Bay I worked in the greenhouse and the packing shed for a while. The tomatoes, potatoes, swedes and other farm produce they grew off the land were not just for the prison itself, but were supplied to other places. We used to have a bit of fun when we packaged up the cucumbers and courgettes. Before they were all packed and sent off to Holloway women's prison, we'd cut the ends of one or two in the shape of a big bell-end – 'that's one for the girlies in the prison!' we'd all laugh.

"Because Hollesley Bay is an open prison and everything is more relaxed compared to tougher places like Norwich, we didn't have to brew our own stuff – we had our alcohol smuggled in. Nothing too excessive, though. I probably had five or six bottles of vodka while I was there.

"People on the outside would throw stuff over fences or tractor drivers would be used as couriers to bring us back things that were strategically hidden in nearby fields, at a marker point.

"One day, they asked six of us to rebuild a fence in a field and to get there we had to walk through Hollesley village. We had to walk right past a pub and it was a killer not being able to pop in for a pint. Even the screw who was accompanying us wanted a drink but it was more than his life was worth to let us enter that pub.

"But I did get to spend three Saturdays at home with my family, on what they call a 'Home Visit'. It was weird coming out at 6.30 in the morning knowing you had to go back to prison again at 5.00pm that night."

Like most subjects, Michael has strong, thought-provoking opinions on the prison system and his insights will be illuminating to some.

"Prison certainly doesn't do what it's supposed to do – it doesn't really reform many prisoners," he claims. "Some people do courses to show willing but there are certain others in there who will just keep going back. While I was there, I saw some people go in and out 10 times.

"Don't get me wrong, there are obviously good reasons to have prisons because some people deserve to be locked away for a long time. But for other offences, prison isn't the answer. It might keep them off the streets and stop them from committing a crime for a few years, but if it's in your head that you're going to come out and carry on doing what you did before on the outside, then spending time in prison will just teach those people better ways of going about their criminal activities. Prisoners talk amongst themselves about better methods and how to avoid detection, and what goes on in there is pretty manic really.

"It's also wrong the way they imprison people who are clearly mentally unstable and put them among others who abuse them and make them much worse. One young bloke in his early 20s honestly thought he was Jesus. He didn't eat for days on end and I tried to help, by putting food aside for him, because I felt sorry for him. I'm not a bad person and I felt for this kid but he was past helping.

"He wasn't too bad when he first came in, fairly intelligent, but in the end he just sat on the edge of his bunk, rocking backwards and forwards. He was a lost soul who needed help but all the other prisoners and screws ever did was laugh at him or ignore him. When he had an argument with someone who was taking the piss out of him, all they did was take him down to solitary confinement.

"While he was there they injected him with powerful drugs to supposedly numb him out and calm him down, but the medication made him even worse. Prison was sending him completely the wrong way. When he came back after five days in solitary, it really hurt me to see the state he was in. He was a bit of a strange character but nowhere near as disturbed as when he left.

"I think he was only due to be in prison for two months for something trivial but the guy didn't even last a month. They took him off to an asylum in the end.

"To see what happened to him in just two months, you felt grateful for being fairly stable. For people who are not stable, it ain't a good place to be.

"I'm not proud of having gone to prison but it was certainly a big experience in my life. Not one I'd like to do again, but it taught me so much about people, the system, the functions of life and also about myself.

"I realised that you're never as badly off as you may think you are – there is always someone worse off than you in prison, like the example I gave with that boy who lost his mind. You realise that you do have a life and it's what you make of it.

"You can also meet interesting people in prison and they're not all villains – well, yes they are, but you know what I mean. I met one nice guy who raced greyhounds at Mildenhall. He got nine years for smuggling cocaine from Spain. He was about 65-years-old and I spent a lot of time with him in his cell chatting about all kinds of things.

"One young bloke, in his early 20s, honestly thought he was Jesus. He didn't eat for days on end and I tried to help, by putting food aside for him, because I felt sorry for him. I'm not a bad person and I felt for this kid but he was past helping."

"You see some pretty gruesome things in there and it wakes you up to what goes on in society, how people behave and, in a way, it can give you more understanding as well. Don't think it's all low life in prison. Jeffrey Archer was at Hollesley Bay – not at the same time as me – but I was disgusted at the privileges it was rumoured he received while he was there."

The last 18-month spell Michael spent in prison only hastened the end of his 25-year relationship with Janet. Michael says: "She gave me a hard time while I was inside and was going to leave me, which I thought was quite nasty. You do feel very lonely and insecure in prison and the only thing you have to hang on to is what is waiting for you on the outside. So that was emotionally very tough.

"We kind of got through that period, although I knew things were never going to be right between us again.

"I tried to go straight and, within reason, I did. But prison didn't stop me taking drugs and if I could make a buck here and there, then I did. But I did try to do the right thing. I'd only sell the bare minimum I needed for me and the family to survive and I'd only deal with the most trusting people.

"Barry Klatt, the former Mildenhall promoter, gave me a full-time job working as an electrician and doing groundwork for his construction company. We were contracted to work at all sorts of places and one of my tasks was to lay pipework as drainage for housing estates, as well as fitting electrical cables.

"I worked my nuts off for him for a year but then Barry sacked me. We were working on site at Basildon in Essex for a week and one night I decided to check out the local nightclub – I had mates from down that way and met up with them to score a bit of Charlie. I took Barry's son with me for company but, of course, we didn't get in until about 3.00am and it was 10 o'clock before I got up to start work, still charged up on the coke.

"Barry came into work that morning and sacked both me and his son on the spot. He told us to find our own way home, so I had to catch a train from Basildon to Harlow, then on to Bishop's Stortford and home.

"I'd managed to put a few quid away during that year – about £2,500 – but it meant scrimping on a lot, which Janet didn't like. We'd gone from a life of luxury before the drugs raid on the bungalow to living like paupers. I'd talked her out of leaving me while I was in prison and though we persevered for about another 18 months after I came out, that was it. It wasn't working.

"I think it was in the last week in January that I drove out to Czecho with Chris Louis for three days to pick up some cheaper Jawa spares. When I came home on the Monday night, I found our house on the Red Lodge estate almost totally empty. Janet had left me and taken virtually everything – even the curtains on the windows had gone!

"I got a call from Stoney's dad, Bryan, asking if I was interested in helping them and becoming part of their GP set-up. To me, that was like a Godsend and I jumped at the chance. It was the perfect opportunity to regain my reputation as a tuner."

"At first I don't think I wanted to admit to myself what was really going on. I went upstairs and saw that she'd even taken the bloody quilt off the bed! The heating was turned off, so it was cold, too.

"By the following morning it had sunk in – and this time I didn't even bother to chase after her or try and find out where she was living. After 25 years, I knew that was the end of it. I was pretty down and depressed at the time but I told myself that I was going to start a new life."

Val Lee recalls: "I got a phone call. He said: 'Mum, I've come back to an empty house'.

"They used to go at it like cat and dog and they both have to take responsibility for the break-up. I had a reasonable relationship with Janet but she could be very jealous. With all the travelling Michael did in his career, he obviously had girls chasing after him and Janet used to feel put out that she was left stuck at home with the kids. 'I know the feeling, I've been through it too,'

I'd tell her. And I can remember her saying to me: 'Yes, and look at you and Andy – you've parted company, haven't you?' It's always difficult for the women when their men are often away for days and weeks on end.

"You couldn't blame Janet for them splitting up in the end. She'd put up with things. She had been off before and they got back together again, but in the end she just disappeared," Val said.

"It was in 2000 that I took the opportunity to go back to tuning speedway engines," says Michael. "Dad let me use his garage at the house in Melbourn, which he still had kitted out, and after about three months work really started to pick up. That's when I started to help Carl Stonehewer, who became the first second division (Premier League) rider to qualify for the Grand Prix series.

"The tools and facilities Dad had weren't adequate enough to cope with all the work I had on but, fortunately, Tim Woodward, the former team sponsor at Ipswich, offered to let me use his workshop on farm land near Stowmarket rent-free. As well as 'Stoney', Lol Hare and Savalas Clouting also became regular customers of mine.

"Tim then offered me all the equipment already in place at his workshop. It had belonged to the American tuner Carl Blomfeldt but as he'd just gone back to the States, I was able to buy it from him. I was chuffed to bits to have a proper workshop with a lathe and everything else I needed to do the job properly.

"I went with 'Johnno' (Steve Johnston) to the GP Challenge in 1999 that Stoney came in third to hand him a Grand Prix slot. Johnno and Stoney were mates and although we got chatting, the possibility of me tuning Carl's engines was not even spoken about. But through that winter, I got a call from Stoney's dad, Bryan, asking if I was interested in helping them and becoming part of their GP set-up. To me, that was like a Godsend and I jumped at the chance. It was the perfect opportunity to regain my reputation as a tuner."

Stonehewer became the pride of the Premier League. The Workington star, Comets' all-time appearance record holder, proved his qualification for the 2000 GP series was no fluke by winning the right to be there again in both 2001 and 2002. During this same peak period of his long career the Mancunian racer was also called up by Great Britain for three consecutive World Cup Finals, winning a silver medal in 2000. He was also among the first Brits to ride regularly in the Polish and Swedish leagues from the start of the new millennium.

"We had a really successful time," continued Michael."My view on Stoney is that he was a very talented rider who never actually achieved his full potential. For a Premier League rider to win a place in the Grand Prix and entertain, which is what's it's all about, and also beat bloody good riders, was tremendous. He was a proper character, too. Stoney stayed in the GPs for three years and did far better than anyone could have imagined. And I was with him throughout most of that period."

The Kids are All Right

The inside story

Chapter 28

A BRIGHT, intelligent and articulate young man, Jordan Lee doesn't blame the break-up of his parents' marriage or his father's drug-fuelled lifestyle for the problems he himself got into in his late teens.

The personable 26-year-old talks with a maturity beyond his years when he recalls the wild days in the big bungalow at Holywell Row, where his Dad would entertain endless friends and run a drugs empire that sustained his family in a luxurious lifestyle before he was busted.

"We never had a bad upbringing," says Jordan, the second eldest of the Lee children who works as a window fitter for A&B Glass in Sudbury, Suffolk. The others are Jody (30), Kurt (22) and daughter Mikaela (20).

"We lived in a nice, big place and always seemed well off," Jordan continued. "There was an acre of land in front of the house for us to play in and another 20 acres or so in a field behind the bungalow where the stables were. There was always plenty of food in the fridge and the cupboards."

One of Michael's few regrets is that his children were exposed to his drug-taking activities in the family home. If it did leave any psychological scars, Jordan certainly doesn't show any.

"I wouldn't change a thing about how we were brought up. I think Dad is right in saying that his behaviour and what happened at home was quite educational for us in a way. I consider myself to have been quite a lucky teenager and I remember being more street-wise than my mates."

"I was quite oblivious to what was going on with the use of drugs at the bungalow until I was about 13-years-old," he says. "There was always a party atmosphere at home in the evenings when Dad's friends would come over. Sometimes a couple of men would visit, other times there would be only one and on other occasions couples would be over.

"During the day, the four of us kids would be at school, while Mum also worked at a local school as a learning support assistant.

"As far as I remember, Mum didn't show any resistance to what was happening but she tended to stay out of the way. She always made visitors feel welcome, though. There would be the odd occasional flare-up between our parents, when Dad's mind wasn't always where it should have been.

"But I wouldn't change a thing about how we were brought up. I think Dad is right in saying that his behaviour and what happened at home was quite educational for us in a way. I consider myself to have been quite a lucky teenager and I remember being more street-wise than my mates."

Thankfully, most of us can only imagine how painful it must be to visit a loved one, especially a parent, in prison and Jordan admits it was difficult when he, along with his two brothers and sister, would travel the 40-plus miles to Norwich and back to see their Dad during his 18-month spell behind bars.

"It was hard to go to the prison and see your Dad, knowing he wouldn't be coming home with you and instead had to go back to his empty cell. Jody and Kaela probably handled it better than me and Kurt."

"It felt very strange and awkward. Mum took us to visit him two or three times and on other occasions one or two of Dad's friends drove us there," he recalls. "But it was hard to go to the prison and see your Dad, knowing he wouldn't be coming home with you and instead had to go back to his empty cell. Jody, the eldest, and Kaela, the youngest, probably handled it better than me and Kurt."

Jordan spoke of his parents' split and, despite all the initial bitterness and heartache, he believes it has been for the best.

"It was awkward for everyone after Mum and Dad split up. When he got busted, she suddenly had a lot of time to herself to think and she realised that she didn't need him anymore. She could cope on her own, although times were a bit tougher for Mum financially when the five of us had to move from the semi-detached in Red Lodge to a flat above a shop in Mildenhall town centre.

"To be honest, though, our parents needed to split up. They have both moved on and are now much happier in their lives."

Within seconds of talking to him Jordan reminded me so much of Michael in that he is lucid and not afraid to open up about his personal feelings and problems that have affected him, even those of his own making.

"Dad and I are quite alike in many ways, so we would clash a lot," he admits. "When I was 15 I went to work for him for about a year in the workshop he had at Grandad's place in Melbourn. I've always worked, right from the age of 13 when I helped out at the go-kart track in Red Lodge in the evenings and at weekends I did landscape gardening.

"One of the reasons Dad and I clashed was because I wanted to have a go at speedway myself but he wasn't keen on it. Even if I went through the safety fence, at least I could say that I've had a go. He has since explained to me that he didn't encourage me to ride because he didn't like the way speedway was going.

"We had a big fall-out when I moved out from Mum's place and I went to live in Cambridge. As teenagers do, I was going out a lot with friends and I got myself into a bit of bother. One night, just before my 19th birthday, I was involved in a big fight and the other bloke fell and split his head open. He was OK afterwards but because we'd had a big row previously, the police thought that what happened was premeditated.

"I was basically arrested on an assault charge and sent to the Young Offenders' Institute at Norwich Prison, where I served 15 months.

"I'd been on a downward spiral for a while and Dad and I still weren't really talking at the time either. I did send him out a Visiting Order so that he could come and see me, although I don't even know if he received it."

The catalyst for the long overdue reunion of father and son was Jordan and Donna's marriage in August 2007. Michael's son explained: "I hadn't had any contact with Dad or his side of the family since our fall-out a few years earlier but I went out of my way to send invitations to Dad, Grandad (Andy) and the others and I was really happy when they turned up at the wedding. It was nice to catch up.

"To be honest, our parents needed to split up. They have both moved on and are now much happier in their lives."

"Out of the four of us, I'm the one who has done the most to try and reunite our family. Life is too short. We're not going to be here forever, so I'd rather we all put our past problems behind us and moved on," says Jordan, who has a 22-month-old son called Georgie.

"I think Mum and Dad are both better off since they parted. Mum's definitely happy again now, living in Mildenhall with Kurt and Kaela, and she has a good job as a nursery school teachers' assessor.

"Kurt is now looking for work, having not been home long since returning from travelling in Australia, while Kaela has just finished a two-year university course and is considering taking a gap year.

"Jody works as an engineer building big power units for a firm on the Mildenhall industrial estate. He lives near me at Red Lodge, so we've all come back to our roots."

Of Michael and Janet's four children, Jordan was the only one born outside Cambridgeshire. He arrived on May 30, 1984 in the midst of another traumatic period for the Lee family, who were living in Dorset at the time following Michael's transfer to Poole. He had just been banned following that infamous incident during the Pirates' match at King's Lynn and, sadly, Jordan has never been at the track in person to see his father race.

He says: “I would love to have seen him race but I’ve watched him in action many times on DVD and old video cassettes. I’ve seen the World Finals many times and it shocked me to see how big the crowds were in those days. I go along with him now to Peterborough and Ipswich as often as possible, so I can compare the size of crowds now to how they were in his day.

“I was with Dad at a speedway convention and Chris Harris’ mechanic told me: ‘Your Dad’s a complete legend’. I’m always being told by people how good he was. And I can see from watching the footage of him that he had so much natural talent.

“Out of the four of us, I’m the one who has done the most to try and reunite our family. Life is too short. We’re not going to be here forever, so I’d rather we all put our past problems behind us and moved on.”

“He doesn’t really talk to me about his racing days but now that I’m going over to his place to help out in the evenings, we sometimes speak about what he’s doing with the likes of Tai Woffinden.

“To me, Dad has always been ‘The Motorcycle Man’. I’ve loved motorcycles, too, since I was very small. I was always tinkering with them in the garage, taking bits apart and putting them back together again. Mum tells me that a motor bike is all I ever asked for as a little kid. My parents would tell me they’d get me one if I behaved myself. The trouble was, I was a naughty child and not good at being good!”

But Jordan hasn’t given up hope of following his father and grandfather into two-wheeled motorsport some time soon. He added: “I’m saving up for a moto-cross bike and if I do get one, I will probably have a go on it around Grandad’s track at Elsworth.”

Nicky

The woman who saved Michael

Chapter 29

THERE is no doubt which person deserves most credit, if not all, for Michael's decision to finally give up drugs. The catalyst for his survival, and for helping him get back to where he is in the speedway world today, is Nicky Parry, a former hairdresser from Brandon in Suffolk, who has since changed her name to Lee by Deed Poll.

The couple met by chance at the Red Lodge Inn at Red Lodge on St. Patrick's Day, March, 2001.

She recalls: "Michael was leaning low on the bar and because he also looked really skinny, at first I thought he was a jockey! I'm quite tall, so I thought: 'Nah, he'll be no good for me, but then he stood up and I realised he was around six-foot.

"I was there that night getting drunk with a friend and Mike and I got talking after he'd accidentally knocked me off my bar stool. I'd been divorced for about 10 years and hadn't dated anyone for about nine months when I met Michael that night.

He says: "Being a gentleman, I picked her up from her fall and apologised. She didn't have a clue who I was.

"Actually, there's a funny story behind how we got chatting. Angie, the barmaid, who had been to Ipswich Speedway before, happened to ask me in front of Nicky when I was going to arrange for her and some other pub regulars to go and watch another meeting at Foxhall.

"Nicky overheard my conversation with the barmaid and then started to ask me what I knew about speedway, and I just played dumb. 'Ange' said to Nicky: 'Don't you know who he is?

"Nick obviously didn't, because the next thing she said to me was: 'Anyway, what happened to that Michael Lee – he got himself in a lot of trouble, didn't he?' I just stood there and replied: 'Er, I think he's OK now!'

"When the barmaid confirmed who I was, Nick said: 'Nah, you can't be him, he had long, blond hair'."

Nicky admits: "I told Michael that I couldn't be involved with somebody like him."

He laughs as he continues to recall their early courtship: "After we'd been out together a few times, Nick's Old Man Bill found out about us and he tried to warn her off me. He told her: 'You're not going near him, he's the biggest f****** pot-head in East Anglia!'

"He's a builder and a big fella with great hands like shovels. It took me two months to find the balls to visit Nick's parent's place. When I finally did, Bill sussed me out but he gave me a chance and now I get on like a house on fire with him and Nick's mum, Janice. In fact, it was Bill who built my workshop. He's a proper country boy, straight down the line and calls a spade a spade.

"I've also got something in common with Nick's brother Arthur, who is into road-racing and runs his own little team. He used to work for moto-crosser Mark Banks, so motorcycles are in Nick's family as well as mine."

Nicky admits she could not have fallen for the 'old' Michael. "I'm just a country girl who's never been far and he would probably have made mincemeat of me."

Michael is in no doubt how important Nicky has been to his everyday life.

"It wasn't doing time in prison that made me give up drugs, it was the day I met Nick," he says without hesitation. "Because she is dead straight, I immediately stopped doing everything.

"Nick's Old Man Bill found out about us and he tried to warn her off me. He told her: 'You're not going near him, he's the biggest f**** pot-head in East Anglia!'"**

"I had to save myself first through my own determination to kick the habit. As I said, I'd stopped doing coke three times and went back to it again. And it would have been easy to have gone back to my old ways when I first met Nick because I still didn't have much. I was living in the same house at Red Lodge that my missus had moved out of. I drove around in an old banger, a Sierra, and I didn't have much going for me.

"But Nick was the reason why I stopped doing drugs, so in that sense she did save my life.

"I'd actually done a line of coke before I went out and met her for the first time that night," Michael confesses. "But from the moment we met we virtually spent the next three days together, so that was it. I'd had enough of drugs. For me it was . . . end of.

"We really hit it off straight away – I knew it and I think we both knew it – and I wasn't going to lie to her. I wasn't willing to jeopardise the fact that I wanted to be with her. I certainly wasn't going to do drugs behind her back.

"She knew about my past and once we got chatting she asked me things and I said, 'yeah, I like a smoke', and then I asked her if she did too. She said: 'I've never touched anything and never will', and because of that I thought, 'I'm not going to try and change her, maybe this is my time to change'.

"Nicky had come from a reasonable lifestyle in her previous marriage and her parents are both as straight as a die too. I'm not stupid. I had a choice and had to ask myself: 'What do I want to do here?' I knew I wasn't going to get a second shot at it, so the decision was made there and then.

"I told Nick I'd stopped doing drugs and she laughed at first. But sure enough,

I did stop. I've not had any Charlie for nine years. I've had it put in front of me and people have made me feel 'that big' for not joining in. Sometimes people are like that. If they're doing it, it somehow makes them feel better if you are too, as if that makes it a cool thing. But I tell people now: 'If you put that shit in front of me, I'll blow it everywhere, so don't waste it. Keep it for yourself'.

"I don't object to what others choose to do and I've taken a close look at some people's Charlie. I'm not scared of it in that sense. At one time, because I was one of the best at getting hold of good quality Charlie, and I was able to determine for others the quality of their coke, they would come to me to find out what percentage of purity it was. I knew exactly what it was straight away simply by tasting a little bit.

"I didn't find it a difficult thing to give up drugs – it's all in the head. And I was on a different kind of high after meeting Nick. I'd felt very down after my relationship with Janet had ended but, suddenly, I had a new beginning.

"But from the point of view of drug withdrawal symptoms, there were none."

Nicky says: "I'm not interested in Michael's past, only our relationship now. The last nine years or so have passed quickly and I think I got him at his best, although he's a good man anyway.

"I don't think I could have handled him as he was before. I'd never been involved in speedway, though, so perhaps the fact that we came from different backgrounds and have been used to different lifestyles – me as a normal country girl and him with his 'celebrity' life as a rider – has brought more balance to our relationship. We have fun together – we have our down times, too, Michael can get a bit bossy over his tuning – but we cope well and work things out.

"It used to annoy me when I overheard people talk about how Michael wasted his life and his speedway career because I can see the different talents he has. But it seems quite funny to me when people come up to me and say how he was once their hero.

"I'd actually done a line of coke before I went out and met her for the first time that night. But from the moment we met we virtually spent the next three days together, so that was it. I'd had enough of drugs. For me it was . . . end of."

"From what I know of Mike's riding career, one part of me wishes I would have known him then. On the other hand, would I have been the same person I am now and could I have handled the 'groupie' side of speedway?

"I fell in love with the man, not the speedway rider.

"People say that I changed Michael for the better but it was Michael who changed himself. He has moved on so far in the nine years I've known him and what we've achieved together is unbelievable.

"I've heard people talk about Mike in the same terms as George Best and at first I thought it was quite a fair comparison. But as the years have gone by, the obvious difference between them is that Mike has pulled himself out of trouble, whereas George Best took somebody else's liver from a donor and still killed himself through alcohol abuse."

Soul-mates Michael and Nicky at home in 2005.

When they have any spare time, which is not too often these days due to the demands of the business, Nicky and Michael are both very much into their gardening. Her favourite hobby is topiary and her hanging baskets not only add touches to their landscape garden, but she is regularly being commissioned to make them for others impressed by her handiwork.

Apart from their shared love of gardening, the man of the house is Worlington's answer to Jamie Oliver. His speciality dishes include Thai and Mexican cuisine – made with chillies grown in their garden.

"People say that I changed Michael for the better but it was Michael who changed himself. He has moved on so far in the nine years I've known him and what we've achieved together is unbelievable."

"We also grow peppers, tomatoes, potatoes, cucumbers, sweet corn, brussel sprouts, celery, lettuce, spring onions, runner beans, peas – it's a bit like the Good Life at our place! I love the quality and taste of what we produce, it's so much better than what you buy in the supermarket," he says.

Before setting up his tuning business, Michael considered becoming a restaurateur. He explains: "We seriously looked at opening our own Thai restaurant in Newmarket, before they became all the rage. We were going to go into partnership with Mitch Shirra and his wife Kim but we were gutted to be gazumped on the deal at the last minute. Perhaps it was for the best, though, because unfortunately Mitch and his missus split up six months later."

Michael and Nicky's newly-renovated through lounge provides a reminder of his most triumphant times in speedway, the walls adorned by two large framed FIM World Championship diplomas to mark his victories in the world speedway and long-track titles.

And to remind him that he is now in his early 50s, there are photographs of his four children and two grandchildren, Georgie and Lilly. He says: "The two eldest kids, Jody and Jordan, have a little kid each so, believe it or not, I'm now a proud grandad!"

Nicky, who is just less than five years younger than Michael, has two grown-up sons from her first marriage – Chris, 23, an electrician, and 22-year-old John who plays full-time in an emerging rock band called This Is Colour. They are on the verge of a recording contract and set to tour the USA.

As well as being soul-mates, Michael and Nicky also work very well together running their tuning business, TSR (Team Speedway Racing). While he spends hours on end in the workshop at the end of their long garden, she takes care of everything behind the scenes, handling all the things that Michael is not good at.

"We work very well as a team and bounce off each other," says Nicky. "He does his tuning and I look after the banking, keep the company books up to date and that sort of thing.

"During the season he is often under unbelievable pressure to get all his engine work done. Sometimes he will be in the workshop for 18 hours a day.

"The business has also been good for us in that it has brought other people into our lives – like Len and Hazal at Rye House, Rick and Julie Frost at Peterborough and the Woffinden family, plus others who have become good friends."

Nicky and Michael travel to most speedway meetings together and it's plain to see how much they have enriched each other's lives over the past decade. Michael's parents recognise just how much sunshine Nicky has brought into their son's life.

"Nicky is excellent for him. Very rational, supportive and we're really pleased that Michael found her," says Andy Lee.

"I'd say that Michael and I have got a brilliant relationship now. And Michael and Nicky also get on really well with my partner, Chris, who I've been with for about 20 years, and it's nice when we all get together as a family."

Val Lee says: "I like Nicky, she's a nice woman. She is a good influence on Michael and helps him a lot. They have their moments, like everybody does, but they are good for each other. It's nice that they travel a lot together.

"She has been a big help to him in helping to run the business – they make a good team.

"Even before I got to meet Nicky, I saw a terrific change in Michael. He came over to our place once or twice and said he'd met this new girlfriend. He seemed to have more bounce in his step. He asked if it would be all right to bring her over for a meal and that's when he introduced Nicky to me. It was lovely from the moment she walked in.

"After they had gone, Michael's sister Susan said: 'Nicky is nice – let's hope it lasts' which, touch-wood, it will. I know they are very busy but I'd like to see them get married."

No matter what she says, it was Nicky, first and foremost, who turned Michael's life around. But since then a number of others deserve credit for helping him to regain his self-respect.

Back from the Brink

Earning respect

Chapter 30

NICKY has been the rock behind Michael's renaissance in the past decade but there are numerous others who have helped him in recent years.

Michael is especially grateful to Rye House boss Len Silver, who showed him respect and reopened the door back into speedway for him at a time when he was still feeling uncertain of himself following all that had gone before.

Nicky and Michael went on a winter skiing holiday booked through Len's company Silverski that brought Michael back into contact with the man who sold him his first speedway bike at Hackney in the early 70s.

But it was not until Danny King, one of Michael's first customers after he set up TSR, joined Premier League (second division) Rye House in 2005 that the Rockets' chief first fully appreciated Lee's worth as an emerging tuner trying to rebuild his tarnished reputation in the sport.

Impressed by his work with King, Silver then approached Michael and asked him to take Steve Boxall, another Rye House youngster at the time, under his wing. "Len asked me to help Steve specifically but I was at Rye House every week with Danny anyway and in the end I gave help to other members of the team whenever they needed it. But for Len to actually phone up and ask me to get involved at Rye meant a hell of a lot to me.

"Steve didn't have good equipment but we managed to turn him around and he became a heat leader, which led Len to get me even more involved there.

"He didn't pay me a salary for what I did for Rye House but he gave Nicky and I free skiing holidays in the winter, which was great and we've been regularly ever since. And it's not just Len who has gone out of his way to help me and Nicky and make us feel very welcome. Hazal, his business partner, has also been a great friend to us and I'd do anything for both of them because of what they've done for us."

"You hear different things said about Hazal but as far as we are concerned she is a brilliant woman," says Nicky, who often works behind the bar at the Hoddesdon track while Michael is busy in the pits. "Even now, when Michael has to be with Tai Woffinden at the GPs on a weekend, she fully understands and remains very supportive of us.

"When Len and Hazal gave Michael that job at Rye House, it gave him so much confidence to know that he was back in the speedway fold."

Michael adds: "I have full respect for Len, not only for the way he runs his own show at Rye House, but also for the way he's helped me regain my self-respect. He's old school and by giving me responsibility and recognising what

I could do, he's been a great influence."

The 'new' Michael was one of the first ex-riders to volunteer his services when George Barclay and his wife Linda toured the nation to raise funds to build the National Speedway Museum within Paradise Park at Broxbourne in 2006. An enthusiastic and reformed Lee donated the leathers he wore to win the World Long-track Final and also a World Team Cup racejacket of his to go on display in the museum at a time when few other top riders showed any interest in the project.

Michael hands over his leathers and racejacket to the Speedway Museum.

Of the current day riders, Ipswich skipper and 2009 Great Britain World Cup racer Danny King has been with Lee the longest. King says: "I wouldn't be where I am today in speedway if it hadn't been for Mike. He's been great for me. I went from the Conference League to the Elite League in two seasons and I've upped my average every year.

"He first took an interest in me when I rode for Mildenhall in the Conference League. I think he could see I was having bike problems, so we got talking – he's never too shy to try and help someone out.

"He continued to help me when I was doubling-up between Mildenhall and Rye House in the Premier League and I've been with him ever since. We get on very well.

"People don't realise how closely we work together. No matter where I'm riding, even in Poland or Sweden, I'll phone him for advice and he's always there for me."

Michael recalls one occasion, in particular, a couple of seasons ago when he wasn't actually attending a meeting involving King but still managed to deliver some choice words in his direction that transformed the youngster's fortune on the night.

He explains: "I was watching a televised match at Swindon on Sky and after two rides Danny had no points. To be honest, he was riding like a prat. We'd spoken the day before the meeting about the best way to ride the Blunsdon track but I could see from watching the telly that what we'd spoken about had all gone out the window.

"Then his mechanic, Rob, phoned me on his mobile from the pits. I'm sitting at home watching and I told Rob to tell Danny exactly what I thought – that he was riding like a prat, he should start blaming himself instead of his bike and do the things we'd talked about before.

"What happens? He won his next two races and looked a totally different rider. To be fair, Danny was interviewed by Sky later in the meeting and he mentioned that we'd 'had words' over the phone."

This is where Michael's relationship with most of the riders he works with differs from that of most other engine tuners. They will often be on hand to consult over mechanical matters affecting the engines they've prepared, especially at the Grand Prix rounds, but that's where their relationship with the rider begins and ends.

"I have full respect for Len, not only for the way he runs his own show at Rye House, but also for the way he's helped me regain my self-respect. He's old school and by giving me responsibility and recognising what I could do, he's been a great influence."

With all due respect to them, the likes of Finn Rune Jensen (who tunes for Jason Crump), Brian Andersen (Nicki Pedersen), Brian Karger (Chris Harris) and Jan Andersson (Andreas Jonsson) are never going to try and advise their employers how to ride because none of them ever attained that level of achievement themselves as riders. But Michael Lee was World Champion, so the riders he tunes engines for will listen to what he has to say – or they would be stupid not to.

Danny King says: "Yes, I remember that night at Swindon . . . and Mike was right in what he said too. It must be frustrating for him at times to watch me and know that I should be doing better. I think that's when he can get on his high horse a bit.

"But I will listen to what he has to say because he has been there and done it all himself and he has so much experience. But after we've chatted about what I need to do differently to improve, he is the first to come over and pat me on the back if I put it into practice."

King also revealed Lee's other strengths beyond his skill in the workshop and in the pits on race night when he added: "Mike knows how shrewd promoters can be with their money, so he has also helped me to do deals at the start of the season. He's come along with me to make sure I always get the going rate, so that's another side to him that perhaps people don't always appreciate. He's been like a manager to me.

Man of many parts, Michael advising Ipswich skipper Danny King.

"Mike knows how shrewd promoters can be with their money, so he has also helped me to do deals at the start of the season. He's come along with me to make sure I always get the going rate, so that's another side to him that perhaps people don't always appreciate. He's been like a manager to me."

"Where Mike is also different from most other tuners is that he will always work with a rider to produce what they need to suit them. Most tuners will simply do you an engine, give it back and say 'get on with it'.

"Mike is a very talented guy who is never afraid to try new things. Sometimes he'll ask me to test an engine after a meeting because he is looking for my feedback. We'll then talk and work together to get the best from it.

"I knew Mike when he was first really just starting to get back into tuning and he wasn't one of the biggest names then. But as his reputation has grown I've noticed more and more top riders going to him for advice, including the GP boys."

As well as the Rye House team members and Danny King, the Elite League riders of Peterborough have also benefited from Michael's mechanical knowledge and expertise in more recent times. Lee was a regular in the pits at the East of England Showground through much of 2009, when he helped Danish GP star Niels Iversen, and the following year he was formally appointed as Technical Advisor by Panthers' owner Rick Frost.

"Michael has certainly bolstered our set-up in many ways. He has immense experience and his knowledge of bike set-ups and other mechanical aspects has been invaluable to our team," says Frost, who was himself a world champion in powerboat racing.

"I first knew Michael vaguely when I met him a couple of times through Danny King, who I sponsored at the time, but his reputation as a former World Champion preceded him. I used to drive Formula One powerboats and I think Michael and I soon realised that we shared the same winning mentality, and this created a bond between us that has grown over the past couple of years. We both like to stand back and observe things from a distance rather than dive in.

"If anyone can spot a rider who is on drugs and doing what he shouldn't be, then it's me, because I've been there and I can recognise the tell-tale warning signs. And if I did think any of the riders I was working closely with were 'at it', I'd come down on them very hard."

"It has grown to the point where he and Nicky have become firm friends of me and my partner Julie. You couldn't wish to meet a nicer couple than them."

Frost's love of speedway dates back to the post-war boom years when he visited Wembley and supported Lions' legends such as Freddie Williams and Bill Kitchen, plus visiting stars Jack and Norman Parker. Now Frost is convinced his riders are in safe hands when it comes to technical back-up and advice.

He says: "I trust Michael totally and hopefully he trusts me. He has a very positive contribution to make at Peterborough Speedway because he is completely committed to the cause."

Michael is aware that some people might question why, given his past long association with drugs, he is now in a position of influence with young riders of an impressionable age. In fact, he appeared before Ipswich Crown Court again in November 2007 and pleaded guilty to producing cannabis plants, for which he was ordered to do 160 hours community service and undergo a supervision order. "It was just weed for my own use," he says, explaining why he escaped another prison term.

He counters any argument about the legitimacy of his role among riders today by saying: "If anyone can spot a rider who is on drugs and doing what he shouldn't be, then it's me, because I've been there and I can recognise the tell-tale warning signs.

"And if I did think any of the riders I was working closely with were 'at it', I'd come down on them very hard.

"Drugs are not a good thing, I will say that. I'm working with a lot of youngsters now. Fortunately for them, I can pass information to them and keep them away from what I got into. There's a good bunch of kids out there and hopefully they will listen and learn from me."

Michael still smokes rolled-up cigarettes – 'rolleys' – but they and the occasional can of lager at the end of a long, hard day, is, he says, all he needs to chill out these days.

"I've had to stop smoking anything stronger than rolleys because I'm at speedway three nights a week during the season and I get my buzz from that now," he says. "I'm totally engrossed down the workshop most of the time and it would be no good to me being stoned.

"I'm not saying I'll never smoke cannabis again, because I don't think there is anything wrong with it – and people can take that as they want. I'm not stupid, I know what's good and bad for me.

"Let's be honest, the reason I don't smoke cannabis anymore is because I don't want people to look upon me badly, I've got my reputation to think about and I wouldn't do anything now to jeopardise that or insult the people who have given me these good opportunities."

Woffy's World

Back in the big time

Chapter 31

WHEN the 2010 Grand Prix season roared into life at Leszno, Poland on April 24, there was a familiar face behind the black framed glasses worn by the tall, slim man in the black Tai Woffinden Racing jacket.

The top 16 riders in world speedway were about to begin a season-long battle for the sport's richest prize but it was Michael Lee who was feeling as nervous as anyone in the pits that night.

He'd invested years of hard graft and cash to build up TSR into the reputable business it is today and at last he was back on the big-time international stage, where he spent almost all of his own racing career.

Those memories are part of the dim and distant past. All he's concerned about now is the present and the future. And at Leszno and throughout the 2010 GP campaign, it's all about Tai Woffinden, Wolverhampton's talented 19-year-old skipper.

'Woffy' is one of only two Brits - along with Coventry's Chris Harris – contesting the star-studded series, alongside big-hitters headed by World Champion Jason Crump, plus former title holder Nicki Pedersen, rising Polish star Jarek Hampel, Danes Kenneth Bjerre and Hans Andersen, Russian whizzkid Emil Sayfutdinov, Polish legend Tomasz Gollob, Sweden's Andreas Jonsson, Magnus Zetterstrom and Freddie Lindgren, Australian youngster Chris Holder, veteran American Greg Hancock and Norwegian Rune Holta.

Woffinden was invited to compete in the 2010 series as a 'wild card' entry by the organisers and is not generally expected to threaten the recognised elite title contenders this year. At 19 and having shot from the Conference League to top class in just four years, he still has much to learn and this first season of GP racing is mainly about gaining experience, although naturally he still wants to win every race he is in and his support team do all they can to try and make that happen.

Alongside Woffinden's regular mechanics, Michael attends the GP rounds to keep an eye on how the youngster's machinery is performing and to offer advice and the benefit of his experience. Another former rider, Louis Carr, who asked Michael to help him with his work for the British Speedway Under-15 Academy earlier in the decade, is also a familiar figure in the Woffy camp.

Michael was very disappointed that the work he and Carr put in with the young Brits all those years ago was largely undone when the authorities turned to alternative 'managers', but the GP series is recognition that Lee still has very much to offer.

Michael and Tai Woffinden on the Grand Prix stage in 2010.

Speedway Star editor Richard Clark, a regular in the GP press box, isn't surprised to see Michael's presence at speedway's top table again after all these years.

"No, I'm not," says Clarkie, "because he's an intelligent man. And he knows what he does best. Get him talking about speedway – and it's not Michael's style to hold court like that – and you quickly realise he knows more than I ever will.

"Maybe he's 'wasted' – that word again – that knowledge in the past. But, where he is at this moment in his life, he's still got huge amounts to offer, if anyone's prepared to listen. And he's out there offering just that."

But, unlike the other tuners who congregate in the pits, Michael is also there as a hands-on mentor to young Tai, advising him on track conditions, race tactics and, just as importantly, to try and rebuild confidence when results don't match his own hopes and expectations. Many speedway races are won in the head and Lee knows it.

But it's a learning curve for everyone involved in Tai Woffinden Racing and for Michael, it's a challenge he relishes. His hardest, most important work is done in the days and weeks between GP rounds (when he also has to keep on the JRM engines Tai uses for his domestic meetings in England, Poland and Sweden, as well as those of his growing list of other regular customers such as Danny King).

"I'm probably doing work for about 15 different riders now, which means taking care of around 60 engines," says Michael, looking exhausted after another long slog in the workshop. He knows he doesn't quite have the facilities to match the top tuners who have been operating at GP level for years but no-one can match him for experience and dedication.

"In an ideal world, I'd charge more and earn my money from just five or six riders but this is the way it is and I don't like letting anybody down," he says.

Engine tuning in speedway is a vulnerable business. None of the riders Lee tunes for is under contract to him, they are free to switch tuners at the drop of a sprocket, so relationships are built on mutual trust – and results.

"I know that if I don't do the business, then people will take their engines elsewhere. It's the nature of the beast. But I put a lot of hard work into it and I expect the same from them in return.

"I like working with riders who have the same hunger and desire to win that I had at their age. I always hated losing and I like to see that same attitude in the people I'm working with now and in the future."

"I like working with riders who have the same hunger and desire to win that I had at their age. I always hated losing and I like to see that same attitude in the people I'm working with now and in the future."

With Woffinden, though, there is also a huge emotional attachment. Michael has been tuning Tai's motors since his Premier League days with Rye House in 2007, not long after the kid left his birthplace in Perth, Western Australia to follow in his father Rob's tyre tracks into the British leagues.

Rob Woffinden was not a big star when he rode in the 80s, he didn't possess the same natural talent as his son, but he had a massive heart and is fondly remembered as one of the great characters of the old National League, where he made his name with Scunthorpe, Middlesbrough, Sheffield and Boston before retiring and emigrating to Australia with his wife Sue in the mid-90s.

'Woffy' senior was the driving force behind Tai Woffinden Racing and remained totally dedicated to it right up until his tragic death, aged 47, on January 30, 2010 after a courageous year-long battle against incurable cancer. He is sadly missed by all who knew him – and especially by Michael and Nicky Lee who became close friends of the Woffindens.

"I still can't believe Rob's gone," says Michael, the sadness audible in his lowered voice. "He wasn't only Tai's Dad and obviously the man who was driving TWR forward all the time, he was a great mate of mine and his loss has been a shattering blow. I feel absolutely gutted about it, so I can only imagine how hard it's been for Tai."

Nicky says: "Rob was such a good communicator and made everyone in the team feel a part of it.

Watching Woffy's back, Michael and Tai viewing from the pits.

"In the hours before he died, he wrote a lovely letter addressed to Michael and me which we got three days after he passed away. It was heartbreaking and it took us three weeks before we were strong enough to read every word of it all the way through."

"It doesn't matter who you talk to about Rob, whether it's someone he knew from his racing days or a person he met him for the first time last year, everyone just says what a nice person he was.

"I'll never forget the day he came here for the first time. Mike was down the workshop and I was working on the computer at that time. All of a sudden, the back door opened and this total stranger, unshaven and with his hair all ruffled, walked into the house – no knock or anything – and he just smiled at me with his gold tooth showing and said: 'G'day, Nick, I'm Woffy, can I put the kettle on?' And that was it – what a character.

"Last year, he still wanted to go to all of Tai's meetings even though he wasn't well enough most of the time and he knew, like we all did, that he only had a short time to live. He and I would spend most of the night sitting in his car, which had a telly, and we'd spend hours nattering about nothing. We obviously got into deep conversations, too, about Sue and Tai and what he wanted for them both.

"It was lovely talking with him like that. And when he came to see Mike, he'd spend half-an-hour in the house chatting to me before Michael even knew he was here. He'd even help to organise our home improvements. Rob was my best friend and I miss him terribly.

"In the hours before he died, he wrote a lovely letter addressed to Michael and me which we got three days after he passed away. It was heartbreaking and it took us three weeks before we were strong enough to read every word of it all the way through.

"In it, Rob apologised for, in his words, 'dumping TWR on us' and basically thanked us for all that we'd done for Tai and the family, and wished us good luck in the future.

"Sue didn't even know he had written the letter and she found it the day after he died.

"He works unbelievably hard, putting in a lot of hours in the workshop that others might not appreciate. I know that I could take him an engine tonight and it would be ready to use the next morning."

"He totally trusted Michael to look after Tai after he'd gone and that's why I like to go and watch Tai ride as often as possible."

Michael says: "Rob gave us a lot of trust to do what we thought was the best for Tai and we promised him we'd look after his son after he was gone. I know how much hard work Rob put into getting Tai's career off the ground and although I'm committed to helping him all I can, I will obviously never be able to replace Rob or do what he did for his son."

Given the pressure of being under the spotlight in the GP series, where each of the 11 rounds is screened live in homes all over the world, the death of his father on the eve of the 2010 season has thrust even more weight on his young shoulders.

He is, though, very glad of all the support he receives from Michael. Woffinden says: "I didn't really know who Michael was or what he'd done in speedway when I first met him at Rye House. Glyn Taylor had tuned my engines for a couple of months and then Dad looked after my bikes until we went with Mike.

"As I've moved up through my career I've made him even busier but he always responds very well. We talk after each meeting about how the engines performed and whether anything needs to be altered to make them go faster. He is constantly looking for ways to improve.

"He will give me engines to use and not tell me what he's done to them, because he's waiting to see what I think and get feedback from me. I might say: 'It's pulling good off the corner' and he'll say 'yep, that's what I set it up to do', so we have constant communication in that way.

"Dad used to be the one to talk to Mike about my engines before and after my meetings but since he passed away I've got more involved in that side of the business.

"I like to know what's inside my engines, the different cams we use for various size tracks and so on, and Mike's good in that he trusts me with this information. He knows I won't take what he's done for me and give it to another tuner.

"He works unbelievably hard, putting in a lot of hours in the workshop that others might not appreciate. I know that I could take him an engine tonight and it would be ready to use the next morning."

Tai continues: "He works well with my regular mechanics and with Michael, everything has to be perfect. He is 100 per cent professional. He's been through it all and done it himself.

"As a person, he's a really cool and chilled out, and we've become really good friends. We have a great relationship."

Despite his rich promise, Tai Woffinden has a long, long way to go before he achieves what Michael Lee did in speedway and very few will ever get that far. But if he does, no-one will be more delighted for him than Michael himself.

Lee says: "I know how tough the first few months of this season have been for Tai but when he won his first-ever GP race at Prague, I don't mind admitting I had a tear in my eye."

When All's Said and Done

Final thoughts

Chapter 32

THE criminal justice system has delivered its verdict on Michael Lee in the past and the speedway authorities did, too, back in 1984. Everyone seems to have an opinion on the rider generally regarded as the most controversial World Champion ever, so what lasting impressions has he left on many of the people who know him best?

Why did it 'all go wrong' for the wonderkid who once had the speedway world at his feet? We all have our own thoughts and opinions obviously vary. Here many of those who have kindly contributed to this book delivered their own personal summing up of this former track giant.

Cyril Crane remembers a "terrific young rider" at Boston who soon had the speedway world at his feet but kicked it away. He says: "Michael was the most naturally talented rider England has ever had. I believe he could have gone on and equalled Ivan Mauger's record of six world titles.

"With all the talent and ability he had, Michael should be a millionaire now," Crane added.

Also from the King's Lynn management perspective, Martin Rogers says: "As a kid and indeed pretty much through his teenage years, Michael was for the most part a delight. (And Lin and I also especially enjoyed the company of Andy and his then wife Val). Unfortunately, while lots of teenagers have a rebellious few years and then wake up to themselves, Michael seemed to do things in reverse and from a speedway perspective, just became more and more of a worry as time went by.

"Most of the time, off the track, he still came across as a nice, polite, mostly measured individual and he still does. For some people he could never do any wrong. But elite performers in any industry inevitably are judged by their performance in that particular area of their life as much, if not more, than the 'private' version.

"On his own admission he did bring some of his troubles upon himself. While he bravely says it was all his own doing, I still think he got some poor advice before making some of those life choices. Sport, however, is a tough gig, so much more so than most people who have never been actively associated with it can begin to imagine, and speedway has never been in the top echelon of sports when it comes to duty of care or guiding young people."

Former Ipswich and England boss John Berry says: "At the age of 14, Michael's life was full of bikes and engines and racing when other lads of the same age were getting on with their school work and letting off steam at weekends. Michael was so busy being a child prodigy he didn't have time to be an adolescent teenager as well.

"Michael was a great kid. He had no bad side, was a pleasure to deal with, was highly professional and had a great manner. I liked him a great deal. I still do. This was in the glory years for Ipswich and I had no need to covet the lad, but I would have loved to have had him riding for me.

"He was close to being the best speedway rider I ever saw and should be enjoying the luxury lifestyle and accolades many of his less talented peers currently enjoy.

"I just hate what happened to him. His racing record stands up for itself. It shows a lad of unbridled talent, dedication and determination to reach the top. Those who saw him at his best simply accept there was nobody like him and that he developed a style entirely his own which has never been copied since.

"Those who raced against him have no bad words to say. He won his races purely by going faster than the other riders, not by over-aggressive riding. He was just an outstanding talent with pretty well no enemies among his peers.

"Michael was a breath of fresh air to the sport. He was a really nice, albeit easily led, bloke and in his short reign he served England proud. Some would have it that he damaged the image of the sport, and this might be true, but it seems to me the only one who was ever really seriously damaged was himself.

"He denies it was the drugs that caused him to lose his way. He prefers to blame his fall from grace on speedway in general and certain people in particular. Well, he would, wouldn't he!

"For me, it was simply a case of a young man with the world at his feet but not being worldly-wise enough to cope. Michael Lee was the George Best of speedway, or any number of overnight stars in the pop music business who couldn't handle the lifestyle and self-destructed.

"There is a whole cottage industry behind young pop stars and footballers these days, helping them cope with the pressures. Michael had none of those things. Looking back, you have to wonder not so much why things went haywire for him, but why it took so long.

"We haven't run across each other for maybe 30 years, but I still think the world of him. I am absolutely thrilled to hear the now mature Michael has a settled lifestyle. He is a smashing bloke and a great person who simply wasn't mature enough to cope with his enormous success at such a young age."

Michael's former Poole boss Reg Fearman has few kind words to say about Michael after the traumas of 1984 but he admits: "He was the most natural and talented speedway rider of his time – what a waste."

One who does appreciate Michael's efforts for Poole in the early 80s is his ex-Pirates team-mate Neil Middleditch. "The first time I saw Michael ride was in a practice session at Peterborough when he was a young teenager and I was just starting. You knew straight away this lanky kid was something special.

"What might have been if not for the ban, nobody will know, but if you saw 'Mike The Bike' ride you knew you were watching something a little special.

"It was an honour to count him as a friend and team-mate. I once said to Michael if he could give me his talent for one year, I'd make him a lot of money.

"Mike was a great team-mate. We had some wonderful times at Poole, on and off the track, and to watch Michael on a bike was brilliant. He was everything a speedway rider shouldn't be – tall and gangly – but he was a pleasure to watch. Some of the moves he pulled on the track were truly amazing.

"Yes, I think he wasted some opportunities over the years – but hell, he had a great time! Does he regret some things? I think, deep down, maybe a few, but the good times far outweighed the bad."

Lee's former team-mates and rivals recall his class and his integrity on the track. Phil Collins says: "I remember once passing Michael on the outside at King's Lynn and he was always safe and fair and square to race against. He's just a decent man and I don't have a bad word to say about him.

"His meteoric rise was probably what caused his downfall. Hangers-on would want to take him off into different directions and maybe he didn't cope with that side of it as well as he could have.

"By comparison, my brother Pete's rise to the top was a lot slower and he had more time than Mike to appreciate how hard it was to reach his goals."

Doug Wyer, Michael's British Lions captain in Australia, says: "I have watched speedway for a long time. I raced for 20 years myself, so I know just how hard it is to get to the top. I've seen all the World Champions during that era and they were all at the top of their game when they had the title. Some had it more than once but Michael had his day too. He was the champion, he was fit, fast and fearless. Today people would say that he had the X factor but most of us back in the late 70s and early 80s knew that anyway.

"He had a great career. Yes, he made a few mistakes along the way and he paid the price. That's life.

"Michael was a friend and still is today. We don't see each other very often these days but the last time I bumped into him at a meeting, we had a long chat about the good times we had together, especially on those tours Down Under.

"He was a character then and he still is today. I wish him well."

Lee's former long-serving mechanic Dennis Hicks, now 79 and still employed at King's Lynn Speedway on the pit gate, remembers happy days with the World Champion: "Working with Michael took me to thousands of places I would never otherwise have seen, so I'm very grateful to him. I've been connected with King's Lynn more or less since the track opened in 1965 and I'm still involved there today. If you ask me who the all-time greatest Lynn rider was, I'd have to say Terry Betts. But Michael is a very close second."

Asked if he thought it was a pity that many people will remember Michael more for his off-track lifestyle and problems rather than for the superb rider he undoubtedly was, *Speedway Star's* Richard Clark said: "Definitely. When I watched the DVD recently released about Michael, it brought home what a fantastic rider he was, and I told him so when I bumped into him in Leszno for the first Grand Prix of 2010."

Reunited and proud, Andy with Michael in 2010.

Given all the tremendous success Michael compressed into his seven or eight years at the very top, does Clark go along with the common perception that Lee 'wasted' his career?

"He was World Champion, and we all know, or can reel off, hundreds of riders who never reached that pinnacle. So, even from that historic perspective, you'll never be able to deny his right to that title. So the 'waste' aspect is what he allegedly threw away to lead the life he chose.

"I can understand it when some argue it was a waste because there have been many great, great riders who never got to enjoy what he achieved.

"Historically, though, he's going to be referred to, more often than not, as 'that World Champion who went astray'.

"I simply feel privileged I was around when he was in his pomp and was able to witness him first-hand, as a supporter and, later, reporter. I saw him ride for King's Lynn, Poole and England frequently. I was at Gothenburg in 1980 – some great, great memories."

Clarkie will be the first to agree that Michael was always very well liked by the pressmen who covered speedway throughout his career – and certainly not just because he gave us so many juicy stories and headlines!

"From a reporter's point of view, he was always so easy to deal with," continues Richard. "But, funnily enough, I don't think Michael and I had that many dealings during his racing career to be honest. I think that was because I was relatively new on the scene at the time, so those with more experience would have handled the 'big guys'.

"But, I do know I always found him friendly and approachable. And, nowadays, that hasn't changed.

"He also has a very lively, inquiring mind, a great sense of humour – qualities I enjoy in others and, it's fair to say, he's the sort of person I know I'll always feel relaxed around. We don't spend much time together at all, but I do know I'd enjoy it if we did."

Some of Michael's revelations in this book concerning the extent of his use of drugs, and especially his admission that he became a very active dealer himself, will probably shock and dismay many. But in terms of brute honesty, no-one involved in speedway has laid bare their life in quite the same 'warts and all' manner that Michael has here. But I wonder if, by talking so openly about his past use of drugs away from speedway, he makes himself an even bigger target for criticism?

Richard Clark says: "No, far from it. That's his choice, but the good thing about the way criticism arrives on your front doorstep nowadays is it's in the ether, and the ether is the easiest thing in the world to ignore. If you don't want to absorb the views, opinions or rants of the internet community, you don't have to. I could never quite grasp why Mary Whitehouse didn't use the television switch that either changed the channel or turned it off completely. I'm on to either of those in a flash when EastEnders appears on the screen, or any politician."

And Clark doesn't subscribe to the common comparison between Lee and football's most famous 'bad boy' George Best.

"No I don't, or at least not entirely. George appeared to be haunted by very specific demons and to the very end. All I've ever read about him suggests the downward spiral was as much to do with the hangers-on surrounding him, as it was his own fault. Only those enjoying his company at the time will ever really know.

"I'm not so sure Michael would have been so easily led. I think he chose a certain lifestyle and, if it didn't conform with what others considered 'normal' – whatever that means – then hard luck.

"And I think that's still part of him to this day.

"The only similarities I've ever drawn when I've had conversations about this in the past are that George Best, Jimi Hendrix, Jack Kerouac, Scott Fitzgerald, Michael and anyone else you care to name have, in the eyes of some, 'wasted' the gift they were given.

"But would they have achieved what they did had they been different, perhaps more stable, personalities? Would those gifts have been so pronounced?

"I'm a huge Hendrix fan. I'm sad he only managed three official studio releases during his lifetime but those three albums remain amongst the greatest as far as I'm concerned. My enjoyment as a fan hasn't been lessened."

Another journalist, Randall Butt, says: "Michael is a regular visitor to Mildenhall Speedway these days and I'm hugely impressed with the way he's battled back after prison to play a major role in the sport as a mechanical man, and aid for the likes of Tai Woffinden. Also very impressive is that speedway did not turn its back on him, but allowed and helped him regain his self respect."

It's interesting to see how Michael's parents reflect on his life and times.

Andy Lee agrees with John Berry's view when he says: "I believe he did miss out on an awful lot. Speedway became serious too quickly for him and he was too young. His whole social life revolved around speedway, which wasn't ideal.

He didn't have a let-off valve because he knew nothing else.

"Sure, he had girlfriends from time to time but always within the framework of speedway. Whether that's why he went off the rails, I doubt, but it's a part of his life that he missed.

"I know from my own point of view because I had three years in the RAF. And those three years were an enjoyable period – a time of learning, going out and, yeah, a few drinks, and all the things you did in the forces. It really did me good. But Michael missed out on all of that and it certainly wasn't a good thing.

"But we've been surrounded by motorcycles our whole lives. When Michael wanted to do moto-cross, it was no problem because I had a bike there for him to ride – he didn't have to go looking for one.

"I don't ride a motorcycle these days – just in case I'm tempted to ride again. I'm 75 this year and I've had some health problems, so I don't think it would be very wise of me to ride. I suffered a stroke a few years ago – only a minor one, from which I think I've fully recovered. Then, about 18 months ago, I had a quadruple heart bypass, but my heart was good so it was worth doing.

"I didn't sell the business until about 15 years ago. I sold the Royton shop back to the people who originally sold it to me – Pepper and Hayward, who actually went bust. I had a huge offer on the shop in Cambridge. I was 61 when I was approached again by a bloke from Hallens, a local motorcycle company, who had been after it for some years. He pushed me and pushed me and we did a deal.

"Mike was upset that I'd sold it outside the family but, to be honest, at that time, I don't think he would have handled it. I really don't. I had to make a decision and I protected my staff – all 15 of them, some of them even stayed on with the new business – and I think I did the right thing."

Turning to thoughts of Michael and what happened after he quit racing in 1991, Andy says: "It all seems such a long time ago. The main thing is that he's OK now and I'm proud of what he has achieved with his tuning. The fact that he has got himself back into speedway and has made the most of his knowledge and experience to do what he does now is excellent.

"Yes, maybe there were some missed opportunities but who doesn't have those? The fact that he has come through it and is now very much involved in speedway again – at many levels, not just in tuning – is, I think, a wonderful achievement."

But Andy knows that people will always remember his son for some of the things that he did off the track as well as on it.

"I wish they would look upon Michael's achievements on the track without always bringing up the black period," he continues. "I think people are now beginning to think that way and he is still pretty popular, certainly among today's riders of all standards.

"That's what I'd like but it's never going to happen. I could be speaking to someone, who doesn't know who I am and my relationship with Michael, and it still happens at my moto-cross track at Elsworth. Somehow Michael's name will come into the conversation – not because I've mentioned him, but because they have. They might say to me: 'Oh, I knew a Lee who did speedway'. And I'll say: 'No, I'm Andy Lee'. I wait . . . and then all of a sudden they find out and go: 'Oh, he's your son' . . . and the first thing they say next is 'didn't he get into trouble?' I say 'yes, he did'.

"So this is it. Instead of saying 'didn't he get into trouble?', they could have said 'wasn't he a brilliant rider'. That would have done for me.

"But hopefully this book will do Michael some good in that more people will appreciate and understand the depth of what he did in speedway. Riding is obviously the biggest part of what he did in his racing career, but there was more to him than that. The mechanical side of it and his expertise in that field is very important too."

Val Lee has a tough inner-strength, which is probably just as well given all that Michael has put her and Andy through! "I've had to be a bit tough – ever since my mum died when I was 15. I had to cope with life, bringing up a younger brother and looking after a dad who had a broken heart," she says. "I had a stepmother who didn't have any time for me and kicked me out when I was 17."

As well as Michael, Val has also brought up his two sisters, who have talents of their own. She says: "All three got on very well together as kids, and they still do. The girls used to come with me to watch Michael ride.

"Belinda was very successful as a showjumper and in three-day eventing. Her and Sue both rode horses from a young age. Belinda could have done well if she had carried on but she went through secretarial college instead and got a very good job in London. Horse riding then became just a fun thing to do at weekends.

"Belinda and her husband Roy Strudwick have a stud farm at Inistioge, County Kilkenny in southern Ireland, where they breed racehorses. They have 15 horses over here in training, with runners at Newmarket plus tracks in France and Germany.

"They also have homes in London, Majorca and Jersey but because they are tax exiles it makes life difficult for her to come in and out of England.

"Sue did a few horse riding events too but mainly for fun and went into hairdressing instead. She only lives a few miles up the road at Bassingbourn, so I see quite a lot of her."

Michael and his sisters also have an adopted brother, John, now 32. "He was five months-old when I collected him from a home in France and brought him back to England. John calls me 'mum' and I brought him up for more than 25 years.

"The girls have been so good for him and Michael also thinks the world of John. I've got a very good relationship with all my kids."

Val has also had her own health battle to contend with. And she knows the Michael Lee very few others do. "He's a very kind hearted boy and takes things to heart," she says.

Val Lee with her photo albums of Michael's racing career.

"Yes, I'd say he is sensitive. If anyone is in trouble, he's there. When I was diagnosed with cancer a few years ago, I could see that it stressed him – though, touch wood, I'm OK now.

"He will stand up for himself and other people if he thinks they have been dealt an injustice, which is something I think he gets from me.

"I'm there if anyone wants me and they're in trouble. I would never have disowned Michael for what he did.

"Whatever happens, I can face life and I just take each day as it comes.

"I'm proud of what Michael has done in speedway – obviously not the other things in between – but it's great to see him doing what he does now. It's hard work and he can get a bit stressed at times with the tough schedules, but he seems to enjoy it.

"I don't have Sky at home but people say to me: 'I saw your Michael on television, so he's still about then?' I say: 'Yes, he's still about'."

Michael's previous drug-related behaviour led to a three-year estrangement from his father, a rift that is now happily healed. Michael says: "We get on great. We've had a good chat about things and he understands me now.

"When Dad and I fell out it was all to do with me rebelling and going off to do my drug thing, which he disagreed with. I fully understand how he felt.

"Mum has also been a bit disappointed in some ways, and I may have embarrassed her or let her down, but we get on well. In fact, we get on better now than for as far back as I can remember. Although my parents split up, I see both of them regularly and we remain very close."

Michael may not be the millionaire Cyril Crane and others reckon he ought to be, but he has come through a lot, regained his self-respect and found a contentment in his life that often money can't buy.

"I'm certainly not rich – it's not about having money – but I'm happy," he says. "I'm a completely different person to what I was before I met Nick. Anyone outside speedway will tell you that. I'm content with what I have now. I no longer feel that there's something missing in my life.

"People will remember me for what they want. I know there are people who hate me for what I've done and who I am, but it really doesn't bug me anymore what others think. I just wish people would say what they think to my face.

"I don't regret what happened to me in any way at all. It was a big experience in my life and if I had my time over again, I can't say I'd do anything differently. As I said, when I did things, I tended to do them full-on.

"It was nothing to do with the people I mixed with that I became hooked. I wanted to be outside speedway, with a new outlet, because everything I'd done since the age of 14 had revolved around the sport. Perhaps that was my biggest mistake – the fact that I didn't have any other interests in life for so many years. On the other hand, maybe I wouldn't have been as successful at speedway if I hadn't started in it so young and been so obsessed by it? Who knows? I don't think that's the case, though, because I'm a spontaneous person anyway and I always did what I wanted to do."

It's been suggested that a stronger promoter whom Michael fully respected – John Berry has been mentioned – might have forced the young Lee to tow the line more. But knowing what a strong personality JB is too, I can't imagine that Michael would have been more inclined to conform under his regime than any other.

What Michael probably needed was his own 'personal manager', not just a business agent-type to organise his bookings and travel arrangements (though that would have helped ease the pressure on him), but someone he trusted, who understood him and could get through to him and act as a confidant while he was at his peak. But where were the suitable candidates for that role in 1980? I can't think of any.

"I don't think anyone would have kept me in line," says Michael. "I'll never blame anyone, because I've always taken full responsibility for all my actions. I've always done what I thought was right at the time – sometimes in anger, other times in stupidity.

"People say I could've gone on for longer in speedway but it doesn't matter to me that I didn't. I had a bloody good time. It could have gone on for another 10 years, but it didn't.

"I've come through my problems and I've still got a good life. I think some people think I live in a box somewhere or under a brick! A lot of people come round here and say: 'Oh, so you didn't do too badly, then?'

"It's often been said that I could've won the world title another five times or whatever but, who knows, I might never have won it again after 1980.

"Sure, I've had hard times. But I'm a survivor and if you're one of them, you'll always come through.

"I wouldn't change a thing. People talk about everything that has happened to me, including prison, but life has been one very big experience.

"When I look back now at what I did years ago, I almost laugh at it. It seems mad but I know that if I was put back into that same situation, at that age, then I'd still do it all again.

"One thing I will say, I'm not ashamed of anything I've done."

Back from the brink . . . and now a widely respected tuner.

Main Honours

World Champion	1980 (3rd in 1979 & 1983)
World Long-track Champion	1981
World Team Cup winner	1977 & 1980 (2nd in 1978 & 1983)
British Champion	1977 & 1978 (2nd in 1979 & 1980)
Inter-Continental Champion	1979
Commonwealth Champion	1979
British Under-21 Champion	1976
World Pairs Final	2nd in 1979
World Masters Series	3rd in 1979
British League Knockout Cup winner	King's Lynn, 1977 (2nd in 1976)
Inter-League Knockout Cup winner	King's Lynn, 1978 & 1980 (2nd in 1979)
SWAPA Rider of the Year	1983

Michael after winning his first British Championship in 1977, with runner-up Dave Jessup (left) and Doug Wyer.

Career Statistics

Season	Team	M	R	Pts	BP	TPts	CMA
1975	Boston (NNL)	39	162	352	14	366	9.04
1975	King's Lynn (BL1)	27	98	169	13	182	7.43
1976	King's Lynn (BL1)	42	179	406	16	422	9.43
1977	King's Lynn (BL1)	44	196	511	8	519	10.59
1978	King's Lynn (BL1)	38	165	414	8	422	10.23
1979	King's Lynn (BL1)	31	134	333	9	342	10.21
1980	King's Lynn (BL1)	30	129	318	9	327	10.14
1981	King's Lynn (BL1)	37	161	459	7	466	10.30
1982	King's Lynn (BL1)	35	155	364	10	374	9.65
1983	Poole (BL1)	42	191	471	14	485	10.16
1984	Poole (BL1)	11	42	97	0	97	9.24
1985	King's Lynn (BL1)	19	80	140	4	144	7.20
1986	King's Lynn (BL1)	15	62	114	6	120	7.74
1991	King's Lynn (BL1)	15	63	66	21	87	5.52

Includes official league and cup matches only. The maximum Calculated Match Average would be 12.00.

Another tough battle with British rival Kenny Carter in 1981.

Timeline

1958
Thursday, December 11 – Michael Andrew Lee is born at Girton, near Cambridge.

1975
Sunday, March 16 – Michael's competitive speedway debut – Boston v Peterborough in the KO Cup. Wins his first race – Heat 2 – from fellow Boston reserve Trevor Whiting and Panthers' Roy Sizmore and Steve Osborn in a time of 69.2. Scores 12 points from five rides in Barracudas' 40-38 first leg victory.
Boston: Rob Hollingworth 12, Michael Lee 12, Trevor Whiting 9, David Gagen 3, Dave Piddock 3, Billy Burton 1, Les Glover 0.
Peterborough: Brian Clark 12, Roy Carter 12, Mike Cake 6, Steve Osborn 4, Roy Sizmore 3, Jack Walker 1, Ken Matthews 0.
Good Friday, March 28 – Sensational debut at senior league level after a last-minute call-up by King's Lynn. Two days after officially leaving school, Michael top-scores with nine points in the 46-32 home Border Trophy win v. Leicester.
King's Lynn: Michael Lee 9, Terry Betts 8, Trevor Hedge 7, Ian Turner 7, Ray Bales 5, Olle Nygren 5, Eddie Reeves 4.
Leicester: Dave Jessup 11, Ray Wilson 8, Rob Hollingworth 7, Frank Auffret 4, Pete Smith 1, Bruce Forrester 1, Keith White 0.
April 13 – Michael top-scores with nine as Boston make history by becoming the first NNL (second division) team to beat a top flight side thanks to their 40-38 home victory v. Hackney in the new Inter-League KO Cup.
June 12 – International Test debut at Div. 2 level. Michael scores eight points for England in their 47-60 defeat by Australasia at Middlesbrough.
England: Joe Owen 15, Alan Emerson 9, Michael Lee 8, Brian Havelock 5, Graham Jones 5, John Jackson 4, Pete Reading 1.
Australasia: Lou Sansom 14, Roger Wright 10, Colin Farquarson 10, Doug Underwood 10, Ron Henderson 8, Jack Millen 5, Kym Amundson 3.
July 26 – First paid maximum in the BL comes in Lynn's home 52-26 win v. Hackney in which Michael scores 11 (paid 12).
July 27 – Within 24 hours, Michael achieves another 'first' with his maiden full maximum for 'Cudas in their 50-28 NNL win against Mildenhall.
August 25 – Michael lands his first individual title with 14 points to win the Lincolnshire Trophy at Boston, one point ahead of team-mate Les Glover who is the only rider to beat Lee.
October 11 – Another top-scoring performance to cap a brilliant first season. A dozen points in Lynn's 48-30 win v. Reading brings him his first, and only, full BL max of the 1975 campaign.

1976
May 8 – World Championship debut. Michael starts on the title trail in the British Quarter-Final at Belle Vue, where he scores 13 points to finish behind Alan Grahame and John Davis in a run-off to decide top spot. Unfortunately, he finishes a point short of the qualifying cut-off in the British Semi-Final at White City – the only time he fails to reach the World Final in the next five years.
September 4 – King's Lynn v. Coventry and he breaks the Saddlebow Road track record for the first time by winning Heat 5 in 65.8.
Saturday, September 25 – His biggest individual honour to date – a maximum to win the British Under-21 Championship at Canterbury, a point clear of Steve Weatherley.
November – Heads to Australia for the first time as a member of Nigel Boocock's unofficial five-man 'England' team and sets another new record by scoring an 18-point maximum on his Down Under debut at Perth's vast Claremont track against a Western Australia Select side.

1977
January – Signs his first works sponsorship deal with engine manufacturer Weslake.
May 11 – Scores 11 (paid 12) on his senior Test debut in England's 63-45 victory v. Rest of the World at White City. Also named Strongbow Man-of-the-Match.
May – His first Golden Helmet challenge proves unsuccessful as he loses 2-1 to Phil Crump at both Lynn and Bristol.
Wednesday, July 13 – Youngest-ever British Champion at 18. Michael drops his only point to Swindon's Bob Kilby in his second ride before going on to lift the much coveted national title.
Friday, September 2 – His World Final debut. Scores 12 points to claim fourth place.
Sunday, September 16 – Becomes the youngest rider to appear in a World Team Cup Final. His first World Championship gold medal is in the bag after he wins his last ride in Wroclaw, Poland to finish with nine points as England regain the trophy.

Timeline

Saturday, October 15 – Another 'youngest-ever' record, as Michael represents Lynn in the British League Riders' Championship at Belle Vue, finishing third on 11 points behind Ole Olsen and Peter Collins. This remains his best BLRC performance.

Wednesday, October 26 – Cup final hero Michael snatches the vital second place in the last yards of the final heat of the KO Cup Final, second leg, at King's Lynn to clinch an aggregate 79-77 victory v. Reading. It's Stars' first national trophy success in their history.

King's Lynn: Terry Betts 10, Richard Hellsen 7, Michael Lee 7, David Gagen 6, Ian Turner 6, Billy Spiers 3, Carl Glover 2.

Reading: Dave Jessup 12, John Davis 8, Bengt Jansson 6, Doug Underwood 4, Bob Humphreys 3, Hans Wasserman 1, Ian Gledhill 0.

1978

May 20 – Fined £50 by the SCB for walking out of the Daily Mirror/Volkswagen GP round at Bristol.

August 16 – British Champion again. With 14 points at Coventry, Michael becomes the first Englishman to win consecutive British titles (New Zealander Ivan Mauger also did it in the days when colonials contested the UK rounds of the World Championship).

Saturday, September 2 – Scores nine points in the World Final on his debut at Wembley after breaking the track record in his second race.

November 17 – Suspected of using an oversize Weslake engine after scoring an 18-point max in the first Australia v British Lions Test at Perth. Michael strips down his motor to prove his innocence.

December – Concludes a deal with Jawa to become the first British rider to be fully works sponsored by the Czech company.

1979

January 6 – Top-scores with Doug Wyer as the British Lions win v. Australia at Brisbane to clinch a whitewash 7-0 series victory. Lee is also overall leading scorer in the series.

March – Appointed captain of King's Lynn at the age of 20 – the youngest skipper in the BL. Michael gets the new season off to a flier by winning the celebratory 500th meeting staged at King's Lynn.

May 28 – Wins the The Embassy Internationale, one of the biggest meetings in the international calendar, with 14 points at Wimbledon.

June 23 – Debut for England in the World Pairs. Riding alongside Poole's Malcolm Simmons, Michael scores 15 of their 24-point total but in the final at Vojens a controversial refereeing decision robs the English duo of a run-off for the title against the victorious Danes, Ole Olsen and Hans Nielsen.

June 24 – Michael fails to return from the World Pairs Final in time to ride for King's Lynn in the IL4TT finals at Sheffield. Threatened with a £1,000 club fine, he reacts by asking for a transfer.

July 1 – Commonwealth Champion at White City.

August 5 – Completes a quick White City double by winning the Inter-Continental Final.

Sunday, September 2 – Despite beating eventual winner Ivan Mauger, has to settle for third place in the World Final at Katowice.

1980

Friday, September 5 – World Champion at 21. This time 14 points is enough to land him the biggest prize of all in the World Final at Gothenburg, Sweden.

September 21 – With a joint top-score of 11 points, he helps England to regain the World Team Cup in the final at Wroclaw. Chris Morton (11), Peter Collins (10), Dave Jessup (8) and non-riding reserve John Davis complete England's unique grand slam-winning squad.

November – His first trip to the USA, to compete in the 'Superbikers' event . . . before moving on to Australia for the Tri-Nations series tour involving England, USA and the host nation.

1981

June 7 – BSPA strip him of the Golden Helmet after failing to defend his title against Gordon Kennett at Eastbourne.

Saturday, June 26 – Stopped by police while speeding at 145mph on the M1. Arrested for a string of driving offences and also fined £75 for possession of 1.7gms of cannabis.

Saturday, September 5 – loses his world crown to Bruce Penhall at Wembley after scoring a dismal five points.

September – Asks King's Lynn for a transfer but it's rejected by promoter Cyril Crane.

Sunday, September 20 – Bounces back in style to become the first Englishman to win the World Long-track Final at Gornja Radgona in the old Yugoslavia.

Timeline

1982
June – Eliminated at the British Final stage of the World Championship – the first time he fails to reach the World Final since 1976.
November – After another transfer request, he really does leave Lynn, having made 447 appearances (fourth highest in club's history) spanning eight seasons. Scored total of 4,540 points (second only to Terry Betts) and took the chequered flag first a remarkable 1,125 times in 1,917 starts – a strike rate of 59 per cent. He scored 85 full and 21 paid maximums.

1983
February – Wanted by Mildenhall but their application to join BL1 is turned down, so joins Poole in a proposed £39,000 transfer deal.
June 1 – Runner-up to Chris Morton in British Final at Coventry.
August 8 – Runner-up to Hans Nielsen in Inter-Continental Final at White City.
August 12 – Top-scores with 11 points on recall to England, who finish runners-up to Denmark in World Team Cup Final at Vojens.
Saturday, September 4 – Finishes third in the World Final at Norden, Germany with 11 points.
October – Voted SWAPA Rider of the Year.

1984
Saturday, March 31 – suspended from Poole's match at King's Lynn after a heated confrontation with referee John Eglese, who fines Michael £100, bans him from the rest of the meeting and reports him to the Speedway Control Board.
Thursday, May 31 – SCB disciplinary tribunal hearing. Given a five-year ban from all racing following earlier events at Lynn in March.
April – Wins British semi-final round of World Championship at Poole with maximum 15 points.
Sunday, April 29 – Match-winning 16 points for England v USA in second Test at Sheffield.
Monday, May 7 – Walks out of England v USA Test at Ipswich after being penalised for tapes infringements.
Wednesday, May 9 – scores seven points for last-ever appearance for England, who lose 50-58 to USA in final Test at Poole.
Wednesday, June 20 – SCB appeal tribunal hearing in London, where the main charge against him is dropped and the suspension is reduced from five years to one. He's ordered to pay £500 court costs plus an extra £50 fine.

1985
Saturday, May 11 – His suspension completed, Michael rejoins King's Lynn and wins Heat 1 before going on to get 10 from five rides at home v Halifax.
May 27 – Fails to turn up for home match v. Belle Vue.
October – Suspended indefinitely by Lynn for failing to appear at various meetings.

1986
June 12 – Fails to turn up for Stars' match at Sheffield, so suspended for a month and then indefinitely by his club.

1988
March – New Lynn promoters Bill Barker and Malcolm Simmons are prevented from fitting Michael into their team due to maximum points limit.

1990
March – Refused ACU racing licence by the SCB due to unpaid £50 fine dating back to non-appearance at Sheffield almost four years earlier.
November – Finally granted licence to resume riding in 1991.

1991
February – Goes to Australia and rides in big meetings at Adelaide and Melbourne to get ready for his UK comeback.
March – Returns for King's Lynn after five years out of the saddle.
Saturday, June 1 – His last-ever appearance for Lynn, at Cradley Heath.
Sunday, June 2 – Standby reserve for the individual Commonwealth Final round of the World Championship at Lynn. Takes one ride (Heat 18), finishes last . . . and never races competitively again.
August – Final comeback bid ends in pain and a broken back while practicing at Poole.

Index

Index

Index

Index

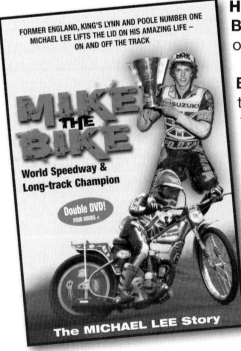